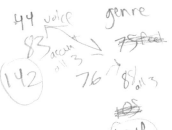

THE WRONGS OF WOMAN; OR MARIA
by Mary Wollstonecraft

and

MEMOIRS OF THE AUTHOR OF A VINDICATION OF THE RIGHTS OF WOMAN
by William Godwin

Eighteenth-Century Literature Series
by College Publishing

Laura L. Runge, Series Editor

This series brings into print significant eighteenth-century literature in pairs or groups that speak to each other. In an age when coffee-houses and salons hummed with the talk of culture, conversation provided a key to urban growth and civilization. Combined with an unprecedented boom in print, the age also witnessed the first widespread success of women and middle class authors. For various reasons, women's part in the cultural conversation became muted over the course of time. The Eighteenth-Century Literature series by College Publishing focuses on restoring that dynamic by making the work of men and women available to today's student in a format that stresses their intertextuality. With informative introductions based in current research and several aids to guide the undergraduate to further reading, this unique series creates an opportunity for a rich and historically based discussion of the work of well-known authors together with their important, but frequently overlooked, contemporaries.

Published Titles

Clara Reeve's *The Old English Baron*
and Horace Walpole's *The Castle of Otranto*,
edited by Laura Runge of the University of South Florida

Mary Wollstonecraft's *The Wrongs of Woman; or Maria*
and William Godwin's *Memoirs of Mary Wollstonecraft Godwin*,
edited by Cynthia Richards of Wittenberg University

THE WRONGS OF WOMAN; OR MARIA
by Mary Wollstonecraft

and

MEMOIRS OF THE AUTHOR OF A VINDICATION OF THE RIGHTS OF WOMAN
by William Godwin

Edited by Cynthia Richards
Wittenberg University

College Publishing
Glen Allen, Virginia

College Publishing books are printed on acid-free paper.

ISBN 0-9679121-6-4
Library of Congress Card Number: 2003108993

College Publishing
12309 Lynwood Drive, Glen Allen, Virginia 23059
T (804) 364-8410 F (804) 364-8408
collegepub@mindspring.com

TABLE OF CONTENTS

Acknowledgements vii
List of Illustrations ix
For Further Exploration xi
Note on the Texts xiii
Introduction 1
Select Bibliography 33
The Wrongs of Woman; or Maria
    Preface 37
    Author's Preface 39
    Text of the 1798 Edition 41
Memoirs of the Author of A Vindication of the Rights of Woman
    Text of the First Edition 202
Appendix
    Excerpts from *The Emigrants* by Gilbert Imlay 302
    Reviews of *The Wrongs of Woman* 320
    Reviews of *The Memoirs* 327
    Combined Review of *The Wrongs of Woman*
    and *Memoirs* 338

Acknowledgements

The work of this edition, as befits its subject matter, has been a family affair. It could not have been accomplished without the unfailing support of my husband, Adam Todd, and the forbearance of my two children, Lily and Samuel, who forgave their mother her many weekends in the office and her commitment to a text they are too young to understand. I must also thank my own mother, Violet Richards, for easing the pressures on all of us by always being willing to help during those busy weekends. The book would not have happened except for the encouragement of Laura Runge to participate in such a worthy series; it would not have been completed except for her careful attention to the details of the text. Along the way, I must also thank Lisa Ottum for her able proofreading skills and Rick Incorvati for his frequent offers to help locate references. My best reader remains Robin Inboden, my good friend and chair, who had time (when she really didn't) to listen to this work in its formative stages and to read it with her unparalleled precision when it was completed. Finally, I thank the students in my English Senior Seminar for reminding me of how important it is to teach Wollstonecraft and to teach her work in a context that conveys the complexity of her accomplishments. I am fortunate to work at a school like Wittenberg University which encourages such connections between teaching and scholarship and in an English department where I receive warm support to do so.

LIST OF ILLUSTRATIONS

Reprint of the title page of *Posthumous Works* 35
Reprint of the contents pages of *Posthumous Works* 36
Portrait of William Godwin. By J.W. Chandler, 1798 198
Reprint of the frontispiece of the first edition
of *Memoirs* 199
Reprint of the title page of the first edition
of *Memoirs* 200

xi

FOR FURTHER EXPLORATION

The Wrongs of Woman; or Maria
Maternal Breastfeeding 42
From *A Vindication of the Rights of Woman*
    On Reason, Madness, and Folly 54
    On Love and Sensibility 77
The American: Gilbert Imlay 71
Employment Opportunities
    "Condemned to Labour": Lower-Class Women 98
    "A Something Betwixt and Between":
    Middle-Class Women 134
The *Feme-Covert*: Marriage Laws in the Eighteenth
Century 144

Memoirs of the Author of A Vindication of the Rights of Woman
    Excerpts from Wollstonecraft's work
        An Exercise in Sensibility: 227
        From *Mary: A Fiction*
        Wollstonecraft and the Revolution Debate: 239
        From *Vindication of the Rights of Man*
        She Speaks of Her Sorrows: 266
        From *Letters Written During A Short Residence*
    On Co-habitation, Love, and Fidelity: 279
    From *An Enquiry Concerning Political Justice*
    Wollstonecraft's Death: The Realities of
    Childbirth in the Late Eighteenth Century 295

A Note on the Texts

The text of *The Wrongs of Woman; or Maria* is taken from the January 1798 collection entitled *The Posthumous Works of the Author of "A Vindication of the Rights of Woman,"* edited by William Godwin. With one exception, I have left the spelling intact. I have also left uncorrected inconsistent punctuation or errors in grammar. The title for this work in the original text reads *The Wrongs of Woman: or, Maria. A Fragment.* I have adopted the standard critical practice when referring to eighteenth-century titles by using the semi-colon instead of the colon and by omitting the comma. Thus, my title reads "The Wrongs of Woman; or Maria." As the work is typically read as a finished piece, I have also dropped the phrase "A Fragment." For *The Memoirs of the Author of "A Vindication of the Rights of Woman,"* I have used the first edition published in 1798. Godwin published a second edition later that year which addressed many of the concerns raised in the mostly negative reviews of this work. The title pages of the January 1798 editions are also reprinted.

The portrait of Mary Wollstonecraft is by John Opie and was painted in 1797 while Wollstonecraft was pregnant with her and Godwin's daughter, Mary Godwin Shelley. National Portrait Gallery, London.

The portrait of William Godwin is by J.W. Chandler and was painted in 1798, the year following Wollstonecraft's death. Tate Gallery, London.

INTRODUCTION

Although this text represents the first time *The Wrongs of Woman; or Maria* and *Memoirs of the Author of "A Vindication of the Rights of Woman"* have been published in the same volume, in the public perception they have always been linked. Both were published in January 1798, less than five months after Mary Wollstonecraft's untimely and unexpected death, and in both cases, the death of this well-known advocate for female equality served as the explicit motive for their publication. Both texts were published by Joseph Johnson, the editor of the radical journal *The Analytical Review* and an established publisher of works questioning the political traditions of England and sympathetic to the profound ideological changes occurring in France, as evidenced by the commencement of the French Revolution in 1789. Yet these other associations paled in contrast to the more obvious connection between these two texts: the two authors were only recently married, less than a year earlier, and that marriage had occasioned much popular interest and speculation. Not surprisingly then, these two texts were reviewed back-to-back or even jointly. For most readers, neither text had an independent life; they both reflected on the short but eventful life of Wollstonecraft. The fact that *The Wrongs of Woman* was published as part of a collection entitled *The Posthumous Works of the Author of "A Vindication of the Rights of Woman"* underscored this perception. As contemporary reviewers saw it, what Wollstonecraft fictionalized in the novel *Wrongs of Woman; or Maria* came to life in the biographical *Memoirs*; what Godwin documented in *The Memoirs* could be traced back to the attitudes represented by the heroine of the novel. One simply could not read one without rereading or reassessing the other.

Although both figures shared political affinities, their literary reputations had not been so wedded in the past. Both authors were famous on their own. Mary Wollstonecraft, as the title of *The Memoirs* suggests, was primarily known for having penned the philosophical work, *A Vindication of the Rights of Woman* (1792). She was not the first to have argued for political, social, and educational equity for women, but she was the first to do so with such urgency and in a context in which she could not be ignored.[1] The reality of the French Revolution, which in its earliest manifestations had resulted in the storming of the political prison the Bastille, the arrest of the French King Louis XVI and his Queen, Marie Antoinette, and the establishment of a republican government based on the Declaration of the Rights of Man, had made all discussions of individual rights in England far from academic. Reactions to the revolution in England were largely negative, with many conservatives fearing that violent protests might soon unsettle their own constitutional monarchy. Even within those liberal circles sympathetic to the revolution's basic principle of individual choice over institutional prerogative, reaction was divided.

In those early years, however, Wollstonecraft was unequivocal in her support of the French Revolution, as her *Vindication of the Rights of Man* (1790), published in response to Edmund Burke's highly critical *Reflections on the Revolution in France* (1790), makes clear.[2] Burke—a respected statesman and advocate of liberal causes, including the American Revolution—had

---

[1] Radical historian Catharine Macaulay published *Letters on Education* in 1790. This work, to which Wollstonecraft was much indebted, also addressed the lack of civil rights for women, and in particular married women. Wollstonecraft favorably reviewed *Letters on Education* for *The Analytical Review*. In 1694, feminist polemicist Mary Astell penned *A Serious Proposal to the Ladies* in order to protest unequal educational opportunities for women and unjust marriage laws.

[2] After living in France from 1793-94 and witnessing first hand the violence instigated by the more extremist factions within the French Revolution, Wollstonecraft became more skeptical of its progress and ultimate outcome. Her *Historical and Moral View of the Origin and Progress of the French Revolution* (1794)— written during her two years of residence in France—remained, however, supportive of its originating ideology and initial actions.

angered many of his former allies with his severe denunciation of the French Revolution. But none responded more quickly and more pointedly than Wollstonecraft. Her *Vindication of the Rights of Man* appeared less than a month after Burke's *Reflections on the Revolution in France*, and a second edition of her work swiftly followed. The first edition was published anonymously, but the second included Wollstonecraft's name on the title page and established her position within the political avant-garde of the period. Wollstonecraft capitalized on that newly achieved status with her *Vindication of the Rights of Woman* (1792), carefully titled to suggest a continuity between that earlier defense of the French Revolution with this even more radical treatise on the need for gender equity. Her title also deliberately evoked Tom Paine's *The Rights of Man* (1791-2), a two-part, exhaustive response to Burke's *Reflections* which sold an unprecedented 200,000 copies, but which in its proposals for an egalitarian society had failed to consider the question of women.[3] Seizing the philosophical moment, Wollstonecraft built upon both her own and Paine's arguments by deploying the Enlightenment faith in reason to argue both for women's inherent equality, and, somewhat paradoxically, for the need to provide educational opportunities for women to insure its cultivation. Responses to her Enlightenment-based argument were predictably mixed, but none in the radical elite could refuse to address it.[4]

Within these politically progressive circles, the chief spokesman for reason and its potential for improving the individual and by implication society at large was William Godwin, who published the very influential *An Enquiry Concerning Political*

---

[3] Estimates of copies sold vary, ranging from 100, 000 to one and a half million, the number suggested by Paine himself. Regardless of the exact numbers, *The Rights of Man* was widely read and highly influential, particularly among the working class. See Marilyn Butler, *Burke, Paine, Godwin, and the Revolution Controversy* (Cambridge: Cambridge University Press, 1984), 108.

[4] Within more liberal journals, her *Vindication of the Rights of Woman* was favorably received and won her many admirers. Interestingly, Godwin was not one of them. As he notes in *The Memoirs*, he found this work strident and unpolished.

Justice (1793) a year after *A Vindication of the Rights of Woman.*
Godwin began this eight-book treatise in the year following
Burke's *Reflections on the Revolution in France* and, although this
work was not explicitly positioned as a rebuttal to Burke, it did
come to represent the most radical, and certainly the most academic, of the philosophical works that followed Burke's *Reflections.* Moreover, at the time of its publication in 1793, the stakes
had become considerably higher. King Louis XVI had been executed in France, war with France declared, and all critiques of
the aristocracy were viewed with deep suspicion and even hostil-
ity. Yet Godwin remained firm in his advocacy of a free society
based on individual reason. Indeed, his optimism regarding the
potential of individual reason became legendary, as it led him to
take as his central tenets that "man is perfectible" and that his
"chief obstacle to happiness is government." By that, he meant
that man could indefinitely improve although never fully reach
perfection, and that human institutions stood in the way of liberty, both of the mind and of the person, rather than facilitating
it. The best government would then be the least felt, and it was
individual reason that would ultimately assure the equality of
all. None made the case more forcibly against government than
Godwin, and none was a stronger advocate for reason.

It was not, however, Wollstonecraft and Godwin's shared
faith in reason or their common association with England's radical circle that had so united them in the public imagination. It
was not even an earlier rumor of their affair. Rather, it was their
reported marriage. For both, their marriage represented something of a scandal. For Godwin, the concern was largely a matter
of principle. In *An Enquiry Concerning Political Justice,* he had
argued quite adamantly against marriage or any form of co-habitation, calling it an "evil" which "checks the individual progress
of mind" and leads to deception and possessiveness. "Marriage is
law," he writes, "and the worst of all laws," and it should be
abolished.[5] Hence, his marriage to Wollstonecraft—so clearly

---

[5] *An Enquiry Concerning Political Justice* (1793) in *The Political and Philosophical*

in violation of his own philosophical ideals—resulted in some embarrassment for him. Yet he did have extenuating circumstances: a baby was on the way, and he would maintain a separate apartment for his work even after his marriage, assuring both Wollstonecraft and him a continued independence. For Wollstonecraft, however, the damage to her reputation could not be so easily addressed. Although in the *Vindication of the Rights of Woman*, she had criticized the prescribed role of women in marriage (which afforded them the primary function of pleasing man), what made the marriage scandalous for her was not philosophical inconsistency. Rather, it revealed her to be radical indeed. Up to this point, Wollstonecraft had been known in public circles as Mary Wollstonecraft Imlay, a name she had taken to insure her safety while living in France and with her lover, the American Gilbert Imlay. At the time, skirmishes had broken out between Britain and France, and Wollstonecraft faced the general threat of imprisonment. Being registered as Imlay's wife at the American embassy gave Wollstonecraft American status and allowed her to remain in France without fear of repercussion. When she returned to England, it also proved a convenient cover, as she had by then given birth to their illegitimate daughter, Fanny. Marrying Godwin made public the fact that she had not been married before; hence, rather than giving her respectability, their marriage de-legitimized her in the eyes of even some of her closest friends. Her marriage to Godwin then was the first in a chain of events that made the details of her life, rather than those of her philosophical or literary work the source of popular interest and speculation.

The publication of the *Posthumous Works of the Author of "A Vindication of the Rights of Woman,"* in which *The Wrongs of Woman* originally appeared, must be seen as another such link in that chain, although its express intention was to pay tribute to her work. Yet when Godwin compiled this four-volume collection,

Writings of William Godwin, 7 vols., ed. Mark Philp (London: Pickering and Chatto, 1993), vol. 3, 453.

his grief was raw. Wollstonecraft had died only a few months earlier, unexpectedly and far too young. At the age of 38, she died from complications arising from the birth of their daughter, Mary. As a result, the choice of pieces included in this collection reads less as a tribute to her work, than to her person. All but one piece were previously unpublished, and the rest were unfinished or represent work we typically assume to be personal. Indeed, the one inclusion which Godwin represents as finished and even equal "in sentiment and passion" to one of the most celebrated novels of the period, *The Sorrows of Werther,* would grossly violate our contemporary sense of what is proper for public presentation. That piece, which became known as *The Letters to Imlay,* in reality had no such formal shape, being rather a series of private letters she wrote to her lover, Imlay. In similar fashion, he includes letters to Joseph Johnson, her friend, employer and frequent publisher, but not in order to testify to the merits of her work. Rather, they demonstrate "the sincerity of his friendship" and become "a valuable and interesting specimen of the mind of the writer." Among the other selections, he includes an oriental tale abandoned by Wollstonecraft and written in her youth and a few "hints for the Second Part of the Rights of Woman." Even these more conventional choices suggest an emphasis on what Wollstonecraft left undone and, hence, what best shows her*self* yet unshaped into public form.

At times, the selections suggest Godwin is paying tribute to his own grief. Why else include the fourteen "Lessons for Children"? As Godwin notes in *The Memoirs,* Wollstonecraft was at work on *Letters on the Management of Infants* at the time of her death, and he himself saw her career as moving toward her becoming an authority on the instruction of children. Yet even he acknowledges that this small fragment from that larger work must seem a "trifle" and have its chief value in its "vividness." Indeed, it is not primarily the promise of a future career that one sees in these lessons, but quite vividly, the profound loss of such a devoted and capable mother. In these lovingly written and almost impressionistic lessons, Wollstonecraft repeatedly addresses a young daughter in her preschool years and assures her of her advancing intellect and skill. Godwin seems to remind the reader of precisely what he and his two girls have lost. Little wonder then that Wollstonecraft's novel and Godwin's memoir were linked in the public perception; both *The Posthumous Works* and *The Memoirs* themselves functioned as a memoir of the author of *A Vindication of the Rights of Woman*, and both were written when Godwin's own grief prevailed.

If, then, *The Wrongs of Woman; or Maria* had trouble claiming an independent life immediately after its publication, it was, in part, because it had none. Although it occupied the first two volumes in this four-volume *Posthumous Works* and was clearly the most substantial of the pieces, it was rarely reviewed apart from the whole. It did not always even merit the most attention, competing with the deeply personal *Letters to Imlay* for public recognition. When it did receive attention, it was largely for how its narrative reflected on Wollstonecraft's life.

Wollstonecraft's earlier fiction had an autobiographical cast as well. Her *Mary: A Fiction* (1788) follows fairly closely the early events of her own development—her unhappy relationship with both her mother and father, her intense devotion to her friend, Fanny Blood, and her journey to Lisbon to comfort Fanny in her final illness. Although there were fictional elements to this story and an attempt to distance it from the author's life through the appended "A Fiction" in the title, few took it that way. What gave it power, even for such a discriminating reader as Godwin, was how it testified to the sensibilities and character of the author herself. To that end, Godwin chose to reread this novel while Wollstonecraft lay dying, as though he could recover her in its fictional heroine. In *The Wrongs of Woman; or Maria*, Wollstonecraft clearly does not disavow such autobiographical connections. She repeats again the difficulties of her relationship with her parents, includes references to the hardships her sisters experience as single, upper middle-class women with few job opportunities, and even makes central to the novel an affair with a man known to have traveled in America, whom those in the know would have certainly taken to be Imlay. In this work as in others, Wollstonecraft invites such scrutiny of her own life, and blurs the distinction between fact and fiction. Its centrality to *The Posthumous Works* only reinforces that; in this context its fragmentary state and unfinished status become almost an emblem of her own too-soon-ended life.

Yet *The Wrongs of Woman; or Maria* also represents a shift in focus for Wollstonecraft in its movement away from the simple recitation of her own life. Although today the novel is more typically referred to as *Maria*, this was clearly not Wollstonecraft's first choice for its title; the "or" preceding this variation on her own name makes it seem almost an afterthought. Other choices in the novel suggest that her initial title is more a deliberate attempt to disengage this narrative from her own identity. In it, she tells not only the story of her heroine Maria, confined in a private madhouse by her cruel and greedy husband, but also that of her keeper, the lower-class Jemima. In the process, she incorporates details that point to the difficulties for middle to upper-middle class women as well as for lower-class women— and she does this not only in Jemima's story, but in other "digressions" within the narrative: the landlady with an abusive husband and the servant forced to take in laundry to feed her children. Even the novel's chief plot element—a woman's flight from an incompatible husband through which she is separated from her daughter—is not her own story, but rather closer to that of her sister, Eliza. Wollstonecraft had been instrumental in orchestrating her sister's escape from an unhappy marriage, but the story was not her own, and her role in it was a secondary one.[7] The "Author's Preface" makes this shift in focus away from the author explicit: "The history," she writes, "ought rather

---

[7] With Wollstonecraft's encouragement, Eliza fled her unhappy marriage soon after the birth of her daughter. She had been suffering from postpartum depression, and found her relationship with the somewhat older and wealthy Meredith Bishop intolerable. Eliza's daughter died before she could arrange a reunion. See Janet Todd, *Mary Wollstonecraft: A Revolutionary Life* (New York: Columbia University Press, 2000), 45-57.

to be considered, more of woman, than of an individual." Wollstonecraft, perhaps for the first time, was not writing her story, but that of woman in general.

Yet ultimately, the publication of *The Memoirs of the Author of "A Vindication of the Rights of Woman"* made such a distinction impossible. It was not Godwin's intention to privilege his own reflections when he penned *The Memoirs* in those painful months following her death. "It has always appeared to me, that to give to the public some account of the life of a person of eminent merit deceased," the opening line of his prefatory remarks reads, "is a duty incumbent on survivors." Nor did he foresee his own work overshadowing that of his subject, Wollstonecraft. In this opening line, he represents himself as merely one "survivor" in a long chain of survivors required to pay homage to the one who predeceases them. It is his own *person* that he wants to disappear in this text, and it is Wollstonecraft's identity that he wants to emerge. Hence, we find the passive voice of this opening sentence, with its impersonal pronoun—a style which disengages him from his own work, but which is intended, his own comments suggest, to allow Wollstonecraft's voice to emerge. "The facts detailed in the following pages," he makes sure we know, "are principally taken from the mouth of the person to whom they relate." Although in this case as in others, Godwin emphasizes how personal and how immediate his details are, it is only to draw attention to how little his own person will dominate the text. Rather, he wants the reader to experience Wollstonecraft's "virtues" for him or herself: "I cannot easily prevail on myself to doubt, that the more fully we are presented with the picture and story of such persons as the subject of the following narrative, the more generally we shall feel in ourselves an attachment to their fate, and a sympathy in their excellencies." The effect, however, of Godwin's "dutiful" attention to the person of Wollstonecraft was to draw attention away from the merit and genesis of her work.

Even the rare sympathetic reviewer of *The Memoirs* saw it this way. The reviewer for *The Analytical Review*, published by

Wollstonecraft's good friend and employer, Joseph Johnson, notes Godwin's attention to Wollstonecraft's person and not her work and, for this reason, offers it "praise," albeit "very limited": "It is indeed a bald narrative of the life of a woman, very eventful and touching."[8] Yet the reviewer still finds it deficient. For one, the emphasis is wrong; it pays little attention to the formation of the writer and her philosophical intellect: "It gives us no correct history of the formation of Mrs. G.'s mind. We are neither informed of her favourite books, her hours of study, nor her attainments in languages and philosophy." Moreover, the reviewer is persuaded, and rightfully so, that it will not promote the sympathy that Godwin envisioned. Yes, it was "very faithful and true." Godwin does present fully her narrative as he intended, but the result of this disclosure will be to "invite many severely to criticize, and some to censure her character."[9]

As this critic predicted, far from promoting sympathy, Godwin's revelations led to open scorn, and condescending expressions of pity. Reviewers are interested in Wolstonecraft's story, but primarily to separate themselves from its "morality" and to proclaim her virtue as nonexistent. Of chief interest to these reviewers are three previously unpublicized events from her private life: her open infatuation with the married painter, Henry Fuseli, the details of her affair with Gilbert Imlay, and the two suicide attempts that coincided with the painful breakup of that relationship. Godwin himself sees great integrity in all three of these events, an ability on Wollstonecraft's part to couple ardent affection with principled, if at times misguided, action. Yet no matter how the reviewers read these events, they condemn her. On one hand, these disclosures of private emotional turmoil put theory into practice: Wollstonecraft proves as disrespectful of established traditions in her private life as she was in her philosophical one. On the other hand, they show how inconsistent her practice was with her theory, "exclaiming against prejudices,

---

[8] *The Analytical Review*, vol. 27 (1798): 238.
[9] *The Analytical Review*, vol. 27 (1798): 238-245.

of some of the most dangerous of which, she was herself per-petually the victim."[10] It was not that Wollstonecraft's life, as represented in Godwin's *Memoirs*, failed to comment on her work; it was that it did so too profoundly for contemporary readers. Her work became but a comment on what was viewed as the true radicalism of her life.

The Wrongs of Woman; or Maria bore the brunt of this reas-sessment. The parallels between the texts were too immediate and too apparent. As *The British Critic* puts it, "The first of these, *The Wrongs of Woman*, represents a specimen of that system of morality in which the writer displayed in her own person, but which is alike offensive to the purity of female virtue, and the precepts of our holy religion."[11] Just as they withheld sympathy from Wollstonecraft, reviewers showed little for Maria and her disastrous marriage. They found her overly critical, not suffi-ciently cognizant of her duties both to husband and to religion, and too quick to attach herself to another. In many ways, it was precisely the criticism the sympathetic reviewer from *The Ana-lytical Reviewer* had feared being leveled against Wollstonecraft herself: "The next charge we expect to hear advanced against the character of Mrs. G., is the versatility of her attachments. It will be said, to-day she loves Mr. Fuseli, tomorrow attaches herself to Mr. Imlay, and, the moment Mr. Imlay abandons her, we find her in the arms of Godwin."[12] Not only Wollstonecraft, but Maria, too, suffered from these accusations of flightiness. Maria's escape from an oppressive marriage, far from being read as representa-tive of the needs of all women, was read as just one more symp-tom of Wollstonecraft's own lack of self –control and emotional restraint.

Thus, Wollstonecraft's explicit objective in her preface to *The Wrongs of Woman*—of telling the story of all women, and not the individual—is largely lost in the initial reception of her

---

[10] *The British Critic*, vol. 12 (1798): 235.
[11] *The British Critic* (1798): 234.
[12] *The Analytical Review*, vol. 27 (1798): 240.

work. The exception, in this case, proves the rule. The review from *The Monthly Mirror* starts to move toward Wollstonecraft's objective—making the lower-class Jemima's tale as central to this story as Maria's—but soon that interest collapses under the weight of Wollstonecraft's true and ultimately more compelling story:

> Both Jemima and Maria seem not only to have continu-
> ally partaken of the bitter cup of misfortune, but to have
> swallowed its very dregs. What catastrophe would have
> ensued, it is impossible now to conjecture; the author of
> the work has had *her* share of afflictions, and is now
> gone, we hope, to that retreat "where the wretched may
> have rest."[13]

In the wake of Godwin's revelations, *The Wrongs of Woman; or Maria* has little chance of claiming its independent life, and almost none of speaking for the fate of all women.

Similarly, Godwin's attempts to expunge himself from the text of Wollstonecraft's life are not entirely successful. His detached tone and passive voice become in at least one review the very mark of his presence. His ability to provide precise detail at a time when his own emotion could have prevailed drew attention to his own philosophical perspective. Describing the final chapter and Godwin's thorough account of Wollstonecraft's death, the reviewer from *The Monthly Mirror* writes, "It is easy for many minds to comprehend the nature of a dangerous and trying labour; and when once we are led into all the minutiae of this state, our pity for the afflicted object is divided between our astonishment at the cool precision of the person who describes it."[14] Thus, for at least one reviewer, *The Memoirs* shows his theory (and not hers) in practice; it demonstrates his ability to sustain an intellectual, almost clinical, detachment, even at the time of his wife's death. For the reviewer at *The Anti-Jacobin*, Godwin's philosophical perspective extends not only to *The Memoirs,* but to *The Wrongs of Woman* as well: "Besides illustration of her own

---

[13] *The Monthly Mirror*, vol. 5 (1798): 154.
[14] Ibid., 153.

opinions, the principles supported and the practices recommended have a very great coincidence with those inculcated by the philosopher himself, in that part of his "Political Justice" in which he describes the promiscuous intercourse of the sexes, as one of the highest improvements to result from *political justice!*"[15] Reviewers see Godwin's influence everywhere, and ultimately, his choices come under the greatest scrutiny, both from Wollstonecraft's detractors and her few remaining advocates.

Hence, the simultaneous publication of these two works did little for either author's immediate reputation. The effect of Godwin's revelations on Wollstonecraft's reputation has become legendary, although to be fair, most accounts also note the changing political attitudes of the period as growing hostilities between France and England fortified the conservative elements in British culture. For nearly 100 years, she slipped out of the lexicon of nameable women writers because of her association with sexual promiscuity and inconsistent feminist ideology. For Godwin, the effects were more subtle, but not less profound. The publication of *The Memoirs* clearly put him on the defensive, somewhat contradictorily marking both the limits of his philosophical optimism and the lived depths of his radicalism. It left him vulnerable, both as a man and as a philosopher. In his grief, he quickly sought to remarry, although initially proving unsuccessful in finding a suitable wife and a mother for his two daughters.[16] Philosophically, he grew more isolated as well. Within the year following Wollstonecraft's death, the attacks on his own *Political Justice* grew in number and intensity as the political landscape shifted underneath him, and his own position became less secure. With military losses to the French mounting and rebellion brewing in Ireland, his views moved from being regarded as radical to nearly treasonous. The scandalous *Mem-*

---

[15] *The Anti-Jacobin Review,* vol. 1 (1798): 91.

[16] In the year following Wollstonecraft's death, Godwin proposed to family friend Maria Reveley and novelist Harriet Lee. Both turned him down. See William St. Clair, *The Godwins and The Shelleys: A Biography of a Family* (Baltimore: Johns Hopkins University Press, 1989), 200-203.

oirs made more concrete the danger of his extremist ideals. His marriage to Mary Jane Clairmont in 1801 did little to alter his connection to Wollstonecraft and her now-troubled legacy, and when their daughter, Mary Wollstonecraft Godwin, eloped with the poet Percy Shelley at the age of 17, while Shelley was still married to another woman, it must have seemed that Wollstonecraft's story had come full circle. In the public perception, Godwin's work and Wollstonecraft's would remain linked.

II

Despite this troubled history, the benefits of pairing these two texts remain obvious. This pairing reproduces the conditions of their original reception. Neither was initially read in isolation of the other, and both become more complex and ultimately more meaningful by how they comment on each other. Moreover, we are no longer likely to read Wollstonecraft's life merely for how it reflects on the morals of an age, nor are we likely to respond in disgust to Godwin's disclosure of such personal details. Rather, we may find his lack of discretion—and even hers—if not endearing, at the very least humanizing. Yet as the history of the original reception for these works also makes apparent, pairing these two texts is not without its dangers. Their initial pairing led to misunderstanding, misreading, and a misappropriation of Wollstonecraft's final novel as a mere coda on her life. It led others to see Godwin's *Memoirs* as an ill-conceived choice of a grieving husband to memorialize his wife, and not as the well-crafted and emotionally moving biographical text that many have subsequently come to see. Indeed, the most recent critical history of these two texts has relied on their *separation* as literary works to restore their respective reputations.

In the case of Wollstonecraft, the need for separation from Godwin's *Memoirs* is most apparent. In drafting her novel, she had clearly imagined a less personal context for her work. Her vision was not one uninfluenced by Godwin, although it was his popular novel *Caleb Williams* (1794) that she had in mind. In that work, Godwin had given fictional shape to the general thrust of his argument in *Political Justice*, that one must question "the modes of domestic and unrecorded despotism by which man becomes the destroyer of man."[17] "No refined and abstract speculation," the novel tells with great suspense the story of Caleb, a peasant's son and secretary to a country squire whose curiosity leads him to discover his master's guilty secret: that he has committed murder. As a result of this discovery, Caleb is relentlessly pursued by an agent of his master, then framed for this murder, and put on trial. Yet ultimately Caleb is cleared and, in the process, Godwin reveals that the squire's true nature, as well as that of social hierarchy, is tyrannical and hence culpable of not only this murder, but also greater civil injustice. In this work, the philosophical becomes concrete, and Godwin's message finds new admirers. Among those admirers is Wollstonecraft herself, and clearly she wants to learn from his example. She shares drafts of *The Wrongs of Woman* with him, and in quite uncharacteristic fashion, labors over questions of tone and balance. By contrast, Wollstonecraft had written *A Vindication of the Rights of Woman* in only six weeks. While Wollstonecraft drafted *The Wrongs of Woman*, her friend, Mary Hays, also successfully composed and published a philosophical novel along the lines of *Caleb Williams*. *Memoirs of Emma Courtney* (1796) is the story of Hays's unrequited love for Cambridge mathematician and reformer William Frend. With Godwin's encouragement, Hays used her correspondence with Frend as well as her letters to Godwin himself to construct a narrative that gave voice to both her own unrequited passion and that of women in general, claiming in both cases that passion could coexist with reason. Wollstonecraft knew then that the novel form could give new urgency to her philosophical ideals and cushion the reception of any personal revelations. Her models were immediate, and never had she been so deliberate in both her philosophical and literary purposes.

As her title makes clear, *The Wrongs of Woman* would be the

---

[17] Preface to *Caleb Williams* (1794), ed. Marilyn Butler (London and New York: Penguin Books, 1988), 3.

narrative companion piece to her earlier *Vindication of the Rights of Woman*. In that work, Wollstonecraft had taken a two-pronged approach. First, she works within the philosophical framework of Enlightenment ideology to argue for women's rights, and secondly, she demonstrates how the current social and political conditions weakened women's capacity to claim and act upon those very rights. At times, the doubleness of her approach led her into seeming contradiction: women are equal, but women are currently inferior as a result of social conditions. On one hand, her argument was simple and largely accepted among radical circles. All men and women were equal in the eyes of God, and equal in large part because of their inherent capacity to reason. To acquire virtue, they need only exercise their reason. Indeed, Wollstonecraft makes this assumption of equality seem almost matter-of-fact in her argument: "In fact, it is a farce to call any being virtuous whose virtues do not result from the exercise of its reason. This was Rousseau's opinion respecting man: I extend it to women."[18] Yet Wollstonecraft is also interested in the conditions which kept women from exercising their reason, namely limited educational and employment opportunities as well as the more pernicious influences of love and marriage. Each weakened women. Lack of opportunity limited the development of women's minds and bodies. Love and marriage forced women to value pleasing men above all else, an objectification that could only render them passive and vain. Wollstonecraft writes:

> It appears to me necessary to dwell on these obvious truths, because females have been insulated, as it were; and, while they have been stripped of the virtues that should clothe humanity, they have been decked with artificial graces that enable them to exercise a short-lived tyranny. Love, in their bosoms, taking place of every nobler passion, their sole ambition is to be fair, to raise

---

[18] *A Vindication of the Rights of Woman* (1792) in *The Works of Mary Wollstonecraft*, vols. 7, ed. Janet Todd and Marilyn Butler (New York: New York University Press, 1989), vol. 5, 90.

emotion instead of inspiring respect; and this ignoble desire, like the servility in absolute monarchies, destroys all strength of character.[19]

What Wollstonecraft protests are the social conditions which curtail the development of women's reason; what she seems most consistently to attack—even paint as a tyrannical figure—is woman herself.

Fiction offered Wollstonecraft a way out of this bind. In *A Vindication of the Rights of Woman*, Wollstonecraft had written disparagingly of novels and their effects on the female mind. Novels reinforced an allegiance to romantic notions, and they did not cultivate the active intellectual engagement so critical to the development of reason. Yet even here, she had allowed that reading novels was better than not reading at all: "For any kind of reading I think better than leaving a blank still a blank, because the mind must receive a degree of enlargement and obtain a little strength by a slight exertion of its thinking powers."[20] The letter to a friend that Godwin includes in "The Author's Preface" of *The Wrongs of Woman* suggests that Wollstonecraft continued to refine her sense of what the novel could accomplish. She remained skeptical of its appeal to high drama, what she calls in this letter its "*stage-effect*," but she was beginning to see other possibilities as well: "It is the delineation of finer sensations, which, in my opinion, constitutes the merits of our best novels." She may have been thinking of Godwin and Hays here—both successful, not only in giving fictional voice to their political ideals, but also in the process, endowing those ideas with greater subtleties. In 1796, Wollstonecraft had herself been successful in delineating the finer sensations of the human heart, not so much in her fictional work, as in her *Letters Written During a Short Residence in Sweden, Norway, and Denmark*, penned shortly after the breakup with Gilbert Imlay. In this series of letters, she presented herself as a deeply compromised figure,

---

[19] Ibid., 105.
[20] Ibid., 256.

like Hays, a woman whose love was not returned, yet who could win the hearts of her readers (chief among them Godwin himself) through her detailing of her own conflicted sensibilities.

Fiction could allow her to enumerate the social conditions which acted to "degrade" women, even expose the weakening effect of those conditions on a woman's mind, yet do so sympathetically. It is clear from her opening page that Wollstonecraft intends us to identify with her heroine, Maria. Her setting evokes the gothic novel, a popular genre of the period involving the harried pursuit of a psychologically naïve, yet highly sympathetic female figure. Wollstonecraft begins her story by comparing the madhouse where Maria is confined to an aging and haunted castle, and, although her heroine is older and more experienced than the standard gothic heroine, she endows her with all the innocence such confinement typically represented.

Yet, as Anne Mellor notes, the "wrongs of women" that this novel enumerates are not only those done to women but also those done *by* women.[21] Once again, Wollstonecraft's setting serves her well. Maria is in a madhouse, and just as her keeper Jemima watches her for any sign of irrationality, so does the reader. We must be wary of her judgment, and of our own judgment of her as well. At times, she seems as susceptible to the "madness and folly" of love as the women Wollstonecraft critiques in *A Vindication*. Her relationship with Henry Darnford, a young man wrongly imprisoned in the private madhouse, takes place when Maria has few choices in her life, and when her desire for love, if not marriage, is acute. Even her reading choices are dictated by his interests, as they first come to know each other through an exchange of his books orchestrated by Jemima. His collection reveals him to be a serious, although fairly conventional, student of literature, including as it does the popular and esteemed moral allegories Dryden's *Fables* and Milton's *Paradise Lost*. Yet it is not a reading list that questions women's pri-

---

[21] Introduction to *Maria or The Wrongs of Woman* (New York: W.W. Norton & Co, 1994), xi.

mary function of pleasing men. Although *The Fables* includes stories of women who choose to act according to their own desires and not those of the men around them, the tone of this work is largely cautionary. In *Paradise Lost*, Milton describes Eve, for all her intelligence, as Adam's natural inferior and makes vanity her chief distinguishing characteristic. Darnford's comment that he finds American women less capable of pleasing men than English ones, although arguably only intended to flatter Maria, suggests that the message of his books is not coincidental. Maria herself likens him to St. Preux, the romantic hero of Jean-Jacques Rousseau's *Julie; or the New Heloise*, which is the very novel Wollstonecraft singles out in *A Vindication* for perpetuating the destructive myth that women's "natural" role is that of pleasing men. That Maria does not acknowledge the danger of her comparison signals to the reader that her new-found love is suspect. Such a characterization indicates that she functions as more than a simple stand-in for the author herself.

At other times, however, Maria appears to operate as our emotional and intellectual guide. Despite confinement in a madhouse, Maria continues to exercise her reason, chiefly through a narrative she addresses to her daughter. Once Maria learns through Jemima that her daughter (from whom she has been forcibly separated) is most likely dead, she shares this narrative with Darnford, and through him, the general reader. The relationship between writer and reader inscribed in the letter, that of a mother addressing her daughter, is one that makes Maria our moral and intellectual superior. Speaking from experience, she cautions her daughter against the wrongs of the world and pleads with her to choose a more enlightened path. Befitting a mother, the tone becomes more didactic in this section of the novel. Wollstonecraft's narrative begins to verge on social realism as it outlines the many inequities, particularly in respect to marriage laws and employment opportunities that await her daughter. Despite its more overtly political tone, the section also follows Wollstonecraft's own life and her own philosophical position most closely. She repeats many of the details of her early years also recorded in *Mary: A Fiction*, yet she deliberately draws comparisons between that personal story and the shape of any woman's story. Moreover, in a shift from *A Vindication*, where Wollstonecraft wrote exclusively of the travails of the middle-class woman (the state she deemed most "natural" to woman), she incorporates parallels with the fate of lower-class women in *The Wrongs of Woman*. Indeed, the very fact that Maria's story follows Jemima's powerful recounting of her far more beleaguered existence suggests a shift in emphasis for Wollstonecraft. Jemima's story frames Maria's, and although it is Darnford who first reads Maria's narrative, it is Maria's sincere sympathy with Jemima's story that prompts her to share this narrative in the first place.

Wollstonecraft's literary career has long made her a contradictory figure. Her first novel is a study in sensibility, embracing a feminized world *"where there was neither marrying,* nor giving in marriage"* (italics Wollstonecraft's)[22] and where the greatest love is that between two female friends. Her *Vindication of the Rights of Woman*, on the other hand, is a paean to reason and the "masculine" virtues, expressing deep reservations about the power of the sensations to improve. Her social agenda is radical, advocating progressive legal, civil, and educational reform, yet she becomes a staunch advocate for what would prove the more conservative agenda of motherhood, home, and hearth. As a person, she could be fiercely independent, supporting herself and much of her family at an early age, and refusing to back down from her political and philosophical point of view even when challenged by friend and foe. Yet in love she is capable of great sacrifice and susceptible to emotional dependency, a tendency which led her to contemplate and twice act upon suicidal urges. With *The Wrongs of Woman; or Maria,* Wollstonecraft finally uses the novel form to embrace what Claudia Johnson has poignantly termed her "equivocal being."[23] The novel form allows her to promote

---

[22] *Mary: A Fiction* (1788) in *The Works of Mary Wollstonecraft*. vol. 1, 73.
[23] Claudia Johnson, *Equivocal Beings: Politics, Gender, and Sentimentality in the 1790s* (Chicago: University of Chicago Press, 1994), 25.

sympathy with her heroine and at the same time force a questioning of her very character. It allows Wollstonecraft to continue to voice her strident objections to the weakened feminine condition, yet do so in the interesting and highly feminized voice of a woman in love. Wollstonecraft never finishes the novel, but it is in the "hints" for its conclusion that Godwin includes that Wollstonecraft's embrace of this doubleness may be most apparent. The possible endings range from the deeply tragic to the resolutely optimistic; Wollstonecraft remains divided until the end.

Such division, however, is not likely to still accusations of inconsistency, even among the feminist critics who "rediscovered" her, first in the early 1900s and then again in the 1970s.[24] Indeed, one of the ironies of Wollstonecraft's legacy is that a woman known for her romantic adventures and a philosopher known for her advocacy of the "masculine" virtue of reason becomes the so-called "mother of feminism." As Cora Kaplan notes, feminists of the 1970s seized upon Wollstonecraft's advocacy of "rationality as the basis of parity between men and women" as a persuasive mechanism for promoting their "ethical claims for full civic subjectivity for women."[25] That motherhood ultimately becomes the primary institution through which Wollstonecraft sees that agenda being realized makes it appealing to both moderates and radicals alike. Her agenda could be read as essentially conservative or deeply destabilizing of this most fundamental

---

[24] As evidence of this rediscovery, six biographies of Wollstonecraft were written within six years. They are: Eleanor Flexnor, *Mary Wollstonecraft: A Biography* (New York: Penguin, 1973); Margaret George, *One Woman's "Situation": A Study of Mary Wollstonecraft* (Urbana: University of Illinois Press, 1970); Edna Nixon, *Mary Wollstonecraft: Her Life and Times* (London: Dent, 1971); Emily Sunstein, *A Different Face: the Life of Mary Wollstonecraft* (Boston and Toronto: Little, Brown, & Co., 1975); Margaret Tims, *Mary Wollstonecraft: A Social Pioneer* (London: Millington, 1976); Claire Tomalin, *The Life and Death of Mary Wollstonecraft* (London: Weidenfeld and Nicolson, 1974).

[25] "Mary Wollstonecraft's Reception and Legacies" in *The Cambridge Companion to Mary Wollstonecraft*, ed. Claudia Johnson (Cambridge: Cambridge University Press, 2002), 254.

relationship between mother and child. Yet feminists of that era remain, according to Kaplan, uncomfortable with the more irrational elements of her life, the ways in which passion and feeling are never fully relegated to the margins, and how these impulses consequently render her work incoherent.

Hence, early appraisals of *The Wrongs of Woman; or Maria* in the context of this rediscovery are divided. For one, this novel becomes central to, even elevated in, Wollstonecraft's canon because it is the text where she addresses her "daughter," a category that now includes the fictional figure, Fanny and Mary, her real daughters, and all latter-day feminists. This is the text where she speaks most directly to this audience. As one critic puts it, "Wollstonecraft's final text is ... a memoir for her own daughters, for all daughters .... She bears the word of an alternative discourse of female experience down through generations of readers who need only be alert enough to embrace the message."[26]

But many of her most admiring readers are disappointed with the novel's effect. It is difficult to say whether Wollstonecraft, according to Mary Poovey in a highly influential work, intended a critique of Maria's "romantic expectations" or whether the author herself succumbed to this very weakness. It is Wollstonecraft's repeated "lapses back into sentimental jargon and romantic idealism" that make any suggestion of irony in her depiction of Maria suspect.[27] Although Poovey's assessment is a great improvement on that of many of her biographers, who had simply asserted her lack of talent as a novelist, she remains suspicious of Wollstonecraft's narrative control. Instead, what critics read in this pseudo-novel are the contradictions of Wollstonecraft's own life and her philosophical perspective writ large. In this respect,

---

[26] Leigh Matthews, "(Un)Confinements: The Madness of Motherhood in Mary Wollstonecraft's *The Wrongs of Woman*," *Mary Wollstonecraft and Mary Shelley: Writing Lives*, ed. Helen Buss, D.L. McDonald, and Anne McWhir (Waterloo, Ontario: Wilfrid Laurier University Press, 2001), 95.

[27] *The Proper Lady and the Woman Writer: Ideology as Style in the Works of Mary Wollstonecraft, Mary Shelley, and Jane Austen* (Chicago: University of Chicago Press, 1984), 105.

such positive reassessment oddly echoes the negative reviews of the work's initial reception. And, as was the case with those reviews, it is the relationship with Gilbert Imlay that brings Wollstonecraft's inconsistencies most clearly into focus. Wollstonecraft, argues Poovey, could not openly acknowledge her own sexuality, and hence she repeatedly veils her desires in the overripe language of sentimentality:

> In the course of her adult life, Wollstonecraft was repeatedly crippled by this collusion between sexuality and sentimentality. Her letters to Imlay reveal the unmistakable pleasure of a woman's first emotionally satisfying and physically stimulating experience. Yet even as she confesses to a "tenderness for [Imlay's] person," Wollstonecraft tries to "purify"—and prolong—their sexual alliance with what she conceded were "romantic" theories of the imagination. [28]

These conflicted sensibilities within the author herself—in Poovey's opinion—result in a literary text that also repeatedly undercuts its own radical agenda.

For Cora Kaplan, the problems within this text are problems within liberal feminism itself. Wollstonecraft sought to isolate artificial passion from reason in her *Vindication of the Rights of Woman*, to cut women off from the claims of desire or sensibility in order to enfranchise them fully as civic subjects. The result was a significant reduction of the psychological territory allowed women in contrast to the more expansive terrain allowed men. In Wollstonecraft's rationalist arguments, for women to be fully human they had to be fully coherent, a condition that forbade them the often fragmentary and contradictory realities of an emotional life. No wonder then that *The Wrongs of Woman; or Maria* seems so uncertain and remains unfinished; the emotional realities and deep desires of its heroine are in many ways taboo within the very system Wollstonecraft advocated for women's liberation from societal constraints.

[28] Ibid., 110-11.

In the most recent wave of reassessment for the novel, Wollstonecraft emerges as more deliberate in her narrative technique, her earlier "mistakes" now read as "startlingly innovative" by one influential critic.[29] Not surprisingly, this shift is accompanied by a de-emphasis on the relationship with Henry Darnford, so often taken to be the figure of Imlay. Rather, it is the mother-daughter pairing that now emerges as the heart of the work and female alliance where Wollstonecraft's truly revolutionary "romance" takes place. In these readings, we are reminded that Wollstonecraft writes this work not while recovering from her breakup with Imlay, or while in the throes of her affair with Godwin, but while pregnant with her daughter, Mary—her pregnancy, the period of her lying-in or so-called "confinement" roughly coinciding with the composition of the novel. In this context, what were once the novel's limitations become its virtues. We no longer see Wollstonecraft through the prism of her failed relationships, and desires that are inconsistent with those professed by Wollstonecraft herself. Rather, we see her through the prism of those desires deeply entwined with the values, and even the body, of Wollstonecraft herself—her love for her children.

As Claudia Johnson argues, there is a "turn toward the female body" in *The Wrongs of Woman; or Maria* and a corresponding turn away from "the emancipatory potential of republican masculinity" promoted in *A Vindication of the Rights of Woman*.[30] This reading does mean that this novel remains significantly inconsistent with the philosophical text that inspired it, but in ways that we can view as progressive. If Wollstonecraft had to deny the female body in the earlier work to claim an equalizing gender neutrality, in this novel she makes that body with all its specificity of femaleness paramount: the image of maternal

---

[29] Claudia Johnson, "Mary Wollstonecraft's Novels" in *The Cambridge Companion to Mary Wollstonecraft* (Cambridge: Cambridge University Press, 2002), 207.
[30] Johnson, "Mary Wollstonecraft: Styles of Radical Maternity" in *Inventing Maternity: Politics, Science, and Literature 1650-1865*, ed. Susan Greenfield and Carol Barash (Lexington: University of Kentucky Press, 1999), 162.

breastfeeding that introduces the novel is one of "a body that can only be female."[31] The shift is profound. Maria does not give up her quest for emancipation (that *is* the novel's central plot device), but thus inscribed as female, she must seek it in "solidarity with other women" and not, as often seemed the case in *Vindication of the Rights of Woman*, in opposition to them. What emerges then is the possibility of a happy ending. Significantly, however, it is not one that unites Maria with Darnford, but one that unites Maria with her friend and protector, Jemima, and the lost daughter, now miraculously recovered. Female alliance replaces the heterosexual couple as the imaginative construct that can liberate the rational and feeling female.

Johnson's assessment seems quite a far cry from the original reviews of this work, which insisted on reading the novel as an exposé of Wollstonecraft's own romantic entanglements and philosophy. By divorcing the novel from its original reading and the figure of Imlay himself, what Wollstonecraft envisioned for this work can be realized. It is not an unfinished novel replete with contradictions, but rather a calculated experiment in matrilineal thinking that rewrites the romance narrative itself.

Ironically, this latest assessment of *The Wrongs of Woman* corresponds with the vision of Wollstonecraft so central to Godwin's *Memoirs*. In *The Memoirs*, he claims that if she had lived, her virtues as a mother would have made her reputation. As mentioned earlier, he saw her becoming an authority on the management of children, and he included excerpts in *The Post-humous Works* from her elliptically-written, and playfully nonsensical "lessons" to prove this point. Even his so-called clinical detachment can be read as paying homage to the specifically female body, i.e., maternal body, so fundamental to the objectives of *The Wrongs of Woman*. As the reviewer from *The Monthly Mirror* explains it, such attention to the aftermath of childbirth and its effect on the female body went beyond proper knowledge: "Surely it is not necessary in a plain simple biographical

[31] Ibid., 162.

composition to alarm one's readers with a recital of circumstances not immediately understood by every head."[32] Thus, in providing this detail, he makes "real a body that can only be female," as Johnson describes it, against the dictates of both his conservative and radical critics who would have preferred to remember only the contested logic of her philosophical work. Indeed, one of his most powerful closing images is one of maternal breastfeeding, the activity with which Wollstonecraft chooses to begin *The Wrongs of Woman*. When Wollstonecraft's fever makes it impossible for her to nurse her infant, puppies are brought in both to ease the pressure of her milk and to insure a continued supply. The absurdity of the situation is not lost on either one of them and they share a moment of laughter. For contemporary reviewers, it must have seemed an inappropriate detail. But for how it speaks to their similar sensibilities and their common commitment to the value of breastfeeding, it suggests that they also shared a vision of what was important, even at this awkward moment, in the political and emotional life of the author of *A Vindication of the Rights of Woman*. Godwin's text did comment on Wollstonecraft's, only not in the singular way that the original reviewers of these two works imagined.

It was precisely Godwin's focus on the body, and in particular the female body, that made contemporary reviewers as well as his friends uncomfortable. He had, as Robert Southey famously accused him, "stripp[ed] his dead wife naked." [33] As Helen Buss argues, this focus on the *female* body was what made his text doomed to initial, albeit "inadvertent failure": "Godwin's mistake was a generic one; he seems to have genuinely believed that he could make a public 'life' of a female person." As Buss explains, a "woman can only have a private existence," having the status—as William Epstein argues—of "a cultural outlaw" and hence proving an unworkable subject for "biographical recognition." [34] With Godwin's frank revelations, Wollstonecraft's

---

[32] *The Monthly Mirror*, vol. 5 (1798): 153.
[33] Quoted in St. Clair, *The Godwins and the Shelleys*, 224.
[34] Helen Buss, "Memoirs Discourse and William Godwin's *Memoirs of the Author*

criminalization in the public eye was quick. For example, *The Anti-Jacobin* indexed its review of this work under "Prostitution: see Mary Wollstonecraft." Once Godwin chose to go public with her story, her status as a "cultural outlaw" was determined.

But if earlier critics saw this choice as either the honorable mistake of a grief-ridden husband or the less honorable one of an amoral philosopher, recent reassessments find it "revolutionary." For Richard Holmes, *The Memoirs* marks a crucial moment in the history of biography: the emergence of the genre's independence from mere memorializing of the subject to objective examination of the person in question.[35] That Wollstonecraft is Godwin's wife makes only more remarkable his courage in exposing the complexities of her character. Moreover, Godwin remains true to his reading of Wollstonecraft even after the initial bout of criticism. In the changes made to the second edition, published the same year as the first, "he removed nothing," writes Holmes, "of real significance from Wollstonecraft's story, and made no attempt to modify his account of her social and political beliefs." For this candor, even in the face of hostile views and criticism, Holmes awards this work an eminent position in the genre of biography and in Godwin's own canon: "In no other subsequent work … did he write with such daring against the conventions of the age."[36] By separating the *literary* effect of this work from its effect on Wollstonecraft's reputation, the value of *The Memoirs* can be reclaimed.

Yet even within the current positive reassessment of this work,

---

of 'A Vindication of the Rights of Woman'" in *Mary Wollstonecraft and Mary Shelley: Writing Lives*, 122.

[35] Holmes's comment fails to take into account the biographies written by Samuel Johnson, composed previous to *The Memoirs*, which also objectively evaluated their subject. Johnson's biographies, however, had far less claim to the personal than Godwin's does. James Boswell's *Life of Johnson* (1787) does combine the personal and impersonal in a manner similar, although not identical, to Godwin's work.

[36] Introduction to *A Short Residence in Sweden, Norway and Denmark* and *Memoirs of an Author of "A Vindication of the Rights of Woman*, ed. Richard Holmes (New York: Penguin Books, 1987), 48.

The Memoirs remains, as Mitzi Myers puts it, "an usual hybrid" in large part because the life of Wollstonecraft and Godwin cannot be readily divided.[37] Buss, for example, writes admiringly of this work, but what she finds "classic" about its form is Godwin's inability to divorce himself from the text. Godwin may be able to resist modifying his wife's actions and character, yet he cannot hold back from defending some of his own behaviors. Writing the memoir rather than a biography necessarily compromises his "objective" stance, as he is a participant in the story he tells. These confessions, both planned and inadvertent, may initially "strip" Wollstonecraft of her power to persuade, but "in the long run," according to Buss, they produce a powerful and revealing portrayal of *both* authors: "The memoir allows this highly complex, often unsatisfying, but very materially real human condition to exist without resolution, and in doing so it empowers readers to participate in the struggle of the contradictory but coexisting stances."[38]

Tillotama Rajan takes this argument even further. The personal assessments and revelations of *The Memoirs* do not "strip" Wollstonecraft of her persuasive power. They rather strengthen it. She argues that this work "has also made possible our own reassessment of Wollstonecraft and how she figures in the political unconscious."[39] Telling all those details about Imlay that late eighteenth-century society deemed "he shouldn't have," for example, allowed the recovery of the passionate, private Wollstonecraft from the partial truth of her public, rationalist face. Only in Godwin's account and in its "twin text" *The Posthumous Works* does the radical doubleness of her feminism fully emerge. In both, Rajan argues, Godwin views Wollstonecraft as "a subject-in-process whose life and ideas are unfinished,"[40] a

---

[37] Mitzi Myers, "Godwin's Memoirs of Wollstonecraft: The Shaping of Self and Subject," *Studies in Romanticism* 20 (1981): 300.

[38] Buss, 119.

[39] Tillotama Rajan, "Framing the Corpus: Godwin's 'Editing' of Wollstonecraft in 1798," *Studies in Romanticism* 39 (2000): 513.

[40] Rajan, 513-14.

reading of Wollstonecraft that can explain and even elevate her so-called inconsistencies. Hence, we need read neither work as "naïve" in its choices, but rather as expert in providing testimony to the fluidity of Wollstonecraft's intelligence and the constant evolution of her ideas. Nor should we lament that neither text has had a fully independent life; their profound symmetry reinforces the individual power of each.

Remarkably, the most recent "reviews" of *The Memoirs* evoke in many ways its initial ones, in that critics unapologetically wed the work of these two writers. But in these "reviews," the "marriage" of these two writers—from both a literal and figurative point of view—is not viewed as a source of scandal but of promise. As was the case in the past, critics continue to note Godwin's positive influence on Wollstonecraft as both a literary model and a thinker. Yet in what marks a significant shift from the earlier assessments, critics point to Wollstonecraft's belated salutary influence on him. Godwin himself, at the conclusion of *The Memoirs,* initially insists on their radical difference as thinkers. In terms that evoke cliché representations of the male and female, he argues that he is the more reasonable one, interested in "metaphysical distinction" and impatient with deception, and she is more a creature of feeling, of spontaneous intuition. This clichéd division would typically make him the superior, yet in a more surprising move, he writes that he regrets not only his personal loss, but also the loss of her example and opportunity for "improvement." Not long after composing *The Memoirs,* Godwin went even further in questioning the division between reason and feeling. He grew suspicious of the artificial distinction between reason and affection, acknowledging that his own logic in *The Enquiry Concerning Political Justice* had been "defective, in … not yielding a proper attention to the empire of feeling."[41] He reverses a key component of that work, making domestic affection and marriage not the worst of associations but instead the best. But as Myers argues, we can find in *The Mem-*

---

[41] Quoted in Myers, 310.

oirs themselves evidence of the very sensibility that he admired in Wollstonecraft; his own imagination and empathy as a writer already breaks down the differences between their characters. His ability to apprehend and convey Wollstonecraft's "intellectual beauty," the ability he ascribes to her, is what ultimately makes his portrait so moving.

The connections between these two writers and these two texts were initially destructive to their reputations in general. Wollstonecraft was first villainized, and then deliberately ignored for nearly a century. Godwin's political thought increasingly became "marginalized," the vulnerabilities he exposed in this text making it easy for some to ignore the rigor of his ideas. Their pairing prompted only the most superficial of observations and led readers to dismiss rather than pursue any meaningful connection. Outside of that immediate context, we can now pursue connections, and the effect of doing so may be to strengthen both their reputations. If nothing else, this pairing can teach us to question the line between reason and feeling, between scandalous iconoclasm and radical promise of change. It can help us appreciate the truly revolutionary effect of their remarkable "marriage" of minds.

III

My choices as an editor seek to reproduce the context in which these two works would have been read originally and, at the same time, remain true to both authors' intentions in crafting the texts. Pairing these works is the obvious first step in constructing such a context. Yet other features of this volume emphasize how interconnected they were for late eighteenth-century readers. I include several contemporary reviews at the back of the book in order to provide a full sense of their respective receptions.

The texts would also have been read in the context of the previous works of both authors, most significantly the philosophical works that had made their reputations, *A Vindication of the Rights of Woman* (1792) and *An Enquiry Concerning Political Justice* (1793). Several text boxes include excerpts from these trea-

tises. Two are from *A Vindication of the Rights of Woman* and
address two concepts central to Wollstonecraft's argument for
women's equity in civil society and her own evolution as a thinker.
"On Reason, Madness, and Folly" looks at how Wollstonecraft
uses reason as the mechanism for women's improvement and for
providing full equity in society, and "On Love and Sensibility"
examines her more conflicted attitude toward the role of sensibility. Godwin's condemnation of marriage in the 1793 edition
of *The Enquiry* is also included and is entitled "On Co-habitation, Love and Fidelity."

Gilbert Imlay, Wollstonecraft's former lover, would also have
been much in the minds of the contemporary readers of these
two works. Hence, I have included a text box exploring his connection to the figure of Henry Darnford in *The Wrongs of Woman*
and his own reputation as a writer and renowned "American."
Somewhat controversially, I have also included a long excerpt from
his novel, *The Emigrants* (1793), published during the first year
of his and Wollstonecraft's courtship. This excerpt includes a plot
remarkably similar to that of *The Wrongs of Woman*. Through a
series of letters, we learn of the unhappy marriage of Eliza, whose
drunken husband arranges for her prostitution. Unlike Maria,
however, Eliza is delivered from this difficult situation by the
death of her husband and the promise of future happiness in
America. Both the similarities and differences between these two
plots are useful for a discussion of Wollstonecraft and Imlay's
politics. They clearly shared political and ideological sympathies,
and a recognition that civil tyrannies complicated a woman's life.[42]

[42] At least two critics have argued that Wollstonecraft wrote *The Emigrants*.
Robert Hare in his 1964 introduction to *The Emigrants* argues that the novel is
too ignorant of American geography and culture to be written by an American
such as Gilbert Imlay, and hence must be written by Wollstonecraft. More
recently, John Cole argues that the novel is too knowledgeable about the plight of
Englishwomen to have been written by an American such as Gilbert Imlay, and
hence must have been written by Wollstonecraft. See Robert Hare, Introduction
to *The Emigrants* (Gainesville: Scholars' Facsimile Press, 1964) and John Cole,
"Imlay's 'Ghost': Wollstonecraft's Authorship of *The Emigrants*," *Eighteenth-Century Women: Studies in Their Lives, Work, and Culture* 1 (2001): 263-98.

As these essays seek to reconstruct the original context, others seek to recover the original intentions of the authors. As Wollstonecraft makes clear in her preface, she intends her novel to tell the story of all women and not simply her own. Her plot consistently directs the reader's attention to the social, political, and economic conditions that affect women's opportunities. Hence, several text boxes address these concerns, including ones on employment opportunities for lower- and middle-class women and the inequities of eighteenth-century marriage law. Maternal breastfeeding was also central to Wollstonecraft's political agenda to empower the domestic woman; in order to explain what made her position radical, I include a text box on contemporary attitudes toward the practice. The text boxes on *A Vindication of the Rights of Woman* also help the modern reader see how the novel builds upon the philosophical tract.

Godwin wanted to pay homage to Wollstonecraft's work and accomplishments. Hence, throughout *The Memoirs*, I include excerpts from various texts of Wollstonecraft, including *Mary: A Fiction* and *Letters Written During A Short Residence*. The text box on the realities of childbirth in the late eighteenth century helps to explain the utter shock of her death for both Godwin and the contemporary reader; even at a time when mortality rates in childbirth were far higher than they are now, her death due to complications arising from childbirth would have been seen as tragic.

Finally, the cover of this volume is intended to reproduce the original context. As the frontispiece of *The Posthumous Works,* Godwin selected the portrait of Wollstonecraft painted by John Opie in 1797 while she was pregnant with their daughter. For Godwin, it was an obvious choice because this same portrait served as his inspiration when he wrote *The Memoirs*. Not long after Wollstonecraft died, Godwin took this portrait and hung it in her study. While ensconced in that room and presumably looking from time to time at this portrait, he composed *The Memoirs*. This was the Wollstonecraft he saw. The cover of this volume reinforces the significance of that originating vision.

SELECT BIBLIOGRAPHY

Wollstonecraft and Godwin
Butler, Marilyn. ed., *Burke, Paine, Godwin, and the Revolution Controversy*. Cambridge University Press, 1984.
Rajan, Tilottama. "Wollstonecraft and Godwin: Reading the Secrets of the Political Novel." *Studies in Romanticism* 27:2 (Summer 1988): 221-251.
St. Clair, William. *The Godwins and the Shelleys: A Biography of a Family*. Baltimore: Johns Hopkins University Press, 1989.
Trott, Nicola. "Sexing the Critic: Mary Wollstonecraft at the Turn of the Century. *1798: The Year of the Lyrical Ballads*. New York: St. Martin's Press, 1998.

Wollstonecraft
Jacobus, Mary. "The Difference of View." *Women Writing and Writing about Women*. Ed. Mary Jacobus. New York: Barnes and Nobel, 1979.
Johnson, Claudia. *Equivocal Beings: Politics, Gender and Sentimentality in the 1790s, Wollstonecraft, Radcliffe, Burney, Austen*. Chicago: University of Chicago Press, 1995.
—. "Mary Wollstonecraft: Styles of Radical Maternity." *Inventing Maternity: Politics, Science, and Literature, 1650-1865*. Eds. Susan C. Greenfield and Carol Barash. Lexington: University of Kentucky Press, 1999.
—. Ed. *The Cambridge Companion to Mary Wollstonecraft*. Cambridge: Cambridge University Press, 2002.
Kaplan, Cora. "Wild Nights: pleasure/sexuality/feminism." *The Ideology of Conduct: Essays in Literature and the History of Sexuality*. Eds. Nancy Armstrong and Leonard Tennenhouse. New York: Methuen, 1987.
Kelly, Gary. *Revolutionary Feminism: the Mind and Career of Mary Wollstonecraft*. New York: St. Martin's Press, 1992.
Langbauer, Laurie. *Women and Romance: The Consolations of Gender in the English Novel*. Ithaca; Cornell University Press, 1990.

Poovey, Mary. *The Proper Lady and the Woman Writer: Ideology as Style in the Works of Mary Wollstonecraft, Mary Shelley, and Jane Austen.* Chicago: University of Chicago Press, 1984.

Sapiro, Virginia. *A Vindication of Political Virtue: The Political Theory of Mary Wollstonecraft.* Chicago: University of Chicago Press, 1992.

Todd, Janet. *Mary Wollstonecraft; A Revolutionary Life.* New York: Columbia University Press, 2000.

Tomalin, Claire. *The Life and Death of Mary Wollstonecraft.* New York: Meridian, 1974.

Godwin

Buss, Helen. "Memoirs Discourse and William Godwin's 'Memoir of the Author of a Vindication of the Rights of Woman'." *Mary Wollstonecraft and Mary Shelley: Writing Lives.* Waterloo, ON: Wilfrid Laurier University Press, 2001.

Myers, Mitzi. "Godwin's Memoirs of Wollstonecraft: The Shaping of Self and Subject." *Studies in Romanticism.* 20:3 (Fall 1981): 299-316.

Rajan, Tilottama. 'Framing the Corpus" Godwin's 'Editing' of Wollstonecraft in 1798. *Studies in Romanticism.* 39:4 (Winter 2000): 511-31.

POSTHUMOUS WORKS

OF THE

AUTHOR

OF A

VINDICATION OF THE RIGHTS OF WOMAN.

IN FOUR VOLUMES.

VOL. L

LONDON:

PRINTED FOR J. JOHNSON, NO. 72, ST. PAUL'S
CHURCH-YARD; AND G. G. AND J. ROBINSON,
PATERNOSTER-ROW.
1798

Title page of *Posthumous Works of the Author of "A Vindication of the Rights of Woman,"* 1798.

C O N T E N T S.

VOL. I. AND II.

The Wrongs of Woman, or Maria; a Fragment: to which is added, the First Book of a Series of Lessons for Children.

VOL. III. AND IV.

Letters and Miscellaneous Pieces.

Contents page of *Posthumous Works of the Author of "A Vindication of the Rights of Woman,"* Volumes I-IV.

PREFACE

The public are here presented with the last literary attempt of an author, whose fame has been uncommonly extensive, and whose talents have probably been most admired, by the persons by whom talents are estimated with the greatest accuracy and discrimination. There are few, to whom her writings could in any case have given pleasure, that would have wished that this fragment should have been suppressed, because it is a fragment. There is a sentiment, very dear to minds of taste and imagination, that finds a melancholy delight in contemplating these unfinished productions of genius, these sketches of what, if they had been filled up in a manner adequate to the writer's conception, would perhaps have given a new impulse to the manners of a world.

The purpose and structure of the following work, had long formed a favourite subject of meditation with its author, and she judged them capable of producing an important effect. The composition had been in progress for a period of twelve months. She was anxious to do justice to her conception, and recommenced and revised the manuscript several different times. So much of it as is here given to the public, she was far from considering as finished, and, in a letter to a friend directly written on the subject, she says, "I am perfectly aware that some of the incidents ought to be transposed, and heightened by a more harmonious shading; and I wished in some degree to avail myself of criticism, before I began to adjust my events into a story, the outline of which I had sketched in my mind* ." The only friends to whom the author communicated her manuscript, were

* A more copious extract of this letter is subjoined to the author's preface [Godwin's note].

Mr. Dyson[1], the translator of the Sorcerer, and the present editor; and it was impossible for the most experienced author to display a stronger desire of profiting by the censures and sentiments that might be suggested.

In revising these sheets for the press, it was necessary for the editor, in some places, to connect the more finished parts with the pages of an older copy, and a line or two in addition sometimes appeared requisite for that purpose. Whenever such a liberty has been taken, the additional phrases will be found inclosed in brackets; it being the editor's most earnest desire, to intrude nothing of himself into the work, but to give to the public the words, as well as ideas, of the real author.

What follows in the ensuing pages, is not a preface regularly drawn out by the author, but merely hints for a preface, which, though never filled up in the manner the writer intended, appeared to be worth preserving.

W. Godwin

---

[1] George Dyson (d. 1822); friend of William Godwin, amateur painter, translator, and addressee of the letter included in the author's preface. He did not respond favorably to an earlier draft of the novel.

AUTHOR'S PREFACE

The Wrongs of Woman, like the wrongs of the oppressed part of mankind, may be deemed necessary by their oppressors: but surely there are a few, who will dare to advance before the improvement of the age, and grant that my sketches are not the abortion of a distempered fancy, or the strong delineations of a wounded heart.

In writing this novel, I have rather endeavoured to pourtray the passions than manners.

In many instances I could have made the incidents more dramatic, would I have sacrificed my main object, the desire of exhibiting the misery and oppression, peculiar to women, that arise out of the partial laws and customs of society.

In the invention of the story, this view restrained my fancy; and the history ought rather to be considered, as of woman, than of an individual.

The sentiments I have embodied.

In many works of this species, the hero is allowed to be mortal, and to become wise and virtuous as well as happy, by a train of events and circumstances. The heroines, on the contrary, are to be born immaculate; and to act like goddesses of wisdom, just come forth highly finished Minervas from the head of Jove. [1]

---

[1] The Roman goddess, Minerva (in Greek mythology known as Athene) emerged fully grown, armed, and "with a mighty shout" from the head of Jove (known in Greek mythology as Zeus). Zeus had earlier swallowed her mother Metis (wisdom) whole in order to avoid a prophecy that her son would depose him. When Zeus later suffers from a headache, Hermes cracks his skull and out emerges Athene [Robert Graves, *The Greek Myths: I* (New York: Penguin, 1955), 46].

[The following is an extract of a letter from the author to a friend, to whom she communicated her manuscript.]

For my part, I cannot suppose any situation more distressing, than for a woman of sensibility, with an improving mind, to be bound to such a man as I have described for life; obliged to renounce all the humanizing affections, and to avoid cultivating her taste, lest her perception of grace and refinement of sentiment, should sharpen to agony the pangs of disappointment. Love, in which the imagination mingles its bewitching colouring, must be fostered by delicacy. I should despise, or rather call her an ordinary woman, who could endure such a husband as I have sketched.

These appear to me (matrimonial despotism of heart and conduct) to be the peculiar Wrongs of Woman, because they degrade the mind. What are termed great misfortunes, may more forcibly impress the mind of common readers; they have more of what may justly be termed *stage-effect*; but it is the delineation of finer sensations, which, in my opinion, constitutes the merit of our best novels. This is what I have in view; and to show the wrongs of different classes of women, equally oppressive, though, from the difference of education, necessarily various.

Wrongs of Woman

Chapter 1

Abodes of horror have frequently been described, and castles, filled with specters and chimeras, conjured up by the magic spell of genius to harrow the soul, and absorb the wondering mind. But, formed of such stuff as dreams are made of, what were they to the mansion of despair, in one corner of which Maria sat, endeavouring to recall her scattered thoughts![1]

Surprise, astonishment, that bordered on distraction, seemed to have suspended her faculties, till, waking by degrees to a keen sense of anguish, a whirlwind of rage and indignation roused her torpid pulse. One recollection with frightful velocity following another, threatened to fire her brain, and make her a fit companion for the terrific inhabitants, whose groans and shrieks were no unsubstantial sounds of whistling winds, or startled birds, modulated by a romantic fancy, which amuse while they affright; but such tones of misery as carry a dreadful certainty directly to the heart. What effect must they then have produced on one, true to the touch of sympathy, and tortured by maternal apprehension!

Her infant's image was continually floating on Maria's sight, and the first smile of intelligence remembered, as none but a mother, an unhappy mother, can conceive. She heard her half speaking half cooing, and felt the little twinkling fingers on her burning bosom—a bosom bursting with the nutriment for which

---

[1] Wollstonecraft makes reference to the vogue for Gothic novels which reached its greatest height in the 1790s and whose fantastic and supernatural plots often took place within the confines of decrepit castles.

this cherished child might now be pining in vain. From a stranger she could indeed receive the maternal aliment, Maria was grieved at the thought—but who would watch her with a mother's tenderness, a mother's self-denial?

MATERNAL BREASTFEEDING

Although somewhat casually addressed in the above paragraph and easy for the modern reader to miss, this reference to maternal breastfeeding would have been highly charged for Wollstonecraft's contemporary readers. Wollstonecraft's insistence on the value of this practice for both the physical and emotional well-being of mother and child would have put her squarely on the side of the medical establishment. Ruth Perry notes that around mid-century, "Medical treatises multiplied on the subject of maternal breast-feeding, urging women to nurse their own children for a variety of medical, social, and psychological reasons....The medical establishment seemed determined to convince women to nurse their own children—for their own sakes, for the health of their children, and often for the good of the nation" (310). This medical advice differed greatly from standard practice in the seventeenth and early eighteenth century, where most middle class and upper class children were assigned to the care of wet-nurses. Maria's obvious disdain for this earlier practice marks her as an "enlightened" woman of the late eighteenth century, but not necessarily an atypical one. As Perry also notes, by the later end of this century, medical treatises had begun to gloat over their success, "observ[ing] that maternal breast-feeding had become a new social expectation for women" (313). According to Toni Bowers, men, rather than women, may have been responsible for this success: "By the 1750s...many fathers had been convinced that, for a variety of material and economic reasons, maternal breastfeeding was preferable to sending a child out to a nurse or even hiring a nurse at home....Accordingly, reluctant mothers were as likely to be pressured *to* breastfeed as formerly they had been forbidden *from* it" (142). Hence, Maria's casual reference to a "burning breast" would have carried with it the force of a cultural mandate, one that "naturalized" an imperative to breastfeed and led to an increased emphasis on the significance of motherhood and the role of the family.

Yet for readers of Wollstonecraft, the context would have been more immediate. Although the above passage associates maternal breastfeeding with a "mother's self-denial," for Wollstonecraft, it is clearly an empowering practice. In *Vindication of the Rights of Woman*, it emerges as both a corrective to women's debilitating vanity and as a new source of sexual appeal. Wollstonecraft writes:

> Cold would be the heart of a husband, were he not rendered unnatural by early debauchery, who did not feel more delight at seeing his child suckled by its mother, than the most artful tricks could ever raise; yet this natural way of cementing the matrimonial tie, and twisting esteem with fonder recollections, wealth leads women to spurn. To preserve their beauty and wear the flowery crown of the day, which gives them a kind of right to reign for a short time over the sex, they neglect to stamp impressions on their husbands' hearts, that would be remembered with more tenderness when the snow on the head began to chill the bosom, than even their virgins charms. (212-13)

Breastfeeding affords women a "natural" power over their husbands, and indeed their families. It is precisely this management of the family that justifies the cultivation of women's reason.

SOURCES

Toni Bowers, " A Point of Conscience": Breastfeeding and Maternal Authority in *Pamela*, Part 2," in *Inventing Maternity: Politics, Science, and Literature 1650-1865*. Edited by Susan C. Greenfield and Carol Barash. Lexington: University of Kentucky Press, 1999. 138-158. Ruth Perry, "Colonizing the Breast: Sexuality and Maternity in Eighteenth-Century England," in *British Literature 1640-1789*. Edited by Robert DeMaria, Jr. Oxford: Blackwell Publishers Inc., 1999. 302-332. Mary Wollstonecraft. *The Works of Mary Wollstonecraft* Vol. 5. Edited by Janet Todd and Marilyn Butler. New York: New York University Press, 1989.

The retreating shadows of former sorrows rushed back in a gloomy train, and seemed to be pictured on the walls of her prison, magnified by the state of mind in which they were viewed—Still she mourned for her child, lamented she was a daughter, and anticipated the aggravated ills of life that her sex rendered almost inevitable, even while dreading she was no more. To think that she was blotted out of existence was agony, when the imagination had been long employed to expand her faculties; yet to suppose her turned adrift on an unknown sea, was scarcely less afflicting.

After being two days the prey of impetuous, varying emotions, Maria began to reflect more calmly on her present situation, for she had actually been rendered incapable of sober reflection, by the discovery of the act of atrocity of which she was the victim. She could not have imagined, that, in all the fermentation of civilized depravity, a similar plot could have entered a human mind. She had been stunned by an unexpected blow; yet life, however joyless, was not to be indolently resigned, or misery endured without exertion, and proudly termed patience. She had hitherto meditated only to point the dart of anguish, and suppressed the heart heavings of indignant nature merely by the force of contempt. Now she endeavoured to brace her mind to fortitude, and to ask herself what was to be her employment in her dreary cell? Was it not to effect her escape, to fly to the succour of her child, and to baffle the selfish schemes of her tyrant—her husband?

These thoughts roused her sleeping spirit, and the self-possession returned, that seemed to have abandoned her in the infernal solitude into which she had been precipitated. The first emotions of overwhelming impatience began to subside, and resentment gave place to tenderness, and more tranquil meditation; though anger once more stopt the calm current of reflection, when she attempted to move her manacled arms. But this was an outrage that could only excite momentary feelings of scorn, which evaporated in a faint smile; for Maria was far from thinking a personal insult the most difficult to endure with magnanimous indifference.

She approached the small grated window of her chamber, and for a considerable time only regarded the blue expanse; though it commanded a view of a desolate garden, and of part of a huge pile of buildings, that, after having been suffered, for half a century, to fall to decay, had undergone some clumsy repairs, merely to render it habitable. The ivy had been torn off the turrets, and the stones not wanted to patch up the breaches of time, and exclude the warring elements, left in heaps in the disordered court. Maria contemplated this scene she knew not how long; or rather gazed on the walls, and pondered on her situation. To the master of this most horrid of prisons, she had, soon after her entrance, raved of injustice, in accents that would have justified his treatment, had not a malignant smile, when she appealed to his judgment, with a dreadful conviction stifled her remonstrating complaints. By force, or openly, what could be done? But surely some expedient might occur to an active mind, without any other employment, and possessed of sufficient resolution to put the risk of life into the balance with the chance of freedom.[2]

---

[2] The conditions Maria describes the cell-like room, her manacled arms, the grated window, and the decaying building—would not have been atypical for private madhouses of the period. Although there were exceptions to this charge, private asylums remained notorious throughout the century for "neglect and corruption" (148). Nor was atypical the charge of "wrongful confinement" (148). Until the Act for Regulating Private Madhouses (1774), these establishments

A woman entered into the midst of these reflections, with a firm, deliberate step, strongly marked features, and large black eyes, which she fixed steadily on Maria's, as if she designed to intimidate her, saying at the same time—"You had better sit down and eat your dinner, than look at the clouds."

"I have no appetite," replied Maria, who had previously determined to speak mildly; "why then should I eat?"

"But, in spite of that, you must and shall eat something. I have had many ladies under my care, who have resolved to starve themselves; but, soon or late, they gave up their intent, as they recovered their senses."

"Do you really think me mad?" asked Maria, meeting the searching glance of her eye.

"Not just now. But what does that prove?—only that you must be the more carefully watched, for appearing at times so reasonable. You have not touched a morsel since you entered the house."—Maria sighed intelligibly.—"Could any thing but madness produce such a disgust for food?"

"Yes, grief; you would not ask the question if you knew what it was." The attendant shook her head; and a ghastly smile of desperate fortitude served as a forcible reply, and made Maria pause, before she added—"Yet I will take some refreshment: I mean not to die.—No; I will preserve my senses; and convince even you, sooner than you are aware of, that my intellects have never been disturbed, though the exertion of them may have been suspended by some infernal drug."

Doubt gathered still thicker on the brow of her guard, as she attempted to convict her of mistake.

"Have patience!" exclaimed Maria, with a solemnity that inspired awe. "My God! how have I been schooled into the practice!" A suffocation of voice betrayed the agonizing emotions

were unregulated, and even after this act, suffered no penalty if abuses were detected. Stories of heiresses and unwanted spouses confined, even drugged, against their will were rampant during this period [Roy Porter, *Mind-Forg'd Manacles: A History of Madness in England from the Restoration to the Regency* (Cambridge: Harvard University Press, 1987)].

she was labouring to keep down; and conquering a qualm of disgust, she calmly endeavoured to eat enough to prove her docility, perpetually turning to the suspicious female, whose observation she courted, while she was making the bed and adjusting the room.

"Come to me often," said Maria, with a tone of persuasion, in consequence of a vague plan that she had hastily adopted, when, after surveying this woman's form and features, she felt convinced that she had an understanding above the common standard; "and believe me mad until, till you are obliged to acknowledge the contrary." The woman was no fool, that is, she was superior to her class; nor had misery quite petrified the life's-blood of humanity, to which reflections on our own misfortunes only give a more orderly course. The manner, rather than the expostulations, of Maria made a slight suspicion dart into her mind with corresponding sympathy, which various other avocations, and the habit of banishing compunction, prevented her, for the present, from examining more minutely.

But when she was told that no person, excepting the physician appointed by her family, was to be permitted to see the lady at the end of the gallery, she opened her keen eyes still wider, and uttered a—"hem!" before she enquired—"Why?" She was briefly told, in reply, that the malady was hereditary, and the fits not occurring but at very long and irregular intervals, she must be carefully watched; for the length of these lucid periods only rendered her more mischievous, when any vexation or caprice brought on the paroxysm of phrensy.

Had her master trusted her, it is probable that neither pity nor curiosity would have made her swerve from the straight line of her interest; for she had suffered too much in her intercourse with mankind, not to determine to look for support, rather to humouring their passions, than courting their approbation by the integrity of her conduct. A deadly blight had met her at the very threshold of existence; and the wretchedness of her mother seemed a heavy weight fastened on her innocent neck, to drag her down to perdition. She could not heroically determine to succour an unfortunate; but, offended at the bare supposition that she could be deceived with the same ease as a common servant, she no longer curbed her curiosity; and, though she never seriously fathomed her own intentions, she would sit, every moment she could steal from observation, listening to the tale, which Maria was eager to relate with all the persuasive eloquence of grief.

It is so cheering to see a human face, even if little of the divinity of virtue beam in it, that Maria anxiously expected the return of the attendant, as of a gleam of light to break the gloom of idleness. Indulged sorrow, she perceived, must blunt or sharpen the faculties to the two opposite extremes; producing stupidity, the moping melancholy of indolence; or the restless activity of a disturbed imagination. She sunk into one state, after being fatigued by the other: till the want of occupation became even more painful than the actual pressure or apprehension of sorrow; and the confinement that froze her into a nook of existence, with an unvaried prospect before her, the most insupportable of evils. The lamp of life seemed to be spending itself to chase the vapours of a dungeon which no art could dissipate.—And to what purpose did she rally all her energy?—Was not the world a vast prison, and woman born slaves?

Though she failed immediately to rouse a lively sense of injustice in the mind of her guard, because it had been sophisticated into misanthropy, she touched her heart. Jemima (she had only a claim to a Christian name, which had not procured her any Christian privileges) could patiently hear of Maria's confinement on false pretenses; she had felt the crushing hand of power, hardened by the exercise of injustice, and ceased to wonder at the perversions of the understanding, which systematize oppression; but, when told that her child, only four months old, had been torn from her, even while she was discharging the tenderest maternal office, the woman awoke in a bosom long estranged from feminine emotions, and Jemima determined to alleviate all in her power, without hazarding the loss of her place, the sufferings of a wretched mother, apparently injured, and certainly unhappy. A sense of right seems to result from the simplest act of reason, and to preside over the faculties of the mind, like the master sense of feeling, to rectify the rest; but (for the comparison may be carried still farther) how often is the exquisite sensibility of both weakened or destroyed by the vulgar occupations, and ignoble pleasures of life?

The preserving her situation was, indeed, an important object to Jemima, who had been hunted from hole to hole, as if she had been a beast of prey, or infected with a moral plague. The wages she received, the greater part of which she hoarded, as her only chance for independence, were much more considerable than she could reckon on obtaining any where else, were it possible that she, an outcast from society, could be permitted to earn a subsistence in a reputable family. Hearing Maria perpetually complain of listlessness, and the not being able to beguile grief by resuming her customary pursuits, she was easily prevailed on, by compassion, and that involuntary respect for abilities, which those who possess them can never eradicate, to bring her some books and implements for writing. Maria's conversation had amused and interested her, and the natural consequence was a desire, scarcely observed by herself, of obtaining the esteem of a person she admired. The remembrance of better days was rendered more lively; and the sentiments then acquired appearing less romantic than they had for a long period, a spark of hope roused her mind to new activity.

How grateful was her attention to Maria! Oppressed by a dead weight of existence, or preyed on by the gnawing worm of discontent, with what eagerness did she endeavour to shorten the long days, which left no traces behind! She seemed to be sailing on the vast ocean of life, without feeling any land-mark to indicate the progress of time; to find employment was then to find variety, the animating principle of nature.

CHAPTER II

Earnestly as Maria endeavoured to soothe, by reading, the anguish of her wounded mind, her thoughts would often wander from the subject she was led to discuss, and tears of maternal tenderness obscured the reasoning page. She descanted on "the ills which flesh is heir to,"[1] with bitterness, when the recollection of her babe was revived by a tale of fictitious woe, that bore any resemblance to her own; and her imagination was continually employed, to conjure up and embody the various phantoms of misery, which folly and vice had let loose on the world. The loss of her babe was the tender string; against other cruel remembrances she laboured to steel her bosom; and even a ray of hope, in the midst of her gloomy reveries, would sometimes gleam on the dark horizon of futurity, while persuading herself that she ought to cease to hope, since happiness was no where to be found.—But of her child, debilitated by the grief with which its mother had been assailed before it saw the light, she could not think without an impatient struggle.

"I, alone, by my active tenderness, could have saved," she would exclaim, "from an early blight, this sweet blossom; and, cherishing it, I should have had something still to love."

In proportion as other expectations were torn from her, this tender one had been fondly clung to, and knit into her heart.

The books she had obtained, were soon devoured, by one who had no other resource to escape from sorrow, and the feverish dreams of ideal wretchedness or felicity, which equally weaken the intoxicated sensibility. Writing was then the only alternative, and she wrote some rhapsodies descriptive of the state of

[1] *Hamlet*, III.i.62-3: "The heart-ache, and the thousand natural shocks/ That flesh is heir to."

her mind; but the events of her past life pressing on her, she resolved circumstantially to relate them, with the sentiments that experience, and more matured reason, would naturally suggest. They might perhaps instruct her daughter, and shield her from the misery, the tyranny, her mother knew not how to avoid.

This thought gave life to her diction, her soul flowed into it, and she soon found the task of recollecting almost obliterated impressions very interesting. She lived again in the revived emotions of youth, and forgot her present in the retrospect of sorrows that had assumed an unalterable character.

Though this employment lightened the weight of time, yet, never losing sight of her main object, Maria did not allow any opportunity to slip of winning on the affections of Jemima: for she discovered in her a strength of mind, that excited her esteem, clouded as it was by the misanthropy of despair.

An insulated being, from the misfortune of her birth, she[2] despised and preyed on the society by which she had been oppressed, and loved not her fellow-creatures, because she had never been beloved. No mother had ever fondled her, no father or brother had protected her from outrage; and the man who had plunged her into infamy, and deserted her when she stood in greatest need of support, deigned not to smooth with kindness the road to ruin. Thus degraded, was she let loose on the world; and virtue, never nurtured by affection, assumed the stern aspect of selfish independence.

This general view of her life, Maria gathered from her exclamations and dry remarks. Jemima indeed displayed a strange mixture of interest and suspicion; for she would listen to her with earnestness, and then suddenly interrupt the conversation, as if afraid of resigning, by giving way to her sympathy, her dear-bought knowledge of the world.

Maria alluded to the possibility of an escape, and mentioned a compensation, or reward; but the style in which she was repulsed made her cautious, and determine not to renew the sub-

---

[2] Jemima.

ject, till she knew more of the character she had to work on. Jemima's countenance, and dark hints, seemed to say, "You are an extraordinary woman; but let me consider, this may only be one of your lucid intervals." Nay, the very energy of Maria's character, made her suspect that the extraordinary animation she perceived might be the effect of madness. "Should her husband then substantiate his charge, and get possession of her estate, from whence would come the promised annuity, or more desired protection? Besides, might not a woman, anxious to escape, conceal some of the circumstances which made against her? Was truth to be expected from one who had been entrapped, kidnapped, in the most fraudulent manner?"

In this train Jemima continued to argue, the moment after compassion and respect seemed to make her swerve; and she still resolved not to be wrought on to do more than soften the rigour of confinement, till she could advance on surer ground.

Maria was not permitted to walk in the garden; but sometimes, from her window, she turned her eyes from the gloomy walls, in which she pined life away, on the poor wretches who strayed along the walks, and contemplated the most terrific of ruins—that of a human soul. What is the view of the fallen column, the mouldering arch, of the most exquisite workmanship,[3] when compared with this living memento of the fragility, the instability, of reason, and the wild luxuriancy of noxious passions? Enthusiasm turned adrift, like some rich stream overflowing its banks, rushes forward with destructive velocity, inspiring a sublime concentration of thought. Thus thought Maria—These are the ravages over which humanity must ever mournfully ponder, with a degree of anguish not excited by crumbling marble, or cankering brass, unfaithful to the trust of monumental fame. It is not over the decaying productions of the mind, embodied with the happiest art, we grieve most bitterly. The view of what has been done by man, produces a

---

[3] The reference is to the late eighteenth-century fad for viewing ruins in the landscape.

melancholy, yet aggrandizing, sense of what remains to be achieved by human intellect; but a mental convulsion, which, like the devastation of an earthquake, throws all the elements of thought and imagination into confusion, makes contemplation giddy, and we fearfully ask on what ground we ourselves stand.

Melancholy and imbecility marked the features of the wretches allowed to breathe at large; for the frantic, those who in a strong imagination had lost a sense of woe, were closely confined. The playful tricks and mischievous devices of their disturbed fancy, that suddenly broke out, could not be guarded against, when they were permitted to enjoy any portion of freedom; for, so active was their imagination, that every new object which accidentally struck their senses, awoke to phrenzy their restless passions; as Maria learned from the burden of their incessant ravings.

Sometimes, with a strict injunction of silence, Jemima would allow Maria, at the close of evening, to stray along the narrow avenues that separated the dungeon-like apartments, leaning on her arm. What a change of scene! Maria wished to pass the threshold of her prison, yet, when by chance she met the eye of rage glaring on her, yet unfaithful to its office, she shrunk back with more horror and affright, than if she had stumbled over a mangled corpse. Her busy fancy pictured the misery of a fond heart, watching over a friend thus estranged, absent, though present—over a poor wretch lost to reason and the social joys of existence; and losing all consciousness of misery in its excess. What a task, to watch the light of reason quivering in the eye, or with agonizing expectation to catch the beam of recollection; tantalized by hope, only to feel despair more keenly, at finding a much loved face or voice, suddenly remembered, or pathetically implored, only to be immediately forgotten, or viewed with indifference or abhorrence!

The heart-rending sigh of melancholy sunk into her soul; and when she retired to rest, the petrified figures she had encountered, the only human forms she was doomed to observe, haunting her dreams with tales of mysterious wrongs, made her wish to sleep to dream no more.

ON REASON, MADNESS AND FOLLY:
FROM *A VINDICATION OF THE RIGHTS OF WOMAN*

As the title suggests, the *Wrongs of Woman* evokes Wollstonecraft's most famous work, indeed the one that made her reputation, *A Vindication of the Rights of Woman* (1792). In seeking to give narrative form to this philosophical treatise, Wollstonecraft follows a practice begun successfully by her then husband, William Godwin (and the author of the *Memoirs*). His *Caleb Williams* (1794) used the novel form, and in particular the gothic conventions of an emotionally-sensitive, pursued hero(ine) and an oppressive, ever-pursuing villain, to expose the political injustices in England and to illustrate the precepts of his far dryer, but influential *Enquiry Concerning Political Justice* (1793). Nowhere does Wollstonecraft use this form more effectively than in her evocation of the madhouse to illustrate the effects of denying reason to women. For Wollstonecraft, the rights of women rested upon their inherent capacity to reason, the cultivation of which—she argues—society had denied them. Her *Vindication* focused on the negative effects of that denial, so grave as to lead potentially to "madness and folly." She writes:

> In short, women, in general, as well as the rich of both sexes, have acquired all the follies and vices of civilization, and missed the useful fruit. ... Their senses are inflamed, and their understandings neglected, consequently they become the prey of their senses, delicately termed sensibility, and are blown about by every momentary gust of feeling. Civilized women are, therefore, so weakened by false refinement, that respecting morals, their condition is much below what it would be were they left in a state nearer to nature. Ever restless and anxious, their over exercised sensibility not only renders them uncom-

fortable to themselves, but troublesome, to use a soft phrase, to others. All their thoughts turn on things calculated to excite emotion; and feeling, when they should reason, their conduct is unstable, and their opinions are wavering—not the wavering produced by deliberation or progressive views, but by contradictory emotions. By fits and starts they are warm in many pursuits; yet this warmth, never concentrated into perseverance, soon exhausts itself; exhaled by its own heat, or meeting with some other fleeting passion, to which reason has never given specific gravity, neutrality ensues. Miserable indeed, must be that being whose cultivation of mind has only tended to inflame its passions! A distinction should be made between inflaming and strengthening them. The passions thus pampered, whilst the judgment is left uninformed, what can be expected to ensue?—Undoubtedly, a mixture of madness and folly!(129-130)

Maria's description then of those "poor wretch[es] lost to reason" makes concrete what Wollstonecraft deemed the fate of all women denied a proper education.

Yet as the title also suggests, Wollstonecraft shifts her focus in this novel. By employing the gothic form and its convention of an emotionally-sensitive heroine besought by *real* danger, she shifts attention from the wrongs done by women (deprived of reason) to the wrongs done *to* women. Compare, for example, Maria's obvious concern for her fellow inmates of the madhouse with the description that comes only a few paragraphs after the passage just cited. In *A Vindication*, the dangers are only imagined:

Fragile in every sense of the word, they are obliged to look up to man for every comfort. In the most trifling dangers they cling to their support, with parasitical tenacity, piteously demanding succour; and their *natural* protector extends his arm, or lifts up his voice, to guard the lovely trembler—from

what? Perhaps the frown of an old cow, or the jump
of a mouse; a rat, would be a serious danger. In the
name of reason, and even common sense, what can
save such beings from contempt; even though they
be soft and fair?

These fears, when not affected, may produce
some pretty attitudes; but they shew a degree of
imbecility which degrades a rational creature in a
way women are not aware of—for love and esteem
are very distinct things. (131)

In *The Wrongs of Woman*, Wollstonecraft replaces contempt
with compassion, the fate of her heroine clearly united with
those "lost to reason." Indeed, as *A Vindication* also makes
clear, it is the shared empowerment of women through the
active use of reason that Wollstonecraft sought. The above
passage concludes with this explanation:

I am fully persuaded that we should hear of none of
these infantine airs, if girls were allowed to take sufficient exercise, and not confined in close rooms till
their muscles are relaxed, and their powers of diges-
tion destroyed. To carry the remark still further, if
fear in girls, instead of being cherished, perhaps,
created, were treated in the same manner as cow-
ardice in boys, we should quickly see women with
more dignified aspects. It is true, they could not
then with equal propriety be termed the sweet flowers that smile in the walk of man; but they would
be more respectable members of society, and discharge the important duties of life by the light of
their own reason. "Educate women like men," says
Rousseau, "and the more they resemble our sex the
less power they will have over us." This is the very
point I aim at. I do not wish them to have power
over men; but over themselves. (131)

Not incidentally, it is precisely this power over herself that
has been denied Maria at the beginning of the novel. Confined, presumed to have no reason, she must struggle to

escape and to prove her own capacity for clear and intelligent thought. The plot of *The Wrongs of Woman* takes us where *A Vindication* ends.

SOURCES

Wollstonecraft, Mary. *A Vindication of the Rights of Woman.* Ed. Janet Todd and Marilyn Butler (New York: New York University Press, 1989).

Day after day rolled away, and tedious as the present moment appeared, they passed in such an unvaried tenor, Maria was surprised to find that she had already been six weeks buried alive, and yet had such faint hopes of effecting her enlargement. She was, earnestly as she had sought for employment, now angry with herself for having been amused by writing her narrative; and grieved to think that she had for an instant thought of any thing, but contriving to escape.

Jemima had evidently pleasure in her society: still, though she often left her with a glow of kindness, she returned with the same chilling air; and, when her heart appeared for a moment to open, some suggestion of reason forcibly closed it, before she could give utterance to the confidence Maria's conversation inspired.

Discouraged by these changes, Maria relapsed into despondency, when she was cheered by the alacrity with which Jemima brought her a fresh parcel of books; assuring her, that she had taken some pains to obtain them from one of the keepers, who attended a gentleman confined in the opposite corner of the gallery.

Maria took up the books with emotion. "They come," said she, "perhaps from a wretch condemned, like me, to reason on the nature of madness, by having wrecked minds continually under his eye; and almost to wish himself—as I do—mad, to escape from the contemplation of it." Her heart throbbed with sympathetic alarm; and she turned over the leaves with awe, as if they had become sacred from passing through the hands of an unfortunate being, oppressed by a similar fate.

Dryden's Fables, Milton's Paradise Lost, with several modern productions, composed the collection.[4] It was a mine of treasure. Some marginal notes, in Dryden's Fables, caught her attention: they were written with force and taste; and in one of the modern pamphlets, there was a fragment left, containing various observations on the present state of society and government, with a comparative view of the politics of Europe and America.[5] These remarks were written with a degree of generous warmth, when alluding to the enslaved state of the labouring majority, perfectly in unison with Maria's mode of thinking.

She read them over and over again; and fancy, treacherous fancy, began to sketch a character, congenial with her own, from these shadowy outlines.—"Was he mad?" She re-perused the marginal notes, and they seemed the production of an animated, but not of a disturbed imagination. Confined to this speculation, every time she re-read them, some fresh refinement of sentiment, or acuteness of thought impressed her, which she was astonished at herself for not having before observed.

What a creative power has an affectionate heart! There are beings who cannot live without loving, as poets love; and who feel the electric spark of genius, wherever it awakens sentiment or grace. Maria had often thought, when disciplining her wayward heart, "that to charm, was to be virtuous." "They who make me wish to appear the most amiable and good in their eyes, must possess in a degree," she would exclaim, "the graces and virtues they call into action."

She took up a book on the powers of the human mind; but, her attention strayed from cold arguments on the nature of what

[4] The gentleman's collection includes two of the more widely read and admired works of the eighteenth century, John Dryden's *Fables Ancient and Modern* (1700) and John Milton's *Paradise Lost* (1667).

[5] This fragment sounds remarkably similar in content to Gilbert Imlay's *A Topographical Description of the Western Territory of North America* (1792). See text box on "Gilbert Imlay: The American," p. 71.

she felt, while she was feeling, and she snapt the chain of the theory to read Dryden's Guiscard and Sigismunda.[6]

Maria, in the course of the ensuing day, returned some of the books, with the hope of getting others—and more marginal notes. Thus shut out from human intercourse, and compelled to view nothing but the prison of vexed spirits, to meet a wretch in the same situation, was more surely to find a friend, than to imagine a countryman one, in a strange land, where the human voice conveys no information to the eager ear.

"Did you ever see the unfortunate being to whom these books belong?" asked Maria, when Jemima brought her supper. "Yes. He sometimes walks out, between five and six, before the family[7] is stirring, in the morning, with two keepers; but even then his hands are confined."

"What! is he so unruly?" enquired Maria, with an accent of disappointment.

"No, not that I perceive," replied Jemima; "but he has an untamed look, a vehemence of eye, that excites apprehension. Were his hands free, he looks as if he could soon manage both his guards: yet he appears tranquil."

"If he be so strong, he must be young," observed Maria.

"Three or four and thirty, I suppose; but there is no judging of a person in his situation."

"Are you sure that he is mad?" interrupted Maria with eagerness. Jemima quitted the room, without replying.

"No, no, he certainly is not!" exclaimed Maria, answering herself; "the man who could write those observations was not disordered in his intellects."

She sat musing, gazing at the moon, and watching its motion as it seemed to glide under the clouds. Then, preparing for

---

[6] Dryden takes from Boccaccio the story of the tragic attempt of a newly widowed princess, Sigismunda, to act upon her own desires and to choose for herself a worthy second husband. Her attempt is foiled when her overly doting father discovers that she has married a suitor below her estate, Guiscard, and subsequently orders his death. In despair, Sigismunda arranges for her own demise.

[7] I.e., the family which owns the private madhouse.

bed, she thought, "Of what use could I be to him, or he to me, if it be true that he is unjustly confined?—Could he aid me to escape, who is himself more closely watched?—Still I should like to see him." She went to bed, dreamed of her child, yet woke exactly at half after five o'clock, and starting up, only wrapped a gown around her, and ran to the window. The morning was chill, it was the latter end of September; yet she did not retire to warm herself and think in bed, till the sound of the servants, moving about the house, convinced her that the unknown would not walk in the garden that morning. She was ashamed at feeling disappointed; and began to reflect, as an excuse, to herself, on the little objects which attract attention when there is nothing to divert the mind; and how difficult it was for women to avoid growing romantic, who had no active duties or pursuits.

At breakfast, Jemima enquired whether she understood French? for, unless she did, the stranger's stock of books was exhausted. Maria replied in the affirmative; but forbore to ask any more questions respecting the person to whom they belonged. And Jemima gave her a new subject for contemplation, by describing the person of a lovely maniac, just brought into an adjoining chamber. She was singing the pathetic ballad of old Rob[8] with the most heart-melting falls and pauses. Jemima had half-opened the door, when she distinguished her voice, and Maria stood close to it, scarcely daring to respire, less a modulation should escape her, so exquisitely sweet, so passionately wild. She began with sympathy to pourtray to herself another victim, when the lovely warbler flew, as it were, from the spray, and a torrent of unconnected exclamations and questions burst from her, interrupted by fits of laughter, so horrid, that Maria shut the door, and, turning her eyes up to heaven, exclaimed—"Gracious God!"

---

[8] "Auld Robin Gray," a Scottish folk song, tells the story of a woman married to a wealthy suitor against her will after her true love has gone to sea. When her lover returns, it is too late and they must forever part.

Several minutes elapsed before Maria could enquire respecting the rumour of the house (for this poor wretch was obviously not confined without a cause); and then Jemima could only tell her, that it was said, "she had been married, against her inclination, to a rich old man, extremely jealous (no wonder, for she was a charming creature); and that, in consequence of his treatment, or something which hung on her mind, she had, during her first lying in, lost her senses."

What a subject of meditation—even to the very confines of madness.

"Woman, fragile flower! why were you suffered to adorn a world exposed to the inroad of such stormy elements?" thought Maria, while the poor maniac's strain was still breathing in her ear, and sinking into her very soul.

Towards the evening, Jemima brought her Rousseau's *Heloise*;[9] and she sat reading with her eyes and heart, till the return of her guard to extinguish the light. One instance of her kindness was, the permitting Maria to have one, till her own hour of retiring to rest. She had read this work long since; but now it seemed to open a new world to her—the only one worth inhabiting. Sleep was not to be wooed; yet, far from being fatigued by the restless rotation of thought, she rose and opened her window, just as the thin watery clouds of twilight made the long silent shadows visible. The air swept across her face with a voluptuous freshness that thrilled to her heart, awakening indefinable emotions; and the sound of a waving branch, or the twittering of a startled bird, alone broke the stillness of reposing nature. Absorbed by the sublime sensibility which renders the consciousness of existence felicity, Maria was happy, till an autumnal scent, wafted by the breeze of morn from the fallen leaves of the adjacent wood, made her recollect that the season had

---

[9] Rousseau, Jean-Jacques, *Julie or the New Heloise* (1761). In this epistolary novel, the noblewoman Julie d'Etange falls in love with her tutor Saint-Preux, but must ultimately marry the wealthy Wolmar, as her overbearing father dictates. Although she remains loyal to her husband and becomes an exemplary mother, she continues to love Saint-Preux until her untimely death.

changed since her confinement; yet life afforded no variety to solace an afflicted heart. She returned dispirited to her couch, and thought of her child till the broad glare of day again invited her to the window. She looked not for the unknown, still how great was her vexation at perceiving the back of a man, certainly he, with his two attendants, as he turned into a side-path which led to the house! A confused recollection of having seen somebody who resembled him, immediately occurred, to puzzle and torment her with endless conjectures. Five minutes sooner, and she should have seen his face, and been out of suspense—was ever any thing so unlucky! His steady, bold step, and the whole air of his person, bursting as it were from a cloud, pleased her, and gave an outline to the imagination to sketch the individual form she wished to recognize.

Feeling the disappointment more severely than she was willing to believe, she flew to Rousseau, as her only refuge from the idea of him, who might prove a friend, could she but find a way to interest him in her fate; still the personification of Saint Preux, or of an ideal lover far superior, was after this imperfect model, of which merely a glance had been caught, even to the minutiae of the coat, and hat of the stranger. But if she lent St. Preux, or the demi-god of her fancy, his form, she richly repaid him by the donation of all St. Preux's sentiments and feelings, culled to gratify her own, to which he seemed to have an undoubted right, when she read on the margin of an impassioned letter, written in the well-known hand—"Rousseau alone, the true Prometheus of sentiment, possessed the fire of genius necessary to pourtray the passion, the truth of which goes so directly to the heart."[10]

Maria was again true to the hour, yet had finished Rousseau, and begun to transcribe some selected passages; unable to quit either the author or the window, before she had a glimpse of the countenance she daily longed to see; and, when seen, it conveyed no distinct idea to her mind where she had seen it before.

---

[10] Prometheus, in Greek mythology, is attributed with making human beings from clay and giving them fire and art.

He must have been a transient acquaintance; but to discover an acquaintance was fortunate, could she contrive to attract his attention, and excite his sympathy.

Every glance afforded colouring for the picture she was delineating on her heart; and once, when the window was half open, the sound of his voice reached her. Conviction flashed on her; she had certainly, in a moment of distress, heard the same accents. They were manly, and characteristic of a noble mind; nay, even sweet—or sweet they seemed to her attentive ear.

She started back, trembling, alarmed at the emotion a strange coincidence of circumstances inspired, and wondering why she thought so much of a stranger, obliged as she had been by his timely interference; [for she recollected, by degrees, all the circumstances of their former meeting.] She found however that she could think of nothing else; or, if she thought of her daughter, it was to wish that she had a father whom her mother could respect and love.

CHAPTER III

When perusing the first parcel of books, Maria had, with her pencil, written in one of them a few exclamations, expressive of compassion and sympathy, which she scarcely remembered, till turning over the leaves of one of the volumes, lately brought to her, a slip of paper dropped out, which Jemima hastily snatched up.

"Let me see it," demanded Maria impatiently, "You surely are not afraid of trusting me with the effusions of a madman?" "I must consider," replied Jemima; and withdrew, with the paper in her hand.

In a life of such seclusion, the passions gain undue force; Maria therefore felt a great degree of resentment and vexation, which she had not time to subdue, before Jemima, returning, delivered the paper.

"Whoever you are, who partake of my fate, accept my sincere commiseration—I would have said protection; but the privilege of man is denied me.

"My own situation forces a dreadful suspicion on my mind— I may not always languish in vain for freedom—say are you—I cannot ask the question; yet I will remember you when my remembrance can be of any use. I will enquire, *why* you are so mysteriously detained—and I *will* have an answer.

"HENRY DARNFORD."

By the most pressing intreaties, Maria prevailed on Jemima to permit her to write a reply to this note. Another and another succeeded, in which explanations were not allowed relative to their present situation; but Maria, with sufficient explicitness, alluded to a former obligation; and they insensibly entered on an interchange of sentiments on the most important subjects. To write these letters was the business of the day, and to receive them the moment of sunshine. By some means, Darnford having discovered Maria's window, when she next appeared at it, he made her, behind his keepers, a profound bow of respect and recognition.

Two or three weeks glided away in this kind of intercourse, during which period Jemima, to whom Maria had given the necessary information respecting her family, had evidently gained some intelligence, which increased her desire of pleasing her charge, though she could not yet determine to liberate her. Maria took advantage of this favourable change, without too minutely enquiring into the cause; and such was her eagerness to hold human converse, and to see her former protector, still a stranger to her, that she incessantly requested her guard to gratify her more than curiosity.

Writing to Darnford, she was led from the sad objects before her, and frequently rendered insensible to the horrid noises around her, which previously had continually employed her feverish fancy. Thinking it selfish to dwell on her own sufferings, when in the midst of wretches, who had not only lost all that endears life, but their very selves, her imagination was occupied with melancholy earnestness to trace the mazes of misery, through which so many wretches must have passed to this gloomy receptacle of disjointed souls, to the grand source of human corruption. Often at midnight was she waked by the dismal shrieks of demoniac rage, or of excruciating despair, uttered in such wild tones of indescribable anguish as proved the total absence of reason, and roused phantoms of horror in her mind, far more terrific than all that dreaming superstition ever drew. Besides, there was frequently something so inconceivably picturesque in the varying gestures of unrestrained passion, so irresistibly comic in their sallies, or so heart-piercingly pathetic in the little airs they would sing, frequently bursting out after an awful silence, as to fascinate the attention, and amuse the fancy, while torturing the soul. It was the uproar of the passions which she was compelled to observe; and to mark the lucid beam of reason, like a light trembling in a socket, or like the flash which divides the threatening clouds of angry heaven only to display the horrors which darkness shrouded.

Jemima would labour to beguile the tedious evenings, by describing the persons and manners of the unfortunate beings, whose figures or voices awoke sympathetic sorrow in Maria's bosom; and the stories she told were the more interesting, for perpetually leaving room to conjecture something extraordinary. Still Maria, accustomed to generalize her observations, was led to conclude from all she heard, that it was a vulgar[1] error to suppose that people of abilities were the most apt to lose the command of reason. On the contrary, from most of the instances she could investigate, she thought it resulted, that the passions only appeared strong and disproportioned, because the judgment was weak and unexercised; and that they gained strength by the decay of reason, as the shadows lengthen during the sun's decline.

Maria impatiently wished to see her fellow-sufferer; but Darnford was still more earnest to obtain an interview. Accustomed to submit to every impulse of passion, and never taught, like women, to restrain the most natural, and acquire, instead of the bewitching frankness of nature, a factitious propriety of behaviour, every desire became a torrent that bore down all opposition.

His travelling trunk, which contained the books lent to Maria, had been sent to him, and with a part of its contents he bribed his principal keeper; who, after receiving the most solemn promise that he would return to his apartment without attempting to explore any part of the house, conducted him, in the dusk of the evening, to Maria's room.

Jemima had apprized her charge of the visit, and she expected with trembling impatience, inspired by a vague hope

---

[1] In common or general use; custom, customary, or ordinary, as a matter of use or practice (*OED*).

that he might again prove her deliverer, to see a man who had before rescued her from oppression. He entered with an animation of countenance, formed to captivate an enthusiast; and, hastily turned his eyes from her to the apartment, which he surveyed with apparent emotions of compassionate indignation. Sympathy illuminated his eye, and, taking her hand, he respectfully bowed on it, exclaiming—"This is extraordinary!—again to meet you, and in such circumstances!" Still, impressive as was the coincidence of events which brought them once more together, their full hearts did not overflow.—*

[And though, after this first visit, they were permitted frequently to repeat their interviews, they were for some time employed in] a reserved conversation, to which all the world might have listened; excepting, when discussing some literary subject, flashes of sentiment, inforced by each relaxing² feature, seemed to remind them that their minds were already acquainted.

[By degrees, Darnford entered into the particulars of his story.] In a few words, he informed her that he had been a thoughtless, extravagant young man; yet, as he described his faults, they appeared to be the generous luxuriancy of a noble mind. Nothing like meanness tarnished the luster of his youth, nor had the worm of selfishness lurked in the unfolding bud, even while he had been the dupe of others. Yet he tardily acquired the experience necessary to guard him against future imposition.

"I shall weary you," continued he, "by my egotism; and did not powerful emotions draw me to you,"—his eyes glistened as he spoke, and a trembling seemed to run through his manly frame,—"I would not waste these precious moments in talking of myself.

---

* The copy which had received the author's last corrections, breaks off in this place, and the pages which follow, to the end of Chap. IV, are printed from a copy in a less finished state [Godwin's note].

² Causing or producing relaxation (*OED*).

"My father and mother were people of fashion; married by their parents. He was fond of the turf, she of the card-table.[3] I, and two or three other children since dead, were kept at home till we became intolerable. My father and mother had a visible dislike to each other, continually displayed; the servants were of the depraved kind usually found in the houses of people of fortune. My brothers and parents all dying, I was left to the care of guardians, and sent to Eton. I never knew the sweets of domestic affection, but I felt the want of indulgence and frivolous respect at school. I will not disgust you with a recital of the vices of my youth, which can scarcely be comprehended by female delicacy. I was taught to love by a creature I am ashamed to mention; and the other women with whom I afterwards became intimate, were of a class of which you can have no knowledge. I formed my acquaintance with them at the theatres; and, when vivacity danced in their eyes, I was not easily disgusted by the vulgarity which flowed from their lips. Having spent, a few years after I was of age, [the whole of] a considerable patrimony, excepting a few hundreds, I had no resource but to purchase a commission[4] in a new-raised regiment, destined to subjugate America. The regret I felt to renounce a life of pleasure, was counterbalanced by the curiosity I had to see America, or rather to travel; [nor had any of those circumstances occurred to my youth, which might have been calculated] to bind my country to my heart. I shall not trouble you with the details of a military life. My blood was still kept in motion; till, towards the close of the contest, I was wounded and taken prisoner.

"Confined to my bed, or chair, by a lingering cure, my only refuge from the preying activity of my mind, was books, which I read with great avidity, profiting by the conversation of my host, a man of sound understanding. My political sentiments now underwent a total change; and, dazzled by the hospitality of the

---

[3] I.e., both his parents enjoyed gambling, his father on horses, his mother at cards.
[4] As was common practice during the time, Darnford becomes an officer in the army by paying a specified fee.

Americans, I determined to take up my adode with freedom. I, therefore, with my usual impetuosity, sold my commission, and traveled into the interior parts of the country, to lay out my money to advantage. Added to this, I did not much like the puritanical manners of the large towns. Inequality of condition was there most disgustingly galling. The only pleasure wealth afforded, was to make an ostentatious display of it; for the cultivation of the fine arts, or literature, had not introduced into the first circles that polish of manners which renders the rich so essentially superior to the poor in Europe. Added to this, an influx of vices had been let in by the Revolution, and the most rigid principles of religion shaken to the centre, before the understanding could be gradually emancipated from the prejudices which led their ancestors undauntedly to seek an inhospitable clime and unbroken soil. The resolution, that led them, in pursuit of independence, to embark on rivers like seas, to search for unknown shores, and to sleep under the hovering mists of endless forests, whose baleful damps agued their limbs, was now turned into commercial speculations, till the national character exhibited a phenomenon in the history of the human mind—a head enthusiastically enterprising, with cold selfishness of heart. And woman, lovely woman!—they charm every where—still there is a degree of prudery, and a want of taste and ease in the manners of the American women, that renders them, in spite of their roses and lilies, far inferior to our European charmers. In the country, they have often a bewitching simplicity of character; but, in the cities, they have all the airs and ignorance of the ladies who give the tone to the circles of the large trading towns in England. They are fond of their ornaments, merely because they are good, and not because they embellish their persons; and are more gratified to inspire the women with jealousy of these exterior advantages, than the men with love. All the frivolity which often (excuse me, Madam) renders the society of modest women so stupid in England, here seemed to throw still more leaden fetters on their charms. Not being an adept in gallantry, I found that I could only keep myself awake in their company by making downright love[5] to them.

"But, not to intrude on your patience, I retired to the track of land which I had purchased in the country, and my time passed pleasantly enough while I cut down the trees, built my house, and planted my different crops. But winter and idleness came, and I longed for more elegant society, to hear what was passing in the world, and to do something better than vegetate with the animals that made a very considerable part of my household. Consequently, I determined to travel. Motion was a substitute for variety of objects; and, passing over immense tracks of country, I exhausted my exuberant spirits, without obtaining much experience. I every where saw industry the fore-runner and not the consequence, of luxury; but this country, every thing being on an ample scale, did not afford those picturesque views, which a certain degree of cultivation is necessary gradually to produce. The eye wandered without an object to fix upon over immeasurable plains, and lakes that seemed replenished by the ocean, whilst eternal forests of small clustering trees, obstructed the circulation of air, and embarrassed the path, without gratifying the eye of taste. No cottage smiling in the waste, no travelers hailed us, to give life to silent nature; or, if perchance we saw the print of a footstep in our path, it was a dreadful warning to turn aside; and the head ached as if assailed by the scalping knife. The Indians who hovered on the skirts of the European settlements had only learned of their neighbors to plunder, and they stole their guns from them to do it with more safety.

"From the woods and back settlements, I returned to the towns, and learned to eat and drink most valiantly; but without entering into commerce (and I detested commerce) I found I could not live there; and, growing heartily weary of the land of liberty and vulgar aristocracy, seated on her bags of dollars, I resolved once more to visit Europe. I wrote to a distant relation in England, with whom I had been educated, mentioning the vessel in which I intended to sail. Arriving in London, my senses

---

[5] I.e., by paying amorous attention to (*OED*).

were intoxicated. I ran from street to street, from theatre to theatre, and the women of the town (again I must beg pardon for my habitual frankness) appeared to me like angels.

"A week was spent in this thoughtless manner, when, returning very late to the hotel in which I had lodged ever since my arrival, I was knocked down in a private street, and hurried, in a state of insensibility, into a coach, which brought me hither, and I only recovered my senses to be treated like one who had lost them. My keepers are deaf to my remonstrances and enquiries, yet assure me that my confinement shall not last long. Still I cannot guess, though I weary myself with conjectures, why I am confined, or in what part of England this house is situated. I imagine sometimes that I hear the sea roar, and wished myself again on the Atlantic, till I had a glimpse of you."*

A few moments were only allowed to Maria to comment on this narrative, when Darnford left her to her own thoughts, to the "never ending, still beginning,"[6] talk of weighing his words, recollecting his tones of voice, and feeling them reverberate on her heart.

"THE AMERICAN:" GILBERT IMLAY

From the novel's initial publication, most readers assumed Henry Darnford to be the rather thinly disguised figure of Gilbert Imlay, Wollstonecraft's lover and the father of her illegitimate daughter Fanny. By giving Darnford this American sojourn, Wollstonecraft courts this reading. She did not, of course, know how notorious their relationship would become following the publication of Godwin's *Mem-*

---

* The introduction of Darnford as the deliverer of Maria in a former instance, appears to have been an afterthought of the author. This has occasioned the omission of any allusion to that circumstance in the preceding narration. EDITOR. [Godwin's note].

6 Dryden, *Alexander's Feast* (1697), l. 97: "War, he sung, is toil and trouble;/ Honour but an empty bubble;/Never ending, still beginning, /Fighting still, and still destroying."

oirs. Yet Gilbert Imlay at the time of their introduction was famous in his own right—and mostly for being an American. His widely read 1792 work *A Topographical Description of the Western Territory of North America* detailed his travels in Kentucky and praised both the virtues of its fertile soil and the simple life its agrarian culture inspired. Imlay's primary audience was the prospective emigrant (and even more to the point, prospective purchasers of the land he was representing), yet his work also struck a resonant chord within Enlightenment circles, most notably gaining him the support of noted Girondist Thomas de Brissot.

And rightfully so. This work, structured as a series of letters to an interested friend, was far from a simple description of this newly chartered state or even an advertisement for these newly acquired lands. From its first paragraph, Imlay makes his politics clear: what begins as simple, descriptive praise for the natural becomes rather quickly a pointed attack on the traditions and laws of the Europeans:

> As it will afford me an opportunity of contrasting the simple manners, and rational life of the Americans, with the distorted and unnatural habits of the Europeans: which have flowed no doubt from the universally bad laws which exist on your continent, and from that pernicious system of blending religion and politics, which has been productive of universal depravity. (1)

Other practitioners of the topographical genre had made America symbolic of the promise of the Enlightenment, yet it was Imlay's unique ability to claim both old and new world allegiances—apart from his land speculation, he also served as a lieutenant or captain in the American revolution—which gave this work unexpected cache at the time of its publication and clearly contributed to its considerable success (The work enjoyed three English reprints, a German translation, and an American reprint.). For his European audience, he was both the "native son" who could speak authoritatively about this new world and an intellectual compatriot who could mirror back their deeply cherished ideals of European radicalism even as these abstractions took new and sometimes threatening shape within the "unexplored" territories of the American wilderness.

Interestingly, Darnford, by contrast, seems remarkably disdainful of American culture, more the jaded European whom Imlay targets in this opening paragraph than the "fresh" American Imlay purports to be. The difference is most notable in Darnford's attitude toward American women, an attitude which from Imlay's work it would appear he did not share. In 1793 (the year of Wollstonecraft's courtship with Imlay), he published *The Emigrants*, another work extolling the virtues of Kentucky and the promises of Republicanism, but this time in the form of a novel and one which centered on the romance between a Captain Arl—ton and Caroline T—N (a couple who bear a striking resemblance to Imlay and Wollstonecraft.) Although Caroline is from an English family, it is her ability to apprehend the virtues of this rugged terrain that make her the object of Capt. Arl—ton's devotion. It is after the following speech which compares her mountainous trek in America with the promenades of London that Arl—ton writes "that I heard with amazement and gazed at her with the most ineffable transports!"

"True, answered Caroline, it is very different: one has a continual sameness which insensibly produces *ennui*, and the others are generally crowded, that it is quite impossible either to enjoy the charms of conversation, or the pleasure of walking. But here is a continual feast for the mind—every rock, every tree, every moss, from their novelty afford subject for contemplation and amusement. Look but at yonder towering hills, (pointing at the same time at a rocky ridge considerably above the others,) whose summits appear to prop the heavens, and then view the various symbols which their chasms produce, and what a sublime imagery does it afford? (25)

These sentiments are not far from Wollstonecraft's own who

herself dreamed of emigrating to America with Imlay and who was instrumental in persuading her favorite brother George to undertake his own journey. Imlay's novel and its final vision of a utopian society on the banks of the Ohio (one that significantly allowed women greater autonomy in marriage) would lead writers as influential as Samuel Taylor Coleridge to fantasize about and, even for a brief time, plan, to join such a community—a vision interestingly unavailable to the Darnford and Maria of this novel.

SOURCES

Verhoeven, W.M. and Amanda Gilroy. Introduction. *The Emigrants* by Gilbert Imlay. New York: Penguin, 1998.

Imlay, Gilbert. *The Emigrants*. Ed. W.M. Verhoeven and Amanda Gilroy. New York: Penguin, 1998.

———. A *Topographical Description of the Western Territory of North America*. London, 1792.

Chapter IV

Pity, and the forlorn seriousness of adversity, have both been considered as dispositions favourable to love, while satirical writers have attributed the propensity to the relaxing effect of idleness; what chance then had Maria of escaping, when pity, sorrow, and solitude all conspired to soften her mind, and nourish romantic wishes, and, from a natural progress, romantic expectations?

Maria was six-and-twenty. But, such was the native soundness of her constitution, that time had only given to her countenance the character of her mind. Revolving thought, and exercised affections had banished some of the playful graces of innocence, producing insensibly that irregularity of features which the struggles of the understanding to trace or govern the strong emotions of the heart, are wont to imprint on the yielding mass. Grief and care had mellowed, without obscuring, the bright tints of youth, and the thoughtfulness which resided on her brow did not take from the feminine softness of her features; nay, such was the sensibility which often mantled over it, that she frequently appeared, like a large proportion of her sex, only born to feel; and the activity of her well-proportioned, and even almost voluptuous figure, inspired the idea of strength of mind, rather than of body. There was a simplicity sometimes indeed in her manner, which bordered on infantine ingenuousness, that led people of common discernment to underrate her talents, and smile at the flights of her imagination. But those who could not comprehend the delicacy of her sentiments, were attached by her unfailing sympathy, so that she was very generally beloved by characters of very different descriptions; still, she was too much under the influence of an ardent imagination to adhere to common rules.

There are mistakes of conduct which at five-and-twenty prove the strength of the mind, that, ten or fifteen years after, would demonstrate its weakness, its incapacity to acquire a sane judgment. The youths who are satisfied with the ordinary pleasures of life, and do not sigh after ideal phantoms of love and friendship, will never arrive at great maturity of understanding; but if these reveries are cherished, as is too frequently the case with women, when experience ought to have taught them in what human happiness consists, they become as useless as they are wretched. Besides, their pains and pleasures are so dependent on outward circumstances, on the objects of their affections, that they seldom act from the impulse of a nerved mind,[1] able to choose its own pursuit.

Having had to struggle incessantly with the vices of mankind, Maria's imagination found repose in pourtraying the possible virtues the world might contain. Pygmalion formed an ivory maid, and longed for an informing soul.[2] She, on the contrary, combined all the qualities of a hero's mind, and fate presented a statue in which she might enshrine them.

We mean not to trace the progress of this passion, or recount how often Darnford and Maria were obliged to part in the midst of an interesting conversation. Jemima ever watched on the tiptoe of fear, and frequently separated them on a false alarm, when they would have given worlds to remain a little longer together.

A magic lamp[3] now seemed to be suspended in Maria's prison, and fairy landscapes flitted round the gloomy walls, late so blank. Rushing from the depth of despair, on the seraph wing of hope, she found herself happy.—She was beloved, and every emotion was rapturous.

[1] Strong, courageous mind.

[2] In Greek mythology, Pygmalion, disappointed in his love for Aphrodite, creates a statue in her image. Ultimately, Aphrodite rewards his devotion by bringing it to life as Galatea.

[3] Also known as a magic lantern. It was a device containing a lamp and lens-like opening used to project and magnify images on a screen.

On Love and Sensibility:
From *A Vindication of the Rights of Woman*

In *A Vindication of the Rights of Woman,* written six years prior to the unfinished *Wrongs of Woman,* Wollstonecraft was unequivocal about love: its overemphasis in the education of women deprived them of reason and made them mere slaves of the senses. She was not, however, unrealistic about how that message would be heard. In a chapter entitled "The Prevailing Opinion of Sexual Character," she writes:

> To speak disrespectfully of love is, I know, high treason against sentiment and fine feelings; but I wish to speak the simple language of truth, and rather to address the head than the heart. To endeavour to reason love out of the world, would be to out Quixote Cervantes, and equally offend against common sense; but an endeavour to restrain this tumultuous passion, and to prove that it should not be allowed to dethrone superior powers, or to usurp the sceptre which the understanding should ever coolly wield, appears less wild. (96)

It was not love per se that troubled her, but rather its shaping effect on the female character. Taught that to be "beloved" was their chief goal, women were required to make its attainment their sole preoccupation. Many "male writers," she contested, "have warmly inculcated that the whole tendency of female education ought to be directed in one point:—to render them pleasing" (96).

The effects of such an "education" could be quite destructive. For one, it made women's own self-worth dependent upon the reaction of others, hence depriving them of their autonomy and even their very character. She writes:

> Love, in their bosoms, taking place of every nobler passion, their sole ambition is to be fair, to raise emotion instead of inspiring respect; and this ignoble desire, like the servility in absolute monarchies, destroys all strength of character. Liberty is the mother

of virtue, and if women, be, by their very constitution, slaves, and not allowed to breathe the sharp
invigorating air of freedom, they must ever languish
like exotics, and be reckoned beautiful flaws in nature. (105)

Thus, rendered merely an object to excite love in others,
women had little to employ them beyond being pleasing,
and this cultivated "idleness" also took its toll on their characters:

… I wish to guard the female heart by exercising
the understanding: for these paradisiacal reveries are
oftener the effect of idleness than of a lively fancy.

Women have seldom sufficient serious employment to silence their feelings; a round of little cares,
or vain pursuits frittering away all strength of mind
and organs, they become naturally only objects of
sense.—In short, the whole tenour of female education (the education of society) tends to render the
best disposed romantic and inconstant; and the remainder vain and mean. (143)

Confined to her room, deprived of employment, Maria in
her madhouse love affair seems in some ways the very em-
bodiment of the woman described above: an "object of sense"
readily susceptible to the "paradisiacal reveries" of love.

Yet in strongly cautioning women against a preoccupation with love and in warning of its disabling effects,
Wollstonecraft did not intend to rule it out altogether. Although at the time of *A Vindication*, she had yet to experience reciprocal love, she held out for the possibility of a
more enobling love even as she lambasted its more common
and, for women, ultimately debasing, form. This longer passage gives voice to the complexity of her position:

Love is, in a great degree, an arbitrary passion, and
will reign, like some other stalking mischiefs, by its
own authority, without deigning to reason: and it
may also be easily distinguished from esteem, the
foundation of friendship, because it is often excited

by evanescent beauties and graces, though, to give an energy to the sentiment, something more solid must deepen their impression and set the imagination to work, to make the most fair—the first good.

Common passions are excited by common qualities.—Men look for beauty and the simper of good-humoured docility: women are captivated by easy manners; a gentleman-like man seldom fails to please them, and their thirsty ears eagerly drink the insinuating nothings of politeness, whilst they turn from the unintelligible sounds of the charmer—reason, charm he never so wisely. With respect to superficial accomplishments, the rake certainly has the advantage; and of these females can form an opinion, for it is their own ground. Rendered gay and giddy by the whole tenor of their lives, the very aspect of wisdom, or the severe graces of virtue, must have a lugubrious appearance to them; and produce a kind of restraint from which they and love, sportive child, naturally revolt. Without taste, excepting of the lighter kind, for taste is the offspring of judgment, how can they discover that true beauty and grace must arise from the play of the mind? and how can they be expected to relish in a lover what they do not, or very imperfectly, possess themselves?

***

Supposing, however, for a moment, that women were, in some future revolution of time, to become, what I sincerely wish them to be, even love would acquire more serious dignity, and be purified in its own fires; and virtue giving true delicacy to their affections, they would turn with disgust from a rake. (188-189)

Ironically, through the publication of William Godwin's *Memoirs*, Wollstonecraft would ultimately become infamous for her own "irrational" love for the rakish Gilbert Imlay; the revelation of her subsequent suicide attempts and her continuing devotion to Imlay despite his many betrayals suggested her own intense vulnerability to these men of "easy manners." Yet her love letters to Godwin himself, her husband at the time of *The Wrongs of Woman*'s composition, suggest that by *this* time that "future revolution in time" where "love would acquire more serious dignity" may have come to pass for herself. In a letter dated October 4, 1796, she writes rapturously of a maturer love, in language reminiscent both of the above passage from *A Vindication* and of Maria's description of her love for Darnford:

> I should have liked to have dined with you to day, after finishing your essays—that my eyes, and lips, I do not exactly mean my voice, might have told you that they had raised you in my *esteem*. What a cold word! I would say love, if you will promise not to dispute about its propriety, when I want to express an increasing affection, founded on a more intimate acquaintance with your heart and understanding.
>
> I shall cork up all my kindness—yet the fine volatile essence may fly off in my walk—you know not how much tenderness for you may escape in a voluptuous sigh, should the air, as is often the case, give a pleasurable movement to the sensations, that have been clustering round my heart, as I read this morning—reminding myself, every now and then, that the writer *loved me*. Voluptuous is often expressive of a meaning I do not now intend to give. I would describe one of those moments, when the senses are exactly tuned by the rising tenderness of the heart, and according reason entices you to live in the present moment, regardless of the past or future—It is not rapture.—It is a sublime tranquility. I have felt it in your arms—Hush! Let not the light see, I was going to say hear it—These confessions

should only be uttered—you know where, when the curtains are up—and all the world shut out—.(41-42)

Sources

Ralph Wardle. *Godwin and Mary: Letters of William Godwin and MaryWollstonecraft.* Lawrence, Kansas: The University of Kansas Press, 1966.
Mary Wollstonecraft. *The Works of Mary Wollstonecraft.* Vol. 5. Edited by Janet Todd and Marilyn Butler. New York: New York University Press, 1989.

To Darnford she had not shown a decided affection; the fear of outrunning his, a sure proof of love, made her often assume a coldness and indifference foreign from her character; and, even when giving way to the playful emotions of a heart just loosened from the frozen bond of grief, there was a delicacy in her manner of expressing her sensibility, which made him doubt whether it was the effect of love.

One evening, when Jemima left them, to listen to the sound of a distant footstep, which seemed cautiously to approach, he seized Maria's hand—it was not withdrawn. They conversed with earnestness of their situation; and, during the conversation, he once or twice gently drew her towards him. He felt the fragrance of her breath, and longed, yet feared, to touch the lips from which it issued; spirits of purity seemed to guard them, while all the enchanting graces of love sported on her cheeks, and languished in her eyes.

Jemima entering, he reflected on his diffidence with poignant regret, and, she once more taking alarm, he ventured, as Maria stood near his chair, to approach her lips with a declaration of love. She drew back with solemnity, he hung down his head abashed; but lifting his eyes timidly, they met her's; she had determined, during that instant, and suffered their rays to mingle. He took, with more ardour, reassured, a half-consenting, half-reluctant kiss, reluctant only from modesty; and there was a sacredness in her dignified manner of reclining her glowing face on his shoulder, that powerfully impressed him. Desire was lost in more ineffable emotions, and to protect her from insult and sorrow—to make her happy, seemed not only the first wish of his heart, but the most noble duty of his life. Such angelic confidence demanded the fidelity of honour; but could he, feeling her in every pulsation, could he ever change, could he be a villain? The emotion with which she, for a moment, allowed herself to be pressed to his bosom, the tear of rapturous sympathy, mingled with a soft melancholy sentiment of recollected disappointment, said—more of truth and faithfulness, than the tongue could have given utterance to in hours! They were silent—yet discoursed, how eloquently? till, after a moment's reflection, Maria drew her chair by the side of his, and, with a composed sweetness of voice, and supernatural benignity of countenance, said, "I must open my whole heart to you; you must be told who I am, why I am here, and why, telling you I am a wife, I blush not to"—the blush spoke the rest.

Jemima was again at her elbow, and the restraint of her presence did not prevent an animated conversation, in which love, sly urchin, was ever at bo-peep.

So much of heaven did they enjoy, that paradise bloomed around them; or they, by a powerful spell, had been transported into Armida's garden.[4] Love, the grand enchanter, "lapt them in Elysium,"[5] and every sense was harmonized to joy and social extacy. So animated, indeed, were their accents of tenderness, in discussing what, in other circumstances, would have been commonplace subjects, that Jemima felt, with surprise, a tear of plea-

---

[4] Torquato Tasso, *Gerusalemme Liberata* (1581). In this work, a group of Christian Knights are enticed into the garden of Armida, a female magician, where they succumb to indolence.

[5] Milton, *Comus* (1637), l. 256: "And lap it in Elysium."

sure trickling down her rugged cheeks. She wiped it away, half ashamed; and when Maria kindly enquired the cause, with all the eager solicitude of a happy being wishing to impart to all nature its overflowing felicity, Jemima owned that it was the first tear that social enjoyment had ever drawn from her. She seemed indeed to breathe more freely; the cloud of suspicion cleared away from her brow; she felt herself, for once in her life, treated like a fellow-creature.

Imagination! who can paint thy power; or reflect the evanescent tints of hope fostered by thee? A despondent gloom had long obscured Maria's horizon—now the sun broke forth, the rainbow appeared, and every prospect was fair. Horror still reigned in the darkened cells, suspicion lurked in the passages, and whispered along the walls. The yells of men possessed, sometimes made them pause, and wonder that they felt so happy, in a tomb of living death. They even chid themselves for such apparent insensibility; still the world contained not three happier beings. And Jemima, after again patrolling the passage, was so softened by the air of confidence which breathed around her, that she voluntarily began an account of herself.

CHAPTER V

"M y father," said Jemima, "seduced my mother, a pretty girl, with whom he lived fellow-servant; and she no sooner perceived the natural, the dreaded consequence, than the terrible conviction flashed on her—that she was ruined. Honesty, and a regard for her reputation, had been the only principles inculcated by her mother; and they had been so forcibly impressed, that she feared shame, more than the poverty to which it would lead. Her incessant importunities to prevail upon my father to screen her from reproach by marrying her, as he had promised in the fervour of seduction, estranged him from her so completely, that her very person became distasteful to him; and he began to hate, as well as despise me,[1] before I was born.

"My mother, grieved to the soul by his neglect, and unkind treatment, actually resolved to famish herself; and injured her health by the attempt; though she had not sufficient resolution to adhere to her project, or renounce it entirely. Death came not at her call; yet sorrow, and the methods she adopted to conceal her condition, still doing the work of a house-maid, had such an effect on her constitution, that she died in the wretched garret, where her virtuous mistress had forced her to take refuge in the very pangs of labour, though my father, after a slight reproof, was allowed to remain in his place—allowed by the mother of six children, who, scarcely permitting a footstep to be heard, during her month's indulgence, felt no sympathy for the poor wretch, denied every comfort required by her situation.

"The day my mother died, the ninth after my birth, I was consigned to the care of the cheapest nurse my father could find;[2]

[1] I.e., her father not only disliked, but also looked down upon her.
[2] A wet nurse: a woman employed to breastfeed an infant.

who suckled her own child at the same time, and lodged as many more as she could get, in two cellar-like apartments.

"Poverty, and the habit of seeing children die off her hands, had so hardened her heart, that the office of a mother did not awaken the tenderness of a woman; nor were the feminine caresses which seem a part of the rearing of a child, ever bestowed on me. The chicken has a wing to shelter under; but I had no bosom to nestle in, no kindred warmth to foster me. Left in dirt, to cry with cold and hunger till I was weary, and sleep without ever being prepared by exercise, or lulled by kindness to rest; could I be expected to become any thing but a weak and rickety babe? Still, in spite of neglect, I continued to exist, to learn to curse existence, [her countenance grew ferocious as she spoke,] and the treatment that rendered me miserable, seemed to sharpen my wits. Confined then in a damp hovel, to rock the cradle of the succeeding tribe, I looked like a little old woman, or a hag shrivelling into nothing. The furrows of reflection and care contracted the youthful cheek, and gave a sort of supernatural wildness to the ever watchful eye. During this period, my father had married another fellow-servant, who loved him less, and knew better how to manage his passion, than my mother. She likewise proving with child, they agreed to keep a shop: my step-mother, if, being an illegitimate offspring, I may venture thus to characterize her, having obtained a sum of rich relation, for that purpose.

"Soon after her lying-in,[3] she prevailed on my father to take me home, to save the expence of maintaining me, and of hiring a girl to assist her in the care of the child. I was young, it was true, but appeared a knowing little thing, and might be made handy. Accordingly I was brought to her house; but not to a home—for a home I never knew. Of this child, a daughter, she was extravagantly fond; and it was a part of my employment, to assist to spoil her, by humouring all her whims, and bearing all her caprices. Feeling her own consequence, before she could

---

[3] A time of confinement or bed rest after childbirth.

speak, she had learned the art of tormenting me, and if I ever dared to resist, I received blows, laid on with no compunctious hand, or was sent to bed dinnerless, as well as supperless.[4] I said that it was a part of my daily labour to attend this child, with the servility of a slave; still it was but a part. I was sent out in all seasons, and from place to place, to carry burdens far above my strength, without being allowed to draw near the fire, or ever being cheered by encouragement or kindness. No wonder then, treated like a creature of another species, that I began to envy, and at length to hate, the darling of the house. Yet, I perfectly remember, that it was the caresses, and kind expressions of my step-mother, which first excited my jealous discontent. Once, I cannot forget it, when she was calling in vain her wayward child to kiss her, I ran to her, saying, 'I will kiss you, ma'am!' and how did my heart, which was in my mouth, sink, what was my de-basement of soul, when pushed away with—'I do not want you, pert thing!' Another day, when a new gown had excited the highest good humour, and she uttered the appropriate *dear*, ad-dressed unexpectedly to me, I thought I could never do enough to please her; I was all alacrity, and rose proportionably in my own estimation.

"As her daughter grew up, she was pampered with cakes and fruit, while I was, literally speaking, fed with the refuse of the table, with her leavings. A liquorish tooth[5] is, I believe, com-mon to children, and I used to steal any thing sweet, that I could catch up with a chance of concealment. When detected, she was not content to chastise me herself at the moment, but, on my father's return in the evening (he was a shopman), the principal discourse was to recount my faults, and attribute them to the wicked disposition which I had brought into the world with me, inherited from my mother. He did not fail to leave the marks of his resentment on my body, and then solaced himself

---

[4] I.e.,without the chief meal of the day, dinner (typically served at midday) or the last meal of the day, supper.
[5] Sweet tooth.

by playing with my sister.—I could have murdered her at those moments. To save myself from these unmerciful corrections, I resorted to falshood, and the untruths which I sturdily maintained, were brought in judgment against me, to support my tyrant's inhuman charge of my natural propensity to vice. Seeing me treated with contempt, and always being fed and dressed better, my sister conceived a contemptuous opinion of me, that proved an obstacle to all affection; and my father, hearing continually of my faults, began to consider me as a curse entailed on him for his sins: he was therefore easily prevailed on to bind me apprentice to one of my step-mother's friends, who kept a slop-shop[6] in Wapping. I was represented (as it was said) in my true colours; but she, 'warranted,' snapping her fingers, 'that she should break my spirit or heart.'

"My mother replied, with a whine, 'that if any body could make me better, it was such a clever woman as herself; though, for her own part, she had tried in vain; but good-nature was her fault.'

"I shudder with horror, when I recollect the treatment I had now to endure. Not only under the lash of my task-mistress, but the drudge of the maid, apprentices and children, I never had a taste of human kindness to soften the rigour of perpetual labour. I had been introduced as an object of abhorrence into the family; as a creature of whom my step-mother, though she had been kind enough to let me live in the house with her own child, could make nothing. I was described as a wretch, whose nose must be kept to the grinding stone—and it was held there with an iron grasp. It seemed indeed the privilege of their superior nature to kick me about, like the dog or cat. If I were attentive, I was called fawning, if refractory, an obstinate mule, and like a mule I received their censure on my loaded back. Often has my mistress, for some instance of forgetfulness, thrown me from one side of the kitchen to the other, knocked my head against the wall, spit in my face, with various refinements on

---

[6] A shop selling cheap and ready-made clothes.

barbarity that I forbear to enumerate, though they were all acted over again by the servant, with additional insults, to which the appellation of *bastard*, was commonly added, with taunts or sneers. But I will not attempt to give you an adequate idea of my situation, lest you, who probably have never been drenched with the dregs of human misery, should think I exaggerate.

"I stole now, from absolute necessity,—bread; yet whatever else was taken, which I had it not in my power to take, was ascribed to me. I was the filching cat, the ravenous dog, the dumb brute, who must bear all; for if I endeavoured to exculpate myself, I was silenced, without any enquiries being made, with 'Hold your tongue, you never tell truth.' Even the very air I breathed was tainted with scorn; for I was sent to the neighbouring shops with Glutton, Liar, or Thief, written on my forehead. This was, at first, the most bitter punishment; but sullen pride, or a kind of stupid desperation, made me, at length, almost regardless of the contempt, which had wrung from me so many solitary tears at the only moments when I was allowed to rest.

"Thus was I the mark of cruelty till my sixteenth year; and then I have only to point out a change of misery; for a period[7] I never knew. Allow me first to make one observation. Now I look back, I cannot help attributing the greater part of my misery, to the misfortune of having been thrown into the world without the grand support of life—a mother's affection. I had no one to love me; or to make me respected, to enable me to acquire respect. I was an egg dropped on the sand; a pauper by nature, hunted from family to family, who belonged to nobody—and nobody cared for me. I was despised from my birth, and denied the chance of obtaining a footing for myself in society. Yes; I had not even the chance of being considered as a fellow-creature—yet all the people with whom I lived, brutalized as they were by the low cunning of trade, and the despicable shifts of poverty, were not without bowels, though they never yearned

[7] I.e., an end.

for me. I was, in fact, born a slave, and chained by infamy to slavery during the whole of existence, without having any companions to alleviate it by sympathy, or to teach me how to rise above it by their example. But, to resume the thread of my tale—

"At sixteen, I suddenly grew tall, and something like comeliness appeared on a Sunday, when I had time to wash my face, and put on clean clothes. My master had once or twice caught hold of me in the passage; but I instinctively avoided his disgusting caresses. One day however, when the family were at a methodist meeting,[8] he contrived to be alone in the house with me, and by blows—yes; blows and menaces, compelled me to submit to his ferocious desire; and, to avoid my mistress's fury, I was obliged in future to comply, and skulk to my loft at his command, in spite of increasing loathing.

"The anguish which was now pent up in my bosom, seemed to open a new world to me: I began to extend my thoughts beyond myself, and grieve for human misery, till I discovered, with horror—ah! what horror!—that I was with child. I know not why I felt a mixed sensation of despair and tenderness, excepting that, ever called a bastard, a bastard appeared to me an object of the greatest compassion in creation.

"I communicated this dreadful circumstance to my master, who was almost equally alarmed at the intelligence; for he feared his wife, and public censure at the meeting. After some weeks of deliberation had elapsed, I in continual fear that my altered shape would be noticed, my master gave me a medicine in a phial, which he desired me to take, telling me, without any circumlocution, for what purpose it was designed. I burst into tears, I thought it was killing myself—yet was such a self as I worth preserving? He cursed me for a fool, and left me to my own reflections. I could not resolve to take this infernal potion; but I

[8] Methodism: an evangelical movement led by John and Charles Wesley and George Whitefield. By mid century, the term "Methodist" had a negative connotation, associated with an overzealous and misguided religious devotion, or enthusiasm.

wrapped it up in an old gown, and hid it in a corner of my box.

"Nobody yet suspected me, because they had been accustomed to view me as a creature of another species. But the threatening storm at last broke over my devoted head—never shall I forget it! One Sunday evening when I was left, as usual, to take care of the house, my master came home intoxicated, and I became the prey of his brutal appetite. His extreme intoxication made him forget his customary caution, and my mistress entered and found us in a situation that could not have been more hateful to her than me. Her husband was 'pot valiant,'[9] he feared her not at the moment, nor had he then much reason, for she instantly turned the whole force of her anger another way. She tore off my cap, scratched, kicked, and buffetted me, till she had exhausted her strength, declaring, as she rested her arm, 'that I had wheedled her husband from her.—But, could any thing better be expected from a wretch, whom she had taken into her house out of pure charity?' What a torrent of abuse rushed out? till, almost breathless, she concluded with saying, 'that I was born a strumpet; it ran in my blood, and nothing good could come to those who harboured me.'

"My situation was, of course, discovered, and she declared that I should not stay another night under the same roof with an honest family. I was therefore pushed out of doors, and my trumpery[10] thrown after me, when it had been contemptuously examined in the passage, lest I should have stolen any thing.

"Behold me then in the street, utterly destitute! Whither could I creep for shelter? To my father's roof I had no claim, when not pursued by shame—now I shrunk back as from death, from my mother's cruel reproaches, my father's execrations. I could not endure to hear him curse the day I was born, though life had been curse to me. Of death I thought, but with a confused emotion of terror, as I stood leaning my head on a post,

---

[9] Courageous through drink.

[10] 'Something of less value than it seems'; hence, 'something of no value'; trifles; worthless stuff, trash, rubbish (*OED*).

and starting at every footstep, lest it should be my mistress coming to tear my heart out. One of the boys of the shop passing by, heard my tale, and immediately repaired to his master, to give him a description of my situation; and he touched the right key—the scandal it would give rise to, if I were left to repeat my tale to every enquirer. This plea came home to his reason, who had been sobered by his wife's rage, the fury of which fell on him when I was out of her reach, and he sent the boy to me with half-a-guinea, desiring him to conduct me to a house, where beggars, and other wretches, the refuse of society, nightly lodged.

"This night was spent in a state of stupefaction, or desperation. I detested mankind, and abhorred myself.

"In the morning I ventured out, to throw myself in my master's way, at his usual hour of going abroad. I approached him, he 'damned me for a b——, declared I had disturbed the peace of the family, and that he had sworn to his wife, never to take any more notice of me.' He left me; but, instantly returning, he told me that he should speak to his friend, a parish-officer, to get a nurse for the brat I laid to him; and advised me, if I wished to keep out of the house of correction, not to make free with his name.

"I hurried back to my hole, and, rage giving place to despair, sought for the potion that was to procure abortion, and swallowed it, with a wish that it might destroy me, at the same time that it stopped the sensations of new-born life, which I felt with indescribable emotion. My head turned round, my heart grew sick, and in the horrors of approaching dissolution, mental anguish was swallowed up. The effect of the medicine was violent, and I was confined to my bed several days; but, youth and a strong constitution prevailing, I once more crawled out, to ask myself the cruel question, 'Whither I should go?' I had but two shillings left in my pocket, the rest had been expended, by a poor woman who slept in the same room, to pay for my lodging, and purchase the necessaries of which she partook.

"With this wretch I went into the neighbouring streets to beg, and my disconsolate appearance drew a few pence from the idle, enabling me still to command a bed; till, recovering from my illness, and taught to put on my rags to the best advantage, I was accosted from different motives, and yielded to the desire of the brutes I met, with the same detestation that I had felt for my still more brutal master. I have since read in novels of the blandishments of seduction, but I had not even the pleasure of being enticed into vice.

"I shall not," interrupted Jemima, "lead your imagination into all the scenes of wretchedness and depravity, which I was condemned to view; or mark the different stages of my debasing misery. Fate dragged me through the very kennels of society; I was still a slave, a bastard, a common property. Become familiar with vice, for I wish to conceal nothing from you, I picked the pockets of the drunkards who abused me; and proved by my conduct that I deserved the epithets, with which they loaded me at moments when distrust ought to cease.

"Detesting my nightly occupation, though valuing, if I may so use the word, my independence, which only consisted in choosing the street in which I should wander, or the roof, when I had money, in which I should hide my head, I was some time before I could prevail on myself to accept of a place in a house of ill fame, to which a girl, with whom I had accidentally conversed in the street, had recommended me. I had been hunted almost into a fever, by the watchmen of the quarter of the town I frequented; one, whom I had unwittingly offended, giving the word to the whole pack. You can scarcely conceive the tyranny exercised by these wretches: considering themselves as the instruments of the very laws they violate, the pretext which steels their conscience, hardens their heart. Not content with receiving from us, outlaws of society (let other women talk of favours) a brutal gratification gratuitously as a privilege of office, they extort a tithe of prostitution, and harass with threats the poor creatures whose occupation affords not the means to silence the growl of avarice. To escape from this persecution, I once more entered into servitude.

"A life of comparative regularity restored my health; and—

do not start—my manners were improved, in a situation where vice sought to render itself alluring, and taste was cultivated to fashion the person, if not to refine the mind. Besides, the common civility of speech, contrasted with the gross vulgarity to which I had been accustomed, was something like the polish of civilization. I was not shut out from all intercourse of humanity. Still I was galled by the yoke of service, and my mistress often flying into violent fits of passion, made me dread a sudden dismission, which I understood was always the case. I was therefore prevailed on, though I felt a horror of men, to accept the offer of a gentleman, rather in the decline of years, to keep his house, pleasantly situated in a little village near Hampstead.

"He was a man of great talents, and of brilliant wit; but, a worn-out voluntary of voluptuousness, his desires became fastidious in proportion as they grew weak, and the native tenderness of his heart was undermined by a vitiated imagination. A thoughtless career of libertinism[11] and social enjoyment, had injured his health to such a degree, that, whatever pleasure his conversation afforded me (and my esteem was ensured by proofs of the generous humanity of his disposition), the being his mistress was purchasing it at a very dear rate. With such a keen perception of the delicacies of sentiment, with an imagination invigorated by the exercise of genius, how could he sink into the grossness of sensuality!

"But, to pass over a subject which I recollect with pain, I must remark to you, as an answer to your often-repeated question, 'Why my sentiments and language were superior to my station?' that I now began to read, to beguile the tediousness of solitude, and to gratify an inquisitive, active mind. I had often, in my childhood, followed a ballad-singer, to hear the sequel of a dismal story, though sure of being severely punished for delaying to return with whatever I was sent to purchase. I could just spell and put a sentence together, and I listened to the various

---

[11]Libertinism: lifestyle associated with sexual promiscuity and free-thinking in religious matters.

arguments, though often mingled with obscenity, which occurred at the table where I was allowed to preside:[12] for a literary friend or two frequently came home with my master, to dine and pass the night. Having lost the privileged respect of my sex, my presence, instead of restraining, perhaps gave the reins to their tongues; still I had the advantage of hearing discussions, from which, in the common course of life, women are excluded.

"You may easily imagine, that it was only by degrees that I could comprehend some of the subjects they investigated, or acquire from their reasoning what might be termed a moral sense. But my fondness of reading increasing, and my master occasionally shutting himself up in this retreat, for weeks together, to write, I had many opportunities of improvement. At first, considering money (I was right!" exclaimed Jemima, altering her tone of voice) "as the only means, after my loss of reputation, of obtaining respect, or even the toleration of humanity, I had not the least scruple to secrete a part of the sums intrusted to me, and to screen myself from detection by a system of falshood. But, acquiring new principles, I began to have the ambition of returning to the respectable part of society, and was weak enough to suppose it possible. The attention of my unassuming instructor, who, without being ignorant of his own powers, possessed great simplicity of manners, strengthened the illusion. Having sometimes caught up hints for thought, from my untutored remarks, he often led me to discuss the subjects he was treating, and would read to me his productions, previous to their publication, wishing to profit by the criticism of unsophisticated feeling. The aim of his writings was to touch the simple springs of the heart; for he despised the would-be oracles, the self-elected philosophers, who fright away fancy, while sifting each grain of thought to prove that slowness of comprehension is wisdom.

"I should have distinguished this as a moment of sunshine, a happy period in my life, had not the repugnance the disgust-

---

[12] Sit at the head of the table.

ing libertinism of my protector inspired, daily become more painful.—And, indeed, I soon did recollect it as such with agony, when his sudden death (for he had recourse to the most exhilarating cordials to keep up the convivial tone of his spirits) again threw me into the desert of human society. Had he had any time for reflection, I am certain he would have left the little property in his power to me: but, attacked by the fatal apoplexy in town, his heir, a man of rigid morals, brought his wife with him to take possession of the house and effects, before I was even informed of his death,—'to prevent,' as she took care indirectly to tell me, 'such a creature as she supposed me to be, from purloining any of them, had I been apprized of the event in time.'

"The grief I felt at the sudden shock the information gave me, which at first had nothing selfish in it, was treated with contempt, and I was ordered to pack up my clothes; and a few trinkets and books, given me by the generous deceased, were contested, while they piously hoped, with a reprobating shake of the head, 'that God would have mercy on his sinful soul!' With some difficulty, I obtained my arrears of wages; but asking—such is the spirit-grinding consequence of poverty and infamy—for a character for honesty and economy, which God knows I merited, I was told by this—why must I call her woman?—'that it would go against her conscience to recommend a kept mistress.' Tears started in my eyes, burning tears; for there are situations in which a wretch is humbled by the contempt they are conscious they do not deserve.

"I returned to the metropolis; but the solitude of a poor lodging was inconceivably dreary, after the society I had enjoyed. To be cut off from human converse, now I had been taught to relish it, was to wander a ghost among the living. Besides, I foresaw, to aggravate the severity of my fate, that my little pittance would soon melt away. I endeavoured to obtain needle-work; but, not having been taught early, and my hands being rendered clumsy by hard work, I did not sufficiently excel to be employed by the ready-made linen shops, when so many women, better qualified, were suing for it. The want of a character prevented my getting a place; for, irksome as servitude would have been to me, I should have made another trial, had it been feasible. Not that I disliked employment, but the inequality of condition to which I must have submitted. I had acquired a taste for literature, during the five years I had lived with a literary man, occasionally conversing with men of the first abilities of the age; and now to descend to the lowest vulgarity, was a degree of wretchedness not to be imagined unfelt. I had not, it is true, tasted the charms of affection, but I had been familiar with the graces of humanity.

"One of the gentlemen, whom I had frequently dined in company with, while I was treated like a companion, met me in the street, and enquired after my health. I seized the occasion, and began to describe my situation; but he was in haste to join, at dinner, a select party of choice spirits; therefore, without waiting to hear me, he impatiently put a guinea into my hand, saying, 'It was a pity such a sensible woman should be in distress—he wished me well from his soul.'

"To another I wrote, stating my case, and requesting advice. He was an advocate for unequivocal sincerity; and had often, in my presence, descanted on the evils which arise in society from the despotism of rank and riches.

"In reply, I received a long essay on the energy of the human mind, with continual allusions to his own force of character. He added, 'That the woman who could write such a letter as I had sent him, could never be in want of resources, were she to look into herself, and exert her powers; misery was the consequence of indolence, and, as to my being shut out from society, it was the lot of man to submit to certain privations.'

"How often have I heard," said Jemima, interrupting her narrative, "in conversation, and read in books, that every person willing to work may find employment? It is the vague assertion, I believe, of insensible indolence, when it relates to men; but, with respect to women, I am sure of its fallacy, unless they will submit to the most menial bodily labour: and even to be employed at hard labour is out of the reach of many, whose reputation misfortune or folly has tainted.

"How writers, professing to be friends to freedom, and the improvement of morals, can assert that poverty is no evil, I cannot imagine."

"No more can I," interrupted Maria; "yet they even expatiate on the peculiar happiness of indigence, though in what it can consist, excepting in brutal rest, when a man can barely earn a subsistence, I cannot imagine. The mind is necessarily imprisoned in its own little tenement; and, fully occupied by keeping it in repair, has not time to rove abroad for improvement. The book of knowledge is closely clasped, against those who must fulfil their daily task of severe manual labour or die; and curiosity, rarely excited by thought or information, seldom moves on the stagnant lake of ignorance."

As far as I have been able to observe," replied Jemima, "prejudices, caught up by chance, are obstinately maintained by the poor, to the exclusion of improvement; they have not time to reason or reflect to any extent, or minds sufficiently exercised to adopt the principles of action, which form perhaps the only basis of contentment in every station."*

"And independence," said Darnford, "they are necessarily strangers to, even the independence of despising their persecutors. If the poor are happy, or can be happy, *things are very well as they are.*[13] And I cannot conceive on what principle those writers contend for a change of system, who support this opinion. The authors on the other side of the question are much more consistent, who grant the fact; yet, insisting that it is the lot of the majority to be oppressed in this life, kindly turn them over to another, to rectify the false weights and measures of this, as the only way to justify the dispensations of Providence. I have not," continued Darnford, "an opinion more firmly fixed by

---

* The copy which appears to have received the author's last corrections, ends at this place [Godwin's note].

[13] Darnford's language echoes the title of William Godwin's novel, *Caleb Williams, Things as They Are* (1794), a work which explores the effect of poverty on the individual.

observation in my mind, than that, though riches may fail to produce proportionate happiness, poverty most commonly excludes it, by shutting up all the avenues to improvement."

"And as for the affections," added Maria, with a sigh, "how gross, and even tormenting do they become, unless regulated by an improving mind! The culture of the heart ever, I believe, keeps pace with that of the mind. But pray go on," addressing Jemima, "though your narrative gives rise to the most painful reflections on the present state of society."

"Not to trouble you," continued she, "with a detailed description of all the painful feelings of unavailing exertion, I have only to tell you, that at last I got recommended to wash in a few families, who did me the favour to admit me into their houses, without the most strict enquiry, to wash from one in the morning till eight at night, for eighteen or twenty-pence a day. On the happiness to be enjoyed over a washing-tub I need not comment; yet you will allow me to observe, that this was a wretchedness of situation peculiar to my sex. A man with half my industry, and, I may say, abilities, could have procured a decent livelihood, and discharged some of the duties which knit mankind together; whilst I, who had acquired a taste for the rational, nay, in honest pride let me assert it, the virtuous enjoyments of life, was cast aside as the filth of society. Condemned to labour, like a machine, only to earn bread, and scarcely that, I became melancholy and desperate.

"CONDEMNED TO LABOUR":
EMPLOYMENT OPPORTUNITIES FOR LOWER CLASS WOMEN

To modern readers, Jemima's account of relentless misery and severely limited economic opportunity can seem exaggerated, reading more like a horror story than an objective social record. Mary Shelley, Wollstonecraft's daughter, surely must have noticed this as well, the plight of her machine-like monster in *Frankenstein* bearing more than a minor resemblance to that of the "condemned" Jemima. Were conditions really this bad for lower-class women in the late eighteenth century?

For the most, yes. Certainly, it could be for an urban woman like Jemima who had neither the advantages of marriage nor that of a learned trade, such as needlework and mantua-making. Jemima's employment history begins somewhat more optimistically, as she enters into two of the more advantageous forms of female labor: domestic service and female apprenticeship. Domestic service, according to Bridget Hill, was "becoming the most important trade for women," as industrialization led to a decline in female agricultural work and participation in "handicraft trades" (125). Hence, lower servants such as house-maids were often recruited from the country (the likely scenario of Jemima's mother) and with even middle-class families increasingly employing servants, work could usually be found. Yet even under the best of circumstances, domestic service was not likely to represent long-term independence, with females beginning service as young as 11 and most completing it by 24. Apprenticeship would represent more long-term stability, as it could lead both to a trade and to the greater likelihood of a favorable marriage. Unlike middle-class and upper-class women, lower-class women were not expected to have a dowry, but it was generally assumed they would contribute to the costs of setting up a home.

Jemima's apprenticeship to a slop-shop would have been a less advantageous position. For one, slops referred to cheap, ready-made clothing, and in particular the clothing and bedding supplied to sailors; hence, Jemima's apprenticeship would not have trained her in the skilled needlework required for the more lucrative positions of seamstress or milliner. Moreover, its clientele would have included sailors, that association most likely posing a risk to a daughter's reputation that one would assume most parents would not want to risk. Regardless, Jemima's pregnancy would have decided her fate, requiring her immediate dismissal both from apprenticeship and domestic service. Moreover, as Hill notes, "For a female servant, pregnancy meant far more than the immediate loss of a place, for without a character reference she was unlikely to get another" (137-138).

Her reputation compromised, Jemima's economic opportunities grow more limited. What is left to her are two of the more common forms of "women's work": prostitution and the washing of linen. Prostitution, according to Hill, "was widespread—and increasing" (173). Surprising is how normalized it had become, often taking "a part-time, seasonal" form and functioning as a kind of "supplemental income" for single mothers and even women between more respectable jobs (173). There was even some talk of licensing prostitution, to which Wollstonecraft was strongly opposed. Although the hardships of prostitution were many, Jemima doesn't really reach bottom until she becomes a washerwoman, one of two jobs exclusively performed by women in the eighteenth century (the other being charwoman) and one notoriously difficult. Indeed, on this point, Wollstonecraft may be underplaying the difficulties: many washerwomen also contracted to do heavy cleaning, such as floors, pots and kettles—and their hours could prove even more onerous than the 1 a.m. to 8 p.m. that Jemima mentions as her typical work day. Despite its physical hardships, the typical washerwoman was an older woman (35-55), usually married or widowed.

The hardships of being a washerwoman were made famous by Mary Collier in her poem "The Woman's Labour" (1739), a response to Stephen Duck's "The Thresher's Labour," where he comments on the idleness of rural women. A washerwoman herself until the age of 63 (as well as being a charwoman), Collier's life—like that of Jemima's—speaks to the frustrations of education and intelligence when opportunity is so limited;

she was taught to read by her parents, but was never able to attend school. Here, her poem addresses the impossible hours, physical and mental challenges, and meager compensation attendant to this position:

At length bright Sol illuminates the skies,
And summons drowsy mortals to arise;
Then comes our mistress to us without fail,
And in her hand, perhaps, a mug of ale
To cheer our hearts, and also to inform
Lays her commands upon us, that we mind
Her linen well, nor leave the dirt behind.
Not this alone, but also to take care
We don't her cambrics nor her ruffles tear;
And these most strictly does of us require,
To save her soap and sparing be of fire;
Tells us her charge is great, nay furthermore,
Her clothes are fewer than the time before.
Now we drive on, resolved our strength to try,
And what we can we do most willingly;
Until with heat and work, 'tis often known,
Not only sweat but blood runs trickling down
Our wrists and fingers: still our work demands
The constant action of our labouring hands.

Now night comes on, from whence you have relief,
But that, alas! does but increase our grief.
With heavy hearts we often view the sun,
Fearing he'll set before our work is done;
For, either in the morning or at night,
We piece the summer's day with candlelight.
Though we all day with our care our work attend,
Such is our fate, we know not when 'twill end.
When evening's come, you homeward take your way;
We, till our work is done, are forced to stay,
And, after all our toil and labour past,
Sixpence or eightpence pays us off at last;
For all our pains no prospect can we see

Attend us, but old age and poverty. (173)
As Mary Collier's poem attests, Jemima's story may be horrific, but it was not exaggerated.

SOURCES

Hill, Bridget. *Women, Work and Sexual Politics in Eighteenth-Century England.* Montreal & Kingston: McGill-Queen's University Press, 1989.

Lonsdale, Roger. *Eighteenth-Century Women Poets.* Oxford: Oxford University Press, 1989.

Wollstonecraft, Mary. *The Works of Mary Wollstonecraft,* Vol 7. Ed. by Janet Todd and Marilyn Butler. New York: New York University Press, 1989.

"I have now to mention a circumstance which fills me with remorse, and fear it will entirely deprive me of your esteem. A tradesman became attached to me, and visited me frequently,—and I at last obtained such a power over him, that he offered to take me home to his house.—Consider, dear madam, I was famishing: wonder not that I became a wolf!—The only reason for not taking me home immediately, was the having a girl in the house, with child by him—and this girl—I advised him—yes, I did! would I could forget it!—to turn out of doors: and one night he determined to follow my advice. Poor wretch! she fell upon her knees, reminded him that he had promised to marry her, that her parents were honest!—What did it avail?—She was turned out.

"She approached her father's door, in the skirts of London,—listened at the shutters,—but could not knock. A watchman had observed her go and return several times—Poor wretch!—[The remorse Jemima spoke of, seemed to be stinging her to the soul, as she proceeded.]

"She left it, and, approaching a tub where horses were watered, she sat down in it, and, with desperate resolution, remained in that attitude—till resolution was no longer necessary!

"I happened that morning to be going out to wash, anticipating the moment when I should escape from such hard labour. I passed by, just as some men, going to work, drew out the still, cold corpse—Let me not recal the horrid moment!—I recognized her pale visage; I listened to the tale told by the spectators, and my heart did not burst. I thought of my own state, and wondered how I could be such a monster!—I worked hard; and, returning home, I was attacked by a fever. I suffered both in body and mind. I determined not to live with the wretch. But he did not try me; he left the neighbourhood. I once more returned to the wash-tub.

"Still this state, miserable as it was, admitted of aggravation. Lifting one day a heavy load, a tub fell against my shin, and gave me great pain. I did not pay much attention to the hurt, till it became a serious wound; being obliged to work as usual, or starve. But, finding myself at length unable to stand for any time, I thought of getting into an hospital. Hospitals, it should seem (for they are comfortless abodes for the sick) were expressly endowed for the reception of the friendless; yet I, who had on that plea a right to assistance, wanted the recommendation of the rich and respectable, and was several weeks languishing for admittance; fees were demanded on entering; and, what was still more unreasonable, security for burying me, that expence not coming into the letter of the charity. A guinea was the stipulated sum—I could as soon have raised a million; and I was afraid to apply to the parish for an order, lest they should have passed me, I knew not whither.[14] The poor woman at whose house I lodged, compassionating my state, got me into the hospital; and the family where I received the hurt, sent me five shillings, three and six-pence of which I gave at my admittance—I know not for what.

"My leg grew quickly better; but I was dismissed before my

---

[14] One could apply for charity only in the area where one legally resided. Hence, Jemima risks being relocated if she applies for help.

cure was completed, because I could not afford to have my linen washed to appear decently, as the virago of a nurse said, when the gentlemen (the surgeons) came. I cannot give you an adequate idea of the wretchedness of an hospital; every thing is left to the care of people intent on gain. The attendants seem to have lost all feeling of compassion in the bustling discharge of their offices; death is so familiar to them, that they are not anxious to ward it off. Every thing appeared to be conducted for the accommodation of the medical men and their pupils, who came to make experiments on the poor, for the benefit of the rich. One of the physicians, I must not forget to mention, gave me half-a-crown, and ordered me some wine, when I was at the lowest ebb. I thought of making my case known to the lady-like matron; but her forbidding countenance prevented me. She condescended to look on the patients, and make general enquiries, two or three times a week; but the nurses knew the hour when the visit of ceremony would commence, and every thing was as it should be.

"After my dismission, I was more at a loss than ever for a subsistence, and, not to weary you with a repetition of the same unavailing attempts, unable to stand at the washing-tub, I began to consider the rich and poor as natural enemies, and became a thief from principle. I could not now cease to reason, but I hated mankind. I despised myself, yet I justified my conduct. I was taken, tried, and condemned to six months' imprisonment in a house of correction. My soul recoils with horror from the remembrance of the insults I had to endure, till, branded with shame, I was turned loose in the street, pennyless. I wandered from street to street, till, exhausted by hunger and fatigue, I sunk down senseless at a door, where I had vainly demanded a morsel of bread. I was sent by the inhabitant to the work-house,[15] to which he had surlily bid me go, saying he 'paid enough in conscience to the poor,' when, with parched tongue,

---

[15] A house established for the provision of work for the unemployed poor of a parish (*OED*).

I implored his charity. If those well-meaning people who exclaim against beggars, were acquainted with the treatment the poor receive in many of these wretched asylums, they would not stifle so easily involuntary sympathy, by saying that they have all parishes to go to, or wonder that the poor dread to enter the gloomy walls. What are the common run of workhouses, but prisons, in which many respectable old people, worn out by immoderate labour, sink into the grave in sorrow, to which they are carried like dogs!"

Alarmed by some indistinct noise, Jemima rose hastily to listen, and Maria, turning to Darnford, said, "I have indeed been shocked beyond expression when I have met a pauper's funeral. A coffin carried on the shoulders of three or four ill-looking wretches, whom the imagination might easily convert into a band of assassins, hastening to conceal the corpse, and quarrelling about the prey on their way. I know it is of little consequence how we are consigned to the earth; but I am led by this brutal insensibility, to what even the animal creation appears forcibly to feel, to advert[16] to the wretched, deserted manner in which they died."

"True," rejoined Darnford, "and, till the rich will give more than a part of their wealth, till they will give time and attention to the wants of the distressed, never let them boast of charity. Let them open their hearts, and not their purses, and employ their minds in the service, if they are really actuated by humanity; or charitable institutions will always be the prey of the lowest order of knaves."

Jemima returning, seemed in haste to finish her tale. "The overseer farmed the poor of different parishes, and out of the bowels of poverty was wrung the money with which he purchased this dwelling, as a private receptacle for madness.[17] He had been a keeper at a house of the same description, and conceived that he could make money much more readily in his old

---

[16] To turn one's attention; to take notice (*OED*).

[17] Private madhouses were quite common in late eighteenth-century England and by some estimates on the rise (Porter, *Mind-Forg'd Manacles*, 137).

occupation. He is a shrewd—shall I say it?—villain. He observed some thing resolute in my manner, and offered to take me with him, and instruct me how to treat the disturbed minds he meant to intrust to my care. The offer of forty pounds a year, and to quit a workhouse, was not to be despised, though the condition of shutting my eyes and hardening my heart was annexed to it.

"I agreed to accompany him; and four years have I been attendant on many wretches, and"—she lowered her voice,—"the witness of many enormities. In solitude my mind seemed to recover its force, and many of the sentiments which I imbibed in the only tolerable period of my life, returned with their full force. Still what should induce me to be the champion for suffering humanity?—Who ever risked any thing for me?—Who ever acknowledged me to be a fellow-creature?"—

Maria took her hand, and Jemima, more overcome by kindness than she had ever been by cruelty, hastened out of the room to conceal her emotions.

Darnford soon after heard his summons, and, taking leave of him, Maria promised to gratify his curiosity, with respect to herself, the first opportunity.

Chapter VI

A
ctive as love was in the heart of Maria, the story she had just heard made her thoughts take a wider range. The opening buds of hope closed, as if they had put forth too early, and the happiest day of her life was overcast by the most melancholy reflections. Thinking of Jemima's peculiar fate and her own, she was led to consider the oppressed state of women, and to lament that she had given birth to a daughter. Sleep fled from her eyelids, while she dwelt on the wretchedness of unprotected infancy, till sympathy with Jemima changed to agony, when it seemed probable that her own babe might even now be in the very state she so forcibly described.

Maria thought, and thought again. Jemima's humanity had rather been benumbed than killed, by the keen frost she had to brave at her entrance into life; an appeal then to her feelings, on this tender point, surely would not be fruitless; and Maria began to anticipate the delight it would afford her to gain intelligence of her child. This project was now the only subject of reflection; and she watched impatiently for the dawn of day, with that determinate purpose which generally insures success.

At the usual hour, Jemima brought her breakfast, and a tender note from Darnford. She ran her eye hastily over it, and her heart calmly hoarded up the rapture a fresh assurance of affection, affection such as she wished to inspire, gave her, without diverting her mind a moment from its design. While Jemima waited to take away the breakfast, Maria alluded to the reflections, that had haunted her during the night to the exclusion of sleep. She spoke with energy of Jemima's unmerited sufferings, and of the fate of a number of deserted females, placed within the sweep of a whirlwind, from which it was next to impossible to escape. Perceiving the effect her conversation produced on the countenance of her guard, she grasped the arm of Jemima with that irresistible warmth which defies repulse, exclaiming— "With your heart, and such dreadful experience, can you lend your aid to deprive my babe of a mother's tenderness, a mother's care? In the name of God, assist me to snatch her from destruction! Let me but give her an education—let me but prepare her body and mind to encounter the ills which await her sex, and I will teach her to consider you as her second mother, and herself as the prop of your age. Yes, Jemima, look at me—observe me closely, and read my very soul; you merit a better fate; "she held out her hand with a firm gesture of assurance; "and I will procure it for you, as a testimony of my esteem, as well as my gratitude."

Jemima had not power to resist this persuasive torrent; and, owning that the house in which she was confined, was situated on the banks of the Thames, only a few miles from London, and not on the sea-coast, as Darnford had supposed, she promised to invent some excuse for her absence, and go herself to trace the situation, and enquire concerning the health, of this abandoned daughter. Her manner implied an intention to do something more, but she seemed unwilling to impart her design; and Maria, glad to have obtained the main point, thought it best to leave her to the workings of her own mind; convinced that she had the power of interesting her still more in favour of herself and child, by a simple recital of facts.

In the evening, Jemima informed the impatient mother, that on the morrow she should hasten to town before the family hour of rising, and received all the information necessary, as a clue to her search. The "Good night!" Maria uttered was peculiarly solemn and affectionate. Glad expectation sparkled in her eye; and, for the first time since her detention, she pronounced the name of her child with pleasureable fondness; and, with all the garrulity of a nurse, described her first smile when she recognized her mother. Recollecting herself, a still kinder "Adieu!" with a "God bless you!"—that seemed to include a maternal benediction, dismissed Jemima.

The dreary solitude of the ensuing day, lengthened by impatiently dwelling on the same idea, was intolerably wearisome. She listened for the sound of a particular clock, which some directions of the wind allowed her to hear distinctly. She marked the shadow gaining on the wall; and, twilight thickening into darkness, her breath seemed oppressed while she anxiously counted nine.—The last sound was a stroke of despair on her heart; for she expected every moment, without seeing Jemima, to have her light extinguished by the savage female who supplied her place. She was even obliged to prepare for bed, restless as she was, not to disoblige her new attendant. She had been cautioned not to speak too freely to her; but the caution was needless, her countenance would still more emphatically have made her shrink back. Such was the ferocity of manner, conspicuous in every word and gesture of this hag, that Maria was afraid to enquire, why Jemima, who had faithfully promised to see her before her door was shut for the night, came not?—and, when the key turned in the lock, to consign her to a night of suspence, she felt a degree of anguish which the circumstances scarcely justified.

Continually on the watch, the shutting of a door, or the sound of a footstep, made her start and tremble with apprehension, something like what she felt, when, at her entrance, dragged along the gallery, she began to doubt whether she were not surrounded by demons?

Fatigued by an endless rotation of thought and wild alarms, she looked like a spectre, when Jemima entered in the morning; especially as her eyes darted out of her head, to read in Jemima's countenance, almost as pallid, the intelligence she dared not trust her tongue to demand. Jemima put down the tea-things, and appeared very busy in arranging the table. Maria took up a cup with trembling hand, then forcibly recovering her fortitude, and restraining the convulsive movement which agitated the muscles of her mouth, she said, "Spare yourself the pain of preparing me for your information, I adjure you!—My child is dead!" Jemima solemnly answered, "Yes;" with a look expressive of compassion and angry emotions. "Leave me," added Maria, making a fresh effort to govern her feelings, and hiding her face in her handkerchief, to conceal her anguish—"It is enough—I know that my babe is no more—I will hear the particulars when I am—*calmer*, she could not utter; and Jemima, without importuning her by idle attempts to console her, left the room.

Plunged in the deepest melancholy, she would not admit Darnford's visits; and such is the force of early associations even on strong minds, that, for a while, she indulged the superstitious notion that she was justly punished by the death of her child, for having for an instant ceased to regret her loss. Two or three letters from Darnford, full of soothing, manly tenderness, only added poignancy to these accusing emotions; yet the passionate style in which he expressed, what he termed the first and fondest wish of his heart, "that his affection might make her some amends for the cruelty and injustice she had endured," inspired a sentiment of gratitude to heaven; and her eyes filled with delicious tears, when, at the conclusion of his letter, wishing to supply the place of her unworthy relations, whose want of principle he execrated, he assured her, calling her his dearest girl, "that it should henceforth be the business of his life to make her happy."

He begged, in a note sent the following morning, to be permitted to see her, when his presence would be no intrusion on her grief; and so earnestly intreated to be allowed, according to promise, to beguile the tedious moments of absence, by dwelling on the events of her past life, that she sent him the memoirs which had been written for her daughter, promising Jemima the perusal as soon as he returned them.

Chapter VII

Addressing these memoirs to you, my child, uncertain whether I shall ever have an opportunity of instructing you, many observations will probably flow from my heart, which only a mother—a mother schooled in misery, could make.

"The tenderness of a father who knew the world, might be great; but could it equal that of a mother—of a mother, labouring under a portion of the misery, which the constitution of society seems to have entailed on all her kind? It is, my child, my dearest daughter, only such a mother, who will dare to break through all restraint to provide for your happiness—who will voluntarily brave censure herself, to ward off sorrow from your bosom. From my narrative, my dear girl, you may gather the instruction, the counsel, which is meant rather to exercise than influence your mind.—Death may snatch me from you, before you can weigh my advice, or enter into my reasoning: I would then, with fond anxiety, lead you very early in life to form your grand principle of action, to save you from the vain regret of having, through irresolution, let the spring-tide of experience pass away, unimproved, unenjoyed.—Gain experience—ah! gain it—while experience is worth having, and acquire sufficient fortitude to pursue your own happiness; it includes your utility, by a direct path. What is wisdom too often, but the owl of the goddess,[1] who sits moping in a desolated heart; around me she shrieks, but I would invite all the gay warblers of spring to nestle in your blooming bosom.—Had I not wasted years in deliberating, after I ceased to doubt, how I ought to have acted—I might now be useful and happy.—For my sake, warned by my example,

---

[1] In Greek mythology, the owl is associated with Athene, the goddess of wisdom.

always appear what you are, and you will not pass through existence without enjoying its genuine blessings, love and respect.

"Born in one of the most romantic parts of England, an enthusiastic fondness for the varying charms of nature is the first sentiment I recollect; or rather it was the first consciousness of pleasure that employed and formed my imagination.

"My father had been a captain of a man of war; but, disgusted with the service, on account of the preferment of men whose chief merit was their family connections or borough interest[2], he retired into the country; and, not knowing what to do with himself—married. In his family, to regain his lost consequence, he determined to keep up the same passive obedience, as in the vessels in which he had commanded. His orders were not to be disputed; and the whole house was expected to fly, at the word of command, as if to man the shrouds, or mount aloft in an elemental strife, big with life or death. He was to be instantaneously obeyed, especially by my mother, whom he very benevolently married for love; but took care to remind her of the obligation, when she dared, in the slightest instance, to question his absolute authority. My eldest brother, it is true, as he grew up, was treated with more respect by my father; and became in due form the deputy-tyrant of the house. The representative of my father, a being privileged by nature—a boy, and the darling of my mother, he did not fail to act like an heir apparent. Such indeed was my mother's extravagant partiality, that, in comparison with her affection for him, she might be said not to love the rest of her children. Yet none of the children seemed to have so little affection for her. Extreme indulgence had rendered him so selfish, that he only thought of himself; and from tormenting insects and animals, he became the despot of his brothers, and still more of his sisters.

"It is perhaps difficult to give you an idea of the petty cares which obscured the morning of my life; continual restraint in the most trivial matters; unconditional submission to orders,

---

[2] Military promotion was often bought in exchange for political favors.

which, as a mere child, I soon discovered to be unreasonable, because inconsistent and contradictory. Thus are we destined to experience a mixture of bitterness, with the recollection of our most innocent enjoyments.

"The circumstances which, during my childhood, occurred to fashion my mind, were various; yet, as it would probably afford me more pleasure to revive the fading remembrance of new-born delight, than you, my child, could feel in the perusal, I will not entice you to stray with me into the verdant meadow, to search for the flowers that youthful hopes scatter in every path; though, as I write, I almost scent the fresh green of spring— of that spring which never returns!

"I had two sisters, and one brother, younger than myself; my brother Robert was two years older, and might truly be termed the idol of his parents, and the torment of the rest of the family. Such indeed is the force of prejudice, that what was called spirit and wit in him, was cruelly repressed as forwardness in me.

"My mother had an indolence of character, which prevented her from paying much attention to our education. But the healthy breeze of a neighbouring heath, on which we bounded at pleasure, volatilized the humours that improper food might have generated. And to enjoy open air and freedom, was paradise, after the unnatural restraint of our fire-side, where we were often obliged to sit three or four hours together, without daring to utter a word, when my father was out of humour, from want of employment, or of a variety of boisterous amusement. I had however one advantage, an instructor, the brother of my father, who, intended for the church, had of course received a liberal education.[3] But, becoming attached to a young lady of great beauty and large fortune, and acquiring in the world some opinions not consonant with the profession for which he was designed, he accepted, with the most sanguine expectations of suc-

---

[3] A presumed career in the church, typical for a second–born son, would have afforded the uncle an education befitting a gentleman and not the professional class. His education would have emphasized broad intellectual understanding, and not technical skill.

cess, the offer of a nobleman to accompany him to India, as his confidential secretary.

"A correspondence was regularly kept up with the object of his affection; and the intricacies of business, peculiarly wearisome to a man of a romantic turn of mind, contributed, with a forced absence to increase his attachment. Every other passion was lost in this master-one, and only served to swell the torrent. Her relations, such were his waking dreams, who had despised him, would court in their turn his alliance, and all the blandishments of taste would grace the triumph of love.—While he basked in the warm sunshine of love, friendship also promised to shed its dewy freshness; for a friend, whom he loved next to his mistress, was the confident, who forwarded the letters from one to the other, to elude the observation of prying relations. A friend false in similar circumstances, is, my dearest girl, an old tale; yet, let not this example, or the frigid caution of cold-blooded moralists make you endeavour to stifle hopes, which are the buds that naturally unfold themselves during the spring of life! Whilst your own heart is sincere, always expect to meet one glowing with the same sentiments; for to fly from pleasure, is not to avoid pain!

"My uncle realized, by good luck, rather than management, a handsome fortune; and returning on the wings of love, lost in the most enchanting reveries, to England, to share it with his mistress and his friend, he found them—united.

"There were some circumstances, not necessary for me to recite, which aggravated the guilt of the friend beyond measure, and the deception, that had been carried on to the last moment, was so base, it produced the most violent effect on my uncle's health and spirits. His native country, the world! lately a garden of blooming sweets, blasted by treachery, seemed changed into a parched desert, the abode of hissing serpents. Disappointment rankled in his heart; and, brooding over his wrongs, he was attacked by a raging fever, followed by a derangement of mind, which only gave place to habitual melancholy, as he recovered more strength of body.

"Declaring an intention never to marry, his relations were

ever clustering about him, paying the grossest adulation to a
man, who, disgusted with mankind, received them with scorn,
or bitter sarcasms. Something in my countenance pleased him,
when I began to prattle. Since his return, he appeared dead to
affection; but I soon, by showing him innocent fondness, became a favorite; and endeavouring to enlarge and strengthen my
mind, I grew dear to him in proportion as I imbibed his sentiments. He had a forcible manner of speaking, rendered more so
by a certain impressive wildness of look and gesture, calculated
to engage the attention of a young and ardent mind. It is not
then surprising that I quickly adopted his opinions in preference, and reverenced him as one of a superior order of beings.
He inculcated, with great warmth, self-respect, and a lofty consciousness of acting right, independent of the censure or applause of the world; nay, he almost taught me to brave, and even
despise its censure, when convinced of the rectitude of my own
intentions.

"Endeavouring to prove to me that nothing which deserved
the name of love or friendship, existed in the world, he drew
such animated pictures of his own feelings, rendered permanent
by disappointment, as imprinted the sentiments strongly on
my heart, and animated my imagination. These remarks are
necessary to elucidate some peculiarities in my character, which
by the world are indefinitely termed romantic.

"My uncle's increasing affection led him to visit me often.
Still, unable to rest in any place, he did not remain long in the
country to soften domestic tyranny; but he brought me books,
for which I had a passion, and they conspired with his conversation, to make me form an ideal picture of life. I shall pass over
the tyranny of my father, much as I suffered from it; but it is
necessary to notice, that it undermined my mother's health; and
that her temper, continually irritated by domestic bickering,
became intolerably peevish.

"My eldest brother was articled[4] to a neighbouring attor-

---

[4] Apprenticed.

ney, the shrewdest, and, I may add, the most unprincipled man in that part of the country. As my brother generally came home every Saturday, to astonish my mother by exhibiting his attainments, he gradually assumed a right of directing the whole family, not excepting my father. He seemed to take a peculiar pleasure in tormenting and humbling me; and if I ever ventured to complain of this treatment to either my father or mother, I was rudely rebuffed for presuming to judge of the conduct of my eldest brother.

"About this period a merchant's family came to settle in our neighbourhood. A mansion-house in the village, lately purchased, had been preparing the whole spring, and the sight of the costly furniture, sent from London, had excited my mother's envy, and roused my father's pride. My sensations were very different, and all of a pleasurable kind. I longed to see new characters, to break the tedious monotony of my life; and to find a friend, such as fancy had pourtrayed. I cannot then describe the emotion I felt, the Sunday they made their appearance at church. My eyes were rivetted on the pillar round which I expected first to catch a glimpse of them, and darted forth to meet a servant who hastily preceded a group of ladies, whose white robes and waving plumes, seemed to stream along the gloomy aisle, diffusing the light, by which I contemplated their figures.

"We visited them in form; and I quickly selected the eldest daughter for my friend. The second son, George, paid me particular attention, and finding his attainments and manners superior to those of the young men of the village, I began to imagine him superior to the rest of mankind. Had my home been more comfortable, or my previous acquaintance more numerous, I should not probably have been so eager to open my heart to new affections.

"Mr. Venables, the merchant, had acquired a large fortune by unremitting attention to business; but his health declining rapidly, he was obliged to retire, before his son, George, had acquired sufficient experience, to enable him to conduct their affairs on the same prudential plan, his father had invariably pursued. Indeed, he had laboured to throw off his authority, having despised his narrow plans and cautious speculation. The eldest son could not be prevailed on to enter the firm; and, to oblige his wife, and have peace in the house, Mr. Venables had purchased a commission for him in the guards.

"I am now alluding to circumstances which came to my knowledge long after; but it is necessary, my dearest child, that you should know the character of your father, to prevent your despising your mother; the only parent inclined to discharge a parent's duty. In London, George had acquired habits of libertinism, which he carefully concealed from his father and his commercial connections. The mask he wore, was so complete a covering of his real visage, that the praise his father lavished on his conduct, and, poor mistaken man! on his principles, con-trasted with his brother's, rendered the notice he took of me peculiarly flattering. Without any fixed design, as I am now convinced, he continued to single me out at the dance, press my hand at parting, and utter expressions of unmeaning passion, to which I gave a meaning naturally suggested by the romantic turn of my thoughts. His stay in the country was short; his manners did not entirely please me; but, when he left us, the colouring of my picture became more vivid—Whither did not my imagination lead me? In short, I fancied myself in love—in love with the disinterestedness, fortitude, generosity, dignity, and humanity, with which I had invested the hero I dubbed. A circumstance which soon after occurred, rendered all these vir-tues palpable. [The incident is perhaps worth relating on other accounts, and therefore I shall describe it distinctly.]

"I had a great affection for my nurse, old Mary, for whom I used often to work, to spare her eyes. Mary had a younger sister, married to a sailor, while she was suckling me; for my mother only suckled my eldest brother, which might be the cause of her extraordinary partiality. Peggy, Mary's sister, lived with her, till her husband, becoming a mate in a West-India trader,[5] got a

---

[5] A sea vessel engaged in trading.

little before-hand in the world. He wrote to his wife from the first port in the Channel, after his most successful voyage, to request her to come to London to meet him; he even wished her to determine on living there for the future, to save him the trouble of coming to her the moment he came on shore; and to turn a penny by keeping a green-stall. It was too much to set out on a journey the moment he had finished a voyage, and fifty miles by land, was worse than a thousand leagues by sea.

"She packed up her alls,[6] and came to London—but did not meet honest Daniel. A common misfortune prevented her, and the poor are bound to suffer for the good of their country— he was pressed in the river—and never came on shore.[7]

"Peggy was miserable in London, not knowing, as she said 'the face of any living soul.'" Besides, her imagination had been employed, anticipating a month or six weeks' happiness with her husband. Daniel was to have gone with her to Sadler's Wells, and Westminster Abbey, and to many sights, which he knew she never heard of in the country. Peggy too was thrifty, and how could she manage to put his plan in execution alone? He had acquaintance; but she did not know the very name of their places of abode. His letters were made up of—How do you does, and God bless yous,—information was reserved for the hour of meeting.

"She too had her portion of information, near at heart. Molly and Jacky were grown such little darlings, she was almost angry that daddy did not see their tricks. She had not half the pleasure she should have had from their prattle, could she have recounted to him each night the pretty speeches of the day. Some stories, however, were stored up—and Jacky could say papa with such a sweet voice, it must delight his heart. Yet when she came, and found no Daniel to greet her, when Jacky called papa, she wept, bidding 'God bless his innocent soul, that did not know what sorrow was.' –But more sorrow was in store for Peggy,

---

[6] Everything that we have, or that concerns or pertains to us (*OED*).

[7] I.e., forced to serve in the army or navy (*OED*). Typically, it was the poor who were forced into service; the practice was not discontinued until 1815.

innocent as she was.—Daniel was killed in the first engagement, and then the *papa* was agony, sounding to the heart.

"She had lived sparingly on his wages, while there was any hope of his return; but, that gone, she returned with a breaking heart to the country, to a little market town, nearly three miles from our village. She did not like to go to service, to be snubbed about, after being her own mistress. To put her children out to nurse was impossible: how far would her wages go? and to send them to her husband's parish, a distant one, was to lose her husband twice over.

"I had heard all from Mary, and made my uncle furnish a little cottage for her, to enable her to sell—so sacred was poor Daniel's advice, now he was dead and gone—a little fruit, toys and cakes. The minding of the shop did not require her whole time, nor even the keeping her children clean, and she loved to see them clean; so she took in washing, and altogether made a shift to earn bread for her children, still weeping for Daniel, when Jacky's arch looks made her think of his father.—It was pleasant to work for her children.—'Yes; from morning till night, could she have had a kiss from their father, God rest his soul! Yes; had it pleased Providence to have let him come back without a leg or an arm, it would have been the same thing to her—for she did not love him because he maintained them—no; she had hands of her own.'

"The country people were honest, and Peggy left her linen out to dry very late. A recruiting party, as she supposed, passing through, made free with a large wash; for it was all swept away, including her own and her children's little stock.

"This was a dreadful blow; two dozen of shirts, stocks,[8] and handkerchiefs. She gave the money which she had laid by for half a year's rent, and promised to pay two shillings a week till all was cleared; so she did not lose her employment. This two shillings a week, and the buying a few necessaries for the children, drove her so hard, that she had not a penny to pay her rent

---

[8] A kind of stiff, close-fitting neck cloth, formerly worn by men generally (*OED*).

with, when a twelvemonth's became due.

"She was now with Mary, and had just told her tale, which Mary instantly repeated—it was intended for my ear. Many houses in this town, producing a borough-interest, were included in the estate purchased by Mr. Venables, and the attorney with whom my brother lived, was appointed his agent, to collect and raise the rents.

"He demanded Peggy's, and, in spite of her intreaties, her poor goods had been seized and sold. So that she had not, and what was worse her children, 'for she had known sorrow enough,' a bed to lie on. She knew that I was good-natured—right charitable, yet not liking to ask for more than needs must, she scorned to petition while people could any how be made to wait. But now, should she be turned out of doors, she must expect nothing less than to lose all her customers, and then she must beg or starve—and what would become of her children?—'had Daniel not been pressed—but God knows best—all this could not have happened.'

"I had two mattresses on my bed; what did I want with two, when such a worthy creature must lie on the ground? My mother would be angry, but I could conceal it till my uncle came down; and then I would tell him all the whole truth, and if he absolved me, heaven would.

"I begged the house-maid to come up stairs with me (servants always feel for the distresses of poverty, and so would the rich if they knew what it was). She assisted me to tie up the mattress; I discovering, at the same time, that one blanket would serve me till winter, could I persuade my sister, who slept with me, to keep my secret. She entering in the midst of the package, I gave her some new feathers, to silence her. We got the mattress down the back stairs, unperceived, and I helped to carry it, taking with me all the money I had, and what I could borrow from my sister.

"When I got to the cottage, Peggy declared that she would not take what I had brought secretly; but, when, with all the eager eloquence inspired by a decided purpose, I grasped her hand with weeping eyes, assuring her that my uncle would screen me from blame, when he was once more in the country, describing, at the same time, what she would suffer in parting with her children, after keeping them so long from being thrown on the parish, she reluctantly consented.

"My project of usefulness ended not here; I determined to speak to the attorney; he frequently paid me compliments. His character did not intimidate me; but, imagining that Peggy must be mistaken, and that no man could turn a deaf ear to such a tale of complicated distress, I determined to walk to the town with Mary the next morning, and request him to wait for the rent, and keep my secret, till my uncle's return.

"My repose was sweet; and, waking with the first dawn of day, I bounded to Mary's cottage. What charms do not a light heart spread over nature! Every bird that twittered in a bush, every flower that enlivened the hedge, seemed placed there to awaken me to rapture—yes; to rapture. The present moment was full fraught with happiness; and on futurity I bestowed not a thought, excepting to anticipate my success with the attorney.

"This man of the world, with rosy face and simpering features, received me politely, nay kindly; listened with complacency to my remonstrances, though he scarcely heeded Mary's tears. I did not then suspect, that my eloquence was in my complexion, the blush of seventeen, or that, in a world where humanity to women is the characteristic of advancing civilization, the beauty of a young girl was so much more interesting than the distress of an old one. Pressing my hand, he promised to let Peggy remain in the house as long as I wished.—I more than returned the pressure—I was so grateful and so happy. Emboldened by my innocent warmth, he then kissed me—and I did not draw back—I took it for a kiss of charity.

"Gay as a lark, I went to dine at Mr. Venables'. I had previously obtained five shillings from my father, towards re-clothing the poor children of my care, and prevailed on my mother to take one of the girls into the house, whom I determined to teach to work and read.

"After dinner, when the younger part of the circle retired to the music-room, I recounted with energy my tale; that is, I mentioned Peggy's distress, without hinting at the steps I had taken to relieve her. Miss Venables gave me half-a-crown; the heir five shillings; but George sat unmoved. I was cruelly distressed by the disappointment—I scarcely could remain on my chair; and, could I have got out of the room unperceived, I should have flown home, as if to run away from myself. After several vain attempts to rise, I leaned my head against the marble chimney-piece, and gazing on the evergreens that filled the fire-place, moralized on the vanity of human expectations; regardless of the company. I was roused by a gentle tap on my shoulder from behind Charlotte's chair. I turned my head, and George slid a guinea into my hand, putting his finger to his mouth, to enjoin me silence.

"What a revolution took place, not only in my train of thoughts, but feelings! I trembled with emotion—now, indeed, I was in love. Such delicacy too, to enhance his benevolence! I felt in my pocket every five minutes, only to feel the guinea; and its magic touch invested my hero with more than mortal beauty. My fancy had found a basis to erect its model of perfection on; and quickly went to work, with all the happy credulity of youth, to consider that heart as devoted to virtue, which had only obeyed a virtuous impulse. The bitter experience was yet to come, that has taught me how very distinct are the principles of virtue, from the casual feelings from which they germinate.

Chapter VIII

I have perhaps dwelt too long on a circumstance, which is only of importance as it marks the progress of a deception that has been so fatal to my peace; and introduces to your notice a poor girl, whom, intending to serve, I led to ruin. Still it is probable that I was not entirely the victim of mistake; and that your father, gradually fashioned by the world, did not quickly become what I hesitate to call him—out of respect to my daughter.

"But, to hasten to the more busy scenes of my life. Mr. Venables and my mother died the same summer; and, wholly engrossed by my attention to her, I thought of little else. The neglect of her darling, my brother Robert, had a violent effect on her weakened mind; for, though boys may be reckoned the pillars of the house without doors, girls are often the only comfort within. They but too frequently waste their health and spirits attending a dying parent, who leaves them in comparative poverty. After closing, with filial piety, a father's eyes, they are chased from the paternal roof, to make room for the first-born, the son, who is to carry the empty family-name down to posterity; though, occupied with his own pleasures, he scarcely thought of discharging, in the decline of his parent's life, the debt contracted in his childhood. My mother's conduct led me to make these reflections. Great as was the fatigue I endured, and the affection my unceasing solicitude evinced, of which my mother seemed perfectly sensible, still, when my brother, whom I could hardly persuade to remain a quarter of an hour in her chamber, was with her alone, a short time before her death, she gave him a little hoard, which she had been some years accumulating.

"During my mother's illness, I was obliged to manage my

father's temper, who, from the lingering nature of her malady, began to imagine that it was merely fancy. At this period, an artful kind of upper servant attracted my father's attention, and the neighbours made many remarks on the finery, not honestly got, exhibited at evening service. But I was too much occupied with my mother to observe any change in her dress or behaviour, or to listen to the whisper of scandal.

"I shall not dwell on the death-bed scene, lively as is the remembrance, or on the emotion produced by the last grasp of my mother's cold hand; when blessing me, she added, 'A little patience, and all will be over!' Ah! my child, how often have those words rung mournfully in my ears—and I have exclaimed— 'A little more patience, and I too shall be at rest!'[1]

"My father was violently affected by her death, recollected instances of his unkindness, and wept like a child.

"My mother had solemnly recommended my sisters to my care, and bid me be a mother to them. They, indeed, became more dear to me as they became more forlorn; for, during my mother's illness, I discovered the ruined state of my father's circumstances, and that he had only been able to keep up appearances, by the sums which he borrowed of my uncle.

"My father's grief, and consequent tenderness to his children, quickly abated, the house grew still more gloomy or riotous; and my refuge from care was again at Mr. Venables'; the young 'squire having taken his father's place, and allowing, for the present, his sister to preside at his table. George, though dissatisfied with his portion of the fortune, which had till lately been all in trade, visited the family as usual. He was now full of speculations in trade, and his brow became clouded by care. He

---

[1] Wollstonecraft's last written words to her husband, William Godwin, echo these of Maria's mother (which themselves echo those of Wollstonecraft's own mother). See Chapter Two, *Memoirs*, p. 213. She writes to Godwin on August 30, 1797, "Mrs. Blenkinsop tells that I am in the most natural state, and can promise me a safe delivery—But that I must have a little patience" [*Godwin and Mary*, Ed. Ralph Wardle (Lawrence, Kansas: University of Kansas Press, 1966), 120]. Wollstonecraft died from complications arising from childbirth on September 10, 1797.

seemed to relax in his attention to me, when the presence of my uncle gave a new turn to his behaviour. I was too unsuspecting, too disinterested, to trace these changes to their source.

My home every day became more and more disagreeable to me; my liberty was unnecessarily abridged, and my books, on the pretext that they made me idle, taken from me. My father's mistress was with child, and he, doating on her, allowed or over-looked her vulgar manner of tyrannizing over us. I was indig-nant, especially when I saw her endeavouring to attract, shall I say seduce? my younger brother. By allowing women but one way of rising in the world, the fostering the libertinism of men, society makes monsters of them, and then their ignoble vices are brought forward as a proof of inferiority of intellect.

The wearisomeness of my situation can scarcely be described. Though my life had not passed in the most even tenour with my mother, it was paradise to that I was destined to endure with my father's mistress, jealous of her illegitimate authority. My father's former occasional tenderness, in spite of his violence of temper, had been soothing to me; but now he only met me with reproofs or portentous frowns. The house-keeper, as she was now termed, was the vulgar despot of the family; and assuming the new char-acter of a fine lady, she could never forgive the contempt which was sometimes visible in my countenance, when she uttered with pomposity her bad English, or affected to be well bred.

To my uncle I ventured to open my heart; and he, with his wonted benevolence, began to consider in what manner he could extricate me out of my present irksome situation. In spite of his own disappointment, or, most probably, actuated by the feel-ings that had been petrified, not cooled, in all their sanguine fervour, like a boiling torrent of lava suddenly dashing into the sea, he thought a marriage of mutual inclination (would envious stars permit it) the only chance for happiness in this disastrous world. George Venables had the reputation of being attentive to business, and my father's example gave great weight to this cir-cumstance; for habits of order in business would, he conceived, extend to the regulation of the affections in domestic life. George seldom spoke in my uncle's company, except to utter a short, judicious question, or to make a pertinent remark, with all due deference to his superior judgment; so that my uncle seldom left his company without observing, that the young man had more in him than people supposed.

In this opinion he was not singular; yet, believe me, and I am not swayed by resentment, these speeches so justly poized, this silent deference, when the animal spirits of other young people were throwing off youthful ebullitions, were not the effect of thought or humanity, but sheer barrenness of mind, and want of imagination. A colt of mettle will curvet[2] and shew his paces. Yes; my dear girl, these prudent young men want all the fire necessary to ferment their faculties, and are characterized as wise, only because they are not foolish. It is true, that George was by no means so great a favourite of mine as during the first year of our acquaintance; still, as he often coincided in opinion with me, and echoed my sentiments; and having myself no other attachment, I heard with pleasure my uncle's proposal; but thought more of obtaining my freedom, than of my lover. But, when George, seemingly anxious for my happiness, pressed me to quit my present painful situation, my heart swelled with gratitude—I knew not that my uncle had promised him five thousand pounds.

Had this truly generous man mentioned his intention to me, I should have insisted on a thousand pounds being settled on each of my sisters; George would have contested; I should have seen his selfish soul; and—gracious God! have been spared the misery of discovering, when too late, that I was united to a heartless, unprincipled wretch. All my schemes of usefulness would not then have been blasted. The tenderness of my heart would not have heated my imagination with visions of the ineffable delight of happy love; nor would the sweet duty of a mother have been so cruelly interrupted.

But I must not suffer the fortitude I have so hardly acquired,

---

[2] I.e., will leap about, frisk.

to be undermined by unavailing regret. Let me hasten forward to describe the turbid stream in which I had to wade—but let me exultingly declare that it is passed—my soul holds fellowship with him no more. He cut the Gordian knot,[3] which my principles, mistaken ones, respected; he dissolved the tie; the fetters rather, that ate into my very vitals—and I should rejoice, conscious that my mind is freed, though confined in hell itself; the only place that even fancy can imagine more dreadful than my present abode.

These varying emotions will not allow me to proceed. I heave sigh after sigh; yet my heart is still oppressed. For what am I reserved? Why was I not born a man, or why was I born at all?

---

[3] To cut a Gordian knot: to get rid of a difficulty by force or by evading the supposed conditions of solution (OED). Alexander the Great "solved" the problem of loosening an intricate knot tied by Gordius, king of Gordium, by cutting through it with a sword.

Chapter IX

I resume my pen to fly from thought. I was married; and we hastened to London. I had purposed taking one of my sisters with me; for a strong motive for marrying, was the desire of having a home at which I could receive them, now their own grew so uncomfortable, as not to deserve the cheering appellation. An objection was made to her accompanying me, that appeared plausible; and I reluctantly acquiesced. I was however willingly allowed to take with me Molly, poor Peggy's daughter. London and preferment, are ideas commonly associated in the country; and, as blooming as May, she bade adieu to Peggy with weeping eyes. I did not even feel hurt at the refusal in relation to my sister, till hearing what my uncle had done for me, I had the simplicity to request, speaking with warmth of their situation, that he would give them a thousand pounds a-piece, which seemed to me but justice. He asked me, giving me a kiss, 'If I had lost my senses?' I started back, as if I had found a wasp in a rose-bush. I expostulated. He sneered; and the demon of discord entered our paradise, to poison with his pestiferous breath every opening joy.

"I had sometimes observed defects in my husband's understanding; but, led astray by prevailing opinion, that goodness of disposition is of the first importance in the relative situations of life, in proportion as I perceived the narrowness of his understanding, fancy enlarged the boundary of his heart. Fatal error! How quickly is the so much vaunted milkiness of nature turned into gall, by an intercourse with the world, if more generous juices do not sustain the vital source of virtue!

"One trait in my character was extreme credulity; but, when my eyes were once opened, I saw but too clearly all I had before overlooked. My husband was sunk in my esteem; still there are youthful emotions, which, for a while, fill up the chasm of love and friendship. Besides, it required some time to enable me to see his whole character in a just light, or rather to allow it to become fixed. While circumstances were ripening my faculties, and cultivating my taste, commerce and gross relaxation were shutting his against any possibility of improvement, till, by stifling every spark of virtue in himself, he began to imagine that it no where existed.

"Do not let me lead you astray, my child, I do not mean to assert, that any human being is entirely incapable of feeling the generous emotions, which are the foundation of every true principle of virtue; but they are frequently, I fear, so feeble, that, like the inflammable quality which more or less lurks in all bodies, they often lie for ever dormant; the circumstances never occurring, necessary to call them into action.

"I discovered however by chance, that, in consequence of some losses in trade, the natural effect of his gambling desire to start suddenly into riches, the five thousand pounds given me by my uncle, had been paid very opportunely. This discovery, strange as you may think the assertion, gave me pleasure; my husband's embarrassments endeared him to me. I was glad to find an excuse for his conduct to my sisters, and my mind became calmer.

"My uncle introduced me to some literary society; and the theatres were a never-failing source of amusement to me. My delighted eye followed Mrs. Siddons,[1] when, with dignified delicacy, she played Calista;[2] and I involuntarily repeated after her, in the same tone, and with a long-drawn sigh,

---

[1] Sarah Siddons (*nee* Kimble) (1775-1830). Siddons, a highly popular actress of the late eighteenth century, was known for her off-stage virtue and her on-stage versatility in both chaste and cross-dressed roles. Once an admirer of Wollstonecraft's, she abandons their friendship after Wollstonecraft's marriage to Godwin and the precipitating pregnancy become known.

[2] The heroine of Nicolas Rowe, *The Fair Penitent* (1703); Calista—one of the great, but controversial roles for eighteenth-century actresses—is seduced and abandoned by her lover, then dutifully marries a man against her inclinations, all the while continuing to protest her fate.

'Hearts like our's were pair'd—not match'd.'[3]

"These were, at first, spontaneous emotions, though, becoming acquainted with men of wit and polished manners, I
could not sometimes help regretting my early marriage; and that,
in my haste to escape from a temporary dependence, and expand my newly fledged wings, in an unknown sky, I had been
caught in a trap, and caged for life. Still the novelty of London,
and the attentive fondness of my husband, for he had some personal regard for me, made several months glide away. Yet, not
forgetting the situation of my sisters, who were still very young,
I prevailed on my uncle to settle a thousand pounds on each;
and to place them in a school near town, where I could frequently visit, as well as have them at home with me.

"I now tried to improve my husband's taste, but we had few
subjects in common; indeed he soon appeared to have little relish for my society, unless he was hinting to me the use he could
make of my uncle's wealth. When we had company, I was disgusted by an ostentatious display of riches, and I have often
quitted the room, to avoid listening to exaggerated tales of money
obtained by lucky hits.

"With all my attention and affectionate interest, I perceived
that I could not become the friend or confident of my husband.
Every thing I learned relative to his affairs I gathered up by accident; and I vainly endeavoured to establish, at our fire-side, that
social converse, which often renders people of different characters dear to each other. Returning from the theatre, or any amusing party, I frequently began to relate what I had seen and highly
relished; but with sullen taciturnity he soon silenced me. I seemed
therefore gradually to lose, in his society, the soul, the energies
of which had just been in action. To such a degree, in fact, did
his cold, reserved manner affect me, that, after spending some
days with him alone, I have imagined myself the most stupid

---

[3] Rowe, *The Fair Penitent*, II.i.103-104: 'Such hearts as ours were never paired
above:/ Ill-suited to each other; joined, not matched." Calista speaks these lines to
Altamont, her father's choice for her husband.

creature in the world, till the abilities of some casual visitor convinced me that I had some dormant animation, and sentiments above the dust in which I had been groveling. The very countenance of my husband changed; his complexion became sallow, and all the charms of youth were vanishing with its vivacity.

"I give you one view of the subject; but these experiments and alterations took up the space of five years; during which period, I had most reluctantly extorted several sums from my uncle, to save my husband, to use his own words, from destruction. At first it was to prevent bills being noted, to the injury of his credit; then to bail him; and afterwards to prevent an execution[4] from entering the house. I began at last to conclude, that he would have made more exertions of his own to extricate himself, had he not relied on mine, cruel as was the task he imposed on me; and I firmly determined that I would make use of no more pretexts.

"From the moment I pronounced this determination, indifference on his part was changed into rudeness, or something worse.

"He now seldom dined at home, and continually returned at a late hour, drunk, to bed. I retired to another apartment; I was glad, I own, to escape from his; for personal intimacy without affection, seemed, to me as the most degrading, as well as the most painful state in which a woman of any taste, not to speak of the peculiar delicacy of fostered sensibility, could be placed. But my husband's fondness for women was of the grossest kind, and imagination was so wholly out of the question, as to render his indulgences of this sort entirely promiscuous, and of the most brutal nature. My health suffered, before my heart was entirely estranged by the loathsome information; could I then have returned to his sullied arms, but as a victim to the prejudices of mankind, who have made women the property of their husbands? I discovered even, by his conversation, when intoxicated, that his favourites were wantons of the lowest class,

---

[4] The seizure of goods by a sheriff's officer (*OED*).

who could by their vulgar, indecent mirth, which he called nature, rouse his sluggish spirits. Meretricious ornaments and manners were necessary to attract his attention. He seldom looked twice at a modest woman, and sat silent in their company; and the charms of youth and beauty had not the slightest effect on his senses, unless the possessors were initiated in vice. His intimacy with profligate women, and his habits of thinking, gave him a contempt for female endowments; and he would repeat, when wine had loosed his tongue, most of the common place sarcasms leveled at them, by men who do not allow them to have minds, because mind would be an impediment to gross enjoyment. Men who are inferior to their fellow men, are always most anxious to establish their superiority over women. But where are these reflections leading me?

"Women who have lost their husband's affection, are justly reproved for neglecting their persons, and not taking the same pains to keep, as to gain a heart; but who thinks of giving the same advice to men, though women are continually stigmatized for being attached to fops;[5] and from the nature of their education, are more susceptible of disgust? Yet why a woman should be expected to endure a sloven, with more patience than a man, and magnanimously to govern herself, I cannot conceive; unless it be supposed arrogant in her to look for respect as well as a maintenance. It is not easy to be pleased, because, after promising to love, in different circumstances, we are told that it is our duty. I cannot, I am sure (though, when attending the sick, I never felt disgust) forget my own sensations, when rising with health and spirit, and after scenting the sweet morning, I have met my husband at the breakfast table. The active attention I had been giving to domestic regulations, which were generally settled before he rose, or a walk, gave a glow to my countenance, that contrasted with his squallid appearance. The squeamishness of stomach alone, produced by the last night's intemperance,

[5] One who is foolishly attentive to and vain of his appearance, dress, or manners; a dandy, an exquisite (*OED*).

which he took no pains to conceal, destroyed my appetite. I think I now see him lolling in an arm-chair, in a dirty powdering gown, soiled linen, ungartered stockings, and tangled hair, yawning and stretching himself. The newspaper was immediately called for, if not brought in on the tea-board, from which he would scarcely lift his eyes while I poured out the tea, excepting to ask for some brandy to put into it, or to declare that he could not eat. In answer to any question, in his best humour, it was a drawling 'What do you say, child?' But if I demanded money for the house expences, which I put off till the last moment, his customary reply, often prefaced with an oath, was, 'Do you think me, madam, made of money?'—The butcher, the baker, must wait; and, what was worse, I was often obliged to witness his surly dismission of tradesmen, who were in want of their money, and whom I sometimes paid with the presents my uncle gave me for my own use.

At this juncture my father's mistress, by terrifying his conscience, prevailed on him to marry her; he was already become a methodist; and my brother, who now practiced for himself, had discovered a flaw in the settlement made on my mother's children, which set it aside, and he allowed my father, whose distress made him submit to any thing, a tithe of his own, or rather our fortune.

My sisters had left school, but were unable to endure home, which my father's wife rendered as disagreeable as possible, to get rid of girls whom she regarded as spies on her conduct. They were accomplished, yet you can (may you never be reduced to the same destitute state!) scarcely conceive the trouble I had to place them in the situation of governesses, the only one in which even a well-educated woman, with more than ordinary talents, can struggle for a subsistence; and even this is a dependence next to menial. Is it then surprising, that so many forlorn women, with human passions and feelings, take refuge in infamy? Alone in large mansions, I say alone, because they had no companions with whom they could converse on equal terms, or from whom they could expect the endearments of affection, they grew melancholy, and the sound of joy made them sad; and the youngest, having a more delicate frame, fell into a decline. It was with great difficulty that I, who now almost supported the house by loans from my uncle, could prevail on the *master* of it, to allow her a room to die in. I watched her sick bed for some months, and then closed her eyes, gentle spirit! for ever. She was pretty, with very engaging manners; yet had never an opportunity to marry, excepting to a very old man. She had abilities sufficient to have shone in any profession, had there been any professions for women, though she shrunk at the name of milliner[6] or mantua-maker[7] as degrading to a gentlewoman. I would not term this feeling false pride to any one but you, my child, whom I fondly hope to see (yes; I will indulge the hope for a moment!) possessed of that energy of character which gives dignity to any station; and with that clear, firm spirit that will enable you to choose a situation for yourself, or submit to be classed in the lowest, if it be the only one in which you can be the mistress of your own actions.

"A Something Betwixt and Between": Employment Opportunities for Middle-Class Women

Being "mistress of [her] own actions"—Maria's fervent wish for her daughter—may seem a humble desire, but economic and social conditions in the late eighteenth century did not make it so. Marriage remained the only acknowledged "success" for women (Hill 226), and although marriage certainly did not represent economic autonomy for women, it at least spared them the social isolation and stigmatized dependency attendant upon its most acceptable alternatives: being a dependent in the father or eldest brother's household, a paid companion, or a governess. Wollstonecraft herself experienced all three of these positions before taking

---

[6] Maker of female apparel, especially bonnets and other head gear (*OED*).
[7] Dressmaker.

the rare and remarkably brave step of embarking on a literary life. For Wollstonecraft, these dependent positions were simply intolerable. Her own reaction to being a governess—considered the best of these options—is strikingly similar to that of Maria's sister, represented in *The Wrongs of Woman* as literally dying from its mental hardships.

Indeed, during her short tenure as a governess for three of the daughters of the Lord and Lady Kingsborough, Wollstonecraft is herself diagnosed with a "nervous disorder" and writes to Joseph Johnson, her soon-to-be employer and the publisher of her *Thoughts on the Education of Daughters* (1787):

> I am still an invalid—and begin to believe that I ought never to expect to enjoy health. My mind preys on my body—and when I endeavour to be useful, I grow too interested for my own peace. Confined almost entirely to the society of children, I am anxiously solicitous for their future welfare, and mortified beyond measure, when counteracted in my endeavours to improve them.—I feel all a mother's fears for the swarm of little ones which surround me, and observe disorders, without having power to apply the proper remedies. How can I be reconciled to life, when it is always a painful warfare, and when I am deprived of all the pleasures I relish?—I allude to rational conversations, and domestic affections. Here, alone, a poor solitary individual in a strange land, tied to one spot, and subject to the caprice of another, can I be contented? (*Collected Letters* 148)

In an earlier letter to her sister Eliza, Wollstonecraft is even more candid, struggling to name the particular kind of dependency and isolation that makes this position so disabling to her:

> All the rest of the females labor to be civil to me; but we move in so different a sphere, I feel grateful for their attention; but not amused. I have scarcely

a moment to collect my thought and *reason* sorrow away…. I am treated like a gentlewoman—but I cannot easily forget my inferior station—and this something betwixt and between is rather awkward. (*Collected Letters* 124)

Not a member of the laboring class, not a gentlewoman, not a mother, yet not unencumbered, the unmarried middle-class woman becomes instead—as Wollstonecraft ultimately coins it—"a something betwixt and between."

Nor would being a paid companion or a dependent in the father or brother's household spare her this marginal status. Although in theory, both positions would seem to allow a surer position within the family, in practice, they often did not. As Wollstonecraft wryly notes, as a companion one must "live with strangers, who are so intolerably tyrannical, that none of their own relations can bear to live with them, though they should even expect a fortune in reversion" (qtd. in Todd 29), and as a dependent in a married brother's household, one "is viewed with averted looks as an intruder, an unnecessary burden on the benevolence of the master of the house, and his new partner" (*Vindication* 65). The practice of "genteel trades" such as millinery or mantua-making were beginning to become acceptable options for unmarried, middle-class women, but cultural resistance was strong, and most unmarried women continued to struggle within these dependent roles (Hill 233).

Such was the case for Wollstonecraft's sisters who alternated among these occupations throughout most of their lifetimes while periodically achieving some independence through the operation of a school for girls. Sadly, the fate of Wollstonecraft's first daughter, Fanny Imlay, proved more tragic. With no promise of dowry or striking looks, her marriage opportunities were limited, and her reputation (compromised by the actions of both her mother and her more adventuresome sisters) made even these more common forms of employment unopen to her. On October 9, 1815, she committed suicide, her own death the only action she saw available to her.

SOURCES

Bridget Hill. *Women, Work, and Sexual Politics in Eighteenth-Century England.* 2ⁿᵈ ed. Montreal & Kingston: McGill-Queen's University Press, 1994.

William St. Clair. *The Godwins and The Shelleys: A Biography of a Family.* Baltimore: Johns Hopkins University Press, 1989.

Janet Todd. *Mary Wollstonecraft: A Revolutionary Life.* New York: Columbia Press, 2000.

Ralph Wardle. Ed. *Collected Letters of Mary Wollstonecraft.* Ithaca: Cornell University Press, 1979.

"Soon after the death of my sister, an incident occurred, to prove to me that the heart of a libertine is dead to natural affection; and to convince me, that the being who has appeared all tenderness, to gratify a selfish passion, is as regardless of the innocent fruit of it, as of the object, when the fit is over. I had casually observed an old, mean-looking woman, who called on my husband every two or three months to receive some money. One day entering the passage of his little counting-house,[8] as she was going out, I heard her say, 'The child is very weak; she cannot live long, she will soon die out of your way, so you need not grudge her a little physic.'

"'So much the better,' he replied, 'and pray mind your own business, good woman.'

"I was struck by his unfeeling, inhuman tone of voice, and drew back, determined when the woman came again, to try to speak to her, not out of curiosity, I had heard enough, but with the hope of being useful to a poor, outcast girl.

---

[8] In this case, either a separate building or a private chamber assigned to business and correspondence.

"A month or two elapsed before I saw this woman again; and then she had a child in her hand that tottered along, scarcely able to sustain her own weight. They were going away, to return at the hour Mr. Venables was expected; he was now from home. I desired the woman to walk into the parlour. She hesitated, yet obeyed. I assured her that I should not mention to my husband (the word seemed to weigh on my respiration), that I had seen her, or his child. The woman stared at me with astonishment; and I turned my eyes on the squalid object [that accompanied her.] She could hardly support herself, her complexion was sallow, her eyes inflamed, with an indescribable look of cunning, mixed with the wrinkles produced by the peevishness of pain.

"Poor child!' I exclaimed. 'Ah! you may well say poor child,' replied the woman. "I brought her here to see whether he would have the heart to look at her, and not get some advice. I do not know what they deserve who nursed her. Why, her legs bent under her like a bow when she came to me, and she has never been well since; but, if they were no better paid than I am, it is not to be wondered at, sure enough.'

"On further enquiry I was informed, that this miserable spectacle was the daughter of a servant, a country girl, who caught Mr. Venables' eye, and whom he seduced. On his marriage he sent her away, her situation being too visible. After her delivery, she was thrown on the town; and died in an hospital within the year. The babe was sent to a parish-nurse,[9] and afterwards to this woman, who did not seem much better; but what was to be expected from such a close bargain? She was only paid three shillings a week for board and washing.

"The woman begged me to give her some old clothes for the child, assuring me, that she was almost afraid to ask master for money to buy even a pair of shoes.

"I grew sick at heart. And, fearing Mr. Venables might enter, and oblige me to express my abhorrence, I hastily enquired

---

[9] A wet nurse provided by the parish in order to aid the poor.

where she lived, promised to pay her two shillings a week more, and to call on her in a day or two; putting a trifle into her hand as a proof of my good intention.

"If the state of this child affected me, what were my feelings at a discovery I made respecting Peggy——?*

---

* The manuscript is imperfect here. An episode seems to have been intended, which was never committed to paper. EDITOR. [Godwin's note].

Chapter X

My father's situation was now so distressing, that I prevailed on my uncle to accompany me to visit him; and to lend me his assistance, to prevent the whole property of the family from becoming the prey of my brother's rapacity; for, to extricate himself out of present difficulties, my father was totally regardless of futurity. I took down with me some presents for my step-mother; it did not require an effort for me to treat her with civility, or to forget the past.

"This was the first time I had visited my native village, since my marriage. But with what different emotions did I return from the busy world, with a heavy weight of experience benumbing my imagination, to scenes, that whispered recollections of joy and hope most eloquently to my heart! The first scent of the wild flowers from the heath, thrilled through my veins, awakening every sense to pleasure. The icy hand of despair seemed to be removed from my bosom; and—forgetting my husband— the nurtured visions of a romantic mind, bursting on me with all their original wildness and gay exuberance, were again hailed as sweet realities. I forgot, with equal facility, that I ever felt sorrow, or knew care in the country; while a transient rainbow stole athwart the cloudy sky of despondency. The picturesque form of several favourite trees, and the porches of rude cottages, with their smiling hedges, were recognized with the gladsome playfulness of childish vivacity. I could have kissed the chickens that pecked on the common; and longed to pat the cows, and frolic with the dogs that sported on it. I gazed with delight on the windmill, and thought it lucky that it should be in motion, at the moment I passed by; and entering the dear green-lane, which led directly to the village, the sound of the well-known rookery gave that sentimental tinge to the varying sensations of

my active soul, which only served to heighten the luster of the
luxuriant scenery. But, spying, as I advanced, the spire, peeping
over the withered tops of the aged elms that composed the rookery, my thoughts flew immediately to the church-yard, and tears
of affection, such was the effect of imagination, bedewed by
mother's grave! Sorrow gave place to devotional feelings. I wandered through the church in fancy, as I used sometimes to do on
a Saturday evening. I recollected with what fervour I addressed
the God of my youth: and once more with rapturous love looked
above my sorrows to the Father of nature. I pause—feeling forcibly all the emotions I am describing; and (reminded, as I regis-
ter my sorrows, of the sublime calm I have felt, when in some
tremendous solitude, my soul rested on itself, and seemed to fill
the universe) I insensibly breathe soft, hushing every wayward
emotion, as if fearing to sully with a sigh, a contentment so
extatic.

"Having settled my father's affairs, and, by my exertions in
his favour, made my brother my sworn foe, I returned to London. My husband's conduct was now changed; I had during
my absence, received several affectionate, penitential letters from
him; and he seemed on my arrival, to wish by his behaviour to
prove his sincerity. I could not then conceive why he acted thus;
and, when the suspicion darted into my head, that it might
arise from observing my increasing influence with my uncle, I
almost despised myself for imagining that such a degree of debasing selfishness could exist.

"He became, unaccountable as was the change, tender and
attentive; and, attacking my weak side, made a confession of his
follies, and lamented the embarrassments in which I, who merited a far different fate, might be involved. He besought me to
aid him with my counsel, praised my understanding, and appealed to the tenderness of my heart.

"This conduct only inspired me with compassion. I wished
to be his friend; but love had spread his rosy pinions, and fled
far, far a way; and had not (like some exquisite perfumes, the fine
spirit of which is continually mingling with the air) left a fra-

grance behind, to mark where he had shook his wings. My husband's renewed caresses then became hateful to me; his brutality was tolerable, compared to his distasteful fondness. Still, compassion, and the fear of insulting his supposed feelings, by a want of sympathy, made me dissemble, and do violence to my delicacy. What a task!

"Those who support a system of what I term false refinement, and will not allow great part of love in the female, as well as male breast, to spring in some respects involuntarily, may not admit that charms are as necessary to feed the passion, as virtues to convert the mellowing spirit into friendship. To such observers I have nothing to say, any more than to the moralists, who insist that women ought to, and can love their husbands, because it is their duty. To you, my child, I may add, with a heart tremblingly alive to your future conduct, some observations, dictated by my present feelings, on calmly reviewing this period of my life. When novelists or moralists praise as a virtue, a woman's coldness of constitution, and want of passion; and make her yield to the ardour of her lover out of sheer compassion, or to promote a frigid plan of future comfort, I am disgusted. They may be good women, in the ordinary acceptance of the phrase, and do no harm; but they appear to me not to have those 'finely fashioned nerves,' which render the senses exquisite. They may possess tenderness; but they want that fire of the imagination, which produces *active* sensibility, and *positive* virtue. How does the woman deserve to be characterized, who marries one man, with a heart and imagination devoted to another? Is she not an object of pity or contempt, when thus sacrilegiously violating the purity of her own feelings? Nay, it is as indelicate, when she is indifferent, unless she be constitutionally insensible; then indeed it is a mere affair of barter; and I have nothing to do with the secrets of trade. Yes; eagerly as I wish you to possess true rectitude of mind, and purity of affection, I must insist that a heartless conduct is the contrary of virtuous. Truth is the only basis of virtue; and we cannot, without depraving our minds, endeavour to please a lover or husband, but in proportion as he pleases us. Men, more effectually to enslave us, may inculcate this partial morality, and lose sight of virtue in subdividing it into the duties of particular stations; but let us not blush for nature without a cause!

"After these remarks, I am ashamed to own, that I was pregnant. The greatest sacrifice of my principles in my whole life, was the allowing my husband again to be familiar with my person, though to this cruel act of self-denial, when I wished the earth to open and swallow me, you owe your birth; and I the unutterable pleasure of being a mother. There was something of delicacy in my husband's bridal attentions; but now his tainted breath, pimpled face, and blood-shot eyes, were not more repugnant to my senses, than his gross manners, and loveless familiarity to my taste.

"A man would only be expected to maintain; yes, barely grant a subsistence, to a woman rendered odious by habitual intoxication; but who would expect him, or think it possible to love her? And unless 'youth, and genial years were flown,'[1] it would be thought equally unreasonable to insist, [under penalty of] forfeiting almost every thing reckoned valuable in life, that he should not love another: whilst woman, weak in reason, impotent in will, is required to moralize, sentimentalize herself to stone, and pine her life away, labouring to reform her embruted mate. He may even spend in dissipation, and intemperance, the very intemperance which renders him so hateful, her property, and by stinting her expences, not permit her to beguile in society, a wearisome, joyless life; for over their mutual fortune she has no power, it must all pass through his hand. And if she be a mother, and in the present state of women, it is a great misfortune to be prevented from discharging the duties, and cultivat-

---

[1] James Thomson, "Song, *For Ever, Fortune, wilt thou prove*" (1730), l. 7: "Bid us sigh on from day to day,/And wish and wish the soul away;/Till youth and genial years are flown,/And all the life is gone?" Wollstonecraft also uses this line to describe the condition of governesses in *Thoughts on the Education of Daughters* (1787).

ing the affections of one, what has she not to endure?—But I have suffered the tenderness of one to lead me into reflections that I did not think of making, to interrupt my narrative—yet the full heart will overflow.

"Mr. Venables' embarrassments did not now endear him to me; still, anxious to befriend him, I endeavoured to prevail on him to retrench his expences; but he had always some plausible excuse to give, to justify his not following my advice. Humanity, compassion, and the interest produced by a habit of living together, made me try to relieve, and sympathize with him; but, when I recollected that I was bound to live with such a being for ever—my heart died within me; my desire of improvement became languid, and baleful, corroding melancholy took possession of my soul. Marriage had bastilled[2] me for life. I discovered in myself a capacity for the enjoyment of the various pleasures existence affords; yet, fettered by the partial laws of society, this fair globe was to me an universal blank.

THE *FEME-COVERT*: MARRIAGE LAWS
IN EIGHTEENTH-CENTURY ENGLAND

Under the "partial laws" of late eighteenth century society, Maria is a *feme-covert,* and as such, is indeed "fettered," having no independent legal standing, and certainly no means by which she can stop her husband's rapid and ill-advised spending. "Upon marriage," writes Gillian Skinner, "a woman's property passed into the control of her husband; she was not able to enter into contracts, to sue or be sued. She had no legal rights over her children, nor did she have the right to leave her husband's house without his permission—if she did so, she gave up her right to his support, but could also be legally compelled to return" (92). As a single

---

[2] The Bastille is the name of the French prison stormed at the onset of the French Revolution in 1798. Wollstonecraft is one of the first to employ this term as a verb, meaning to confine or imprison.

woman or *feme sole*, she would have retained the right to own property and make contracts, but as a married woman she became the protectorate of her husband, her independent desires presumably subsumed by their shared fortune. Sir William Blackstone in 1771 describes this symbiotic relationship thus:

> By marriage the husband and wife are one person in law: that is, the very being or legal existence of the woman is suspended during the marriage, or at least is incorporated and consolidated into that of the husband; under whose wing, protection, and *cover*, she performs every thing; and is therefore called in our law-french a *fem-covert* [*sic*]. (qtd. in Skinner, 92)

In theory, husband and wife were one; in practice, however, some provision was typically made for the wife's separate maintenance. This separate income, known by the popular name of "pin money," was an annual sum paid by the husband to the wife, specifically designed for her personal expenses and usually negotiated at the time of the marriage contract. One of its intentions was to prevent excesses on the part of the husband from infringing on the well-being of the wife, but as Maria's story makes clear, it did not guarantee this result. Courts still hesitated to regard this separate maintenance as a contractural obligation (as it would then call into question the male's social and moral duty to his wife), and thus when George Venables hits hard financial times it is Maria's expenses which are "stint[ed]" and she who must practice economy. A separate estate put in trust for her at the time of her marriage settlement—an "estate," explains Susan Staves, "which the wife is to possess 'for her sole and separate use,' not subject to the control of her husband and not available to her husband's creditors"—would have given Maria somewhat more recourse under these conditions, although often women were physically and emotionally bullied out of these incomes as well. Establishing such an estate would have been an available option to Maria's uncle, and most likely he would have served as its trustee. Of course, at the time of the marriage contract, Maria would have had a jointure settled upon her, but that income would have been available only upon her husband's death, and could be forfeited upon separation or divorce.

SOURCES

Gillian Skinner. "Women's status as legal and civic subjects: 'A worse condition than slavery itself'?" in *Women and Literature in Britain, 1700-1800*, Cambridge: Cambridge University Press, 2000.

Susan Staves. *Married Women's Separate Property in England, 1660-1833*. Cambridge: Harvard University Press, 1990.

"When I exhorted my husband to economy, I referred to himself. I was obliged to practice the most rigid, or contract debts, which I had too much reason to fear would never be paid. I despised this paltry privilege of a wife, which can only be of use to the vicious or inconsiderate, and determined not to increase the torrent that was bearing him down. I was then ignorant of the extent of his fraudulent speculations, whom I was bound to honour and obey.

"A woman neglected by her husband, or whose manners form a striking contrast with his, will always have men on the watch to soothe and flatter her. Besides, the forlorn state of a neglected woman, not destitute of personal charms, is particularly interesting, and rouses that species of pity, which is so near akin, it easily slides into love. A man of feeling thinks not of seducing, he is himself seduced by all the noblest emotions of his soul. He figures to himself all the sacrifices a woman of sensibility must make, and every situation in which his imagination places her, touches his heart, and fires his passions. Longing to take to his bosom the shorn lamb, and bid the drooping buds of hope revive, benevolence changes into passion: and should he then discover that he is beloved, honour binds him fast, though foreseeing that he may afterwards be obliged to pay severe damages to the man, who never appeared to value his wife's society, till he found that there was a chance of his being indemnified for the loss of it.[3]

"Such are the partial laws enacted by men; for, only to lay a stress on the dependent state of a woman in the grand question of the comforts arising from the possession of property, she is [even in this article] much more injured by the loss of the husband's affection, than he by that of his wife; yet where is she, condemned to the solitude of a deserted home, to look for a compensation from the woman, who seduces him from her? She cannot drive an unfaithful husband from his house, nor separate, or tear, his children from him, however culpable he may be; and he, still the master of his own fate, enjoys the smiles of a world, that would brand her with infamy, did she, consolation, venture to retaliate.

"These remarks are not dictated by experience; but merely by the compassion I feel for many amiable women, the *out-laws* of the world. For myself, never encouraging any of the advances that were made to me, my lovers dropped off like the untimely shoots of spring. I did not even coquet with them; because I found, on examining myself, I could not coquet with a man without loving him a little; and I perceived that I should not be able to stop at the line of what are termed *innocent freedoms*, did I suffer any. My reserve was then the consequence of delicacy. Freedom of conduct has emancipated many women's minds; but my conduct has most rigidly been governed by my principles, till the improvement of my understanding has enabled me to discern the fallacy of prejudices at war with nature and reason.

"Shortly after the change I have mentioned in my husband's

---

[3] In the eighteenth century, a husband whose wife commits adultery can sue for damages.

conduct, my uncle was compelled by his declining health, to seek the succour of a milder climate, and embark for Lisbon. He left his will in the hands of a friend, an eminent solicitor; he had previously questioned me relative to my situation and state of mind, and declared very freely, that he could place no reliance on the stability of my husband's professions. He had been deceived in the unfolding of his character; he now thought it fixed in a train of actions that would inevitably lead to ruin and disgrace.

"The evening before his departure, which we spent alone together, he folded me to his heart, uttering the endearing appellation of 'child.'—My more than father! why was I not permitted to perform the last duties of one, and smooth the pillow of death? He seemed by his manner to be convinced that he should never see me more; yet requested me, most earnestly, to come to him, should I be obliged to leave my husband. He had before expressed his sorrow at hearing of my pregnancy, having determined to prevail on me to accompany him, till I informed him of that circumstance. He expressed himself unfeignedly sorry that any new tie should bind me to a man whom he thought so incapable of estimating my value; such was the kind language of affection.

"I must repeat his own words; they made an indelible impression on my mind:

"'The marriage state is certainly that in which women, generally speaking, can be most useful; but I am far from thinking that a woman, once married, ought to consider the engagement as indissoluble (especially if there be no children to reward her for sacrificing her feelings) in case her husband merits neither her love, nor esteem. Esteem will often supply the place of love; and prevent a woman from being wretched, though it may not make her happy. The magnitude of a sacrifice ought always to bear some proportion to the utility in view; and for a woman to live with a man, for whom she can cherish neither affection nor esteem, or even be of any use to him, excepting in the light of a house-keeper, is an abjectness of condition, the enduring of which no concurrence of circumstances can ever make a duty in the sight of God or just men. If indeed she submits to it merely to be maintained in idleness, she has no right to complain bitterly of her fate; or to act, as a person of independent character might, as if she had a title to disregard general rules.

"But the misfortune is, that many women only submit in appearance, and forfeit their own respect to secure their reputation in the world. The situation of a woman separated from her husband, is undoubtedly very different from that of a man who has left his wife. He, with lordly dignity, has shaken of a clog; and the allowing her food and raiment, is thought sufficient to secure his reputation from taint. And, should she have been inconsiderate, he will be celebrated for his generosity and forbearance. Such is the respect paid to the master-key of property! A woman, on the contrary, resigning what is termed her natural protector (though he was never so, but in name) is despised and shunned, for asserting the independence of mind distinctive of a rational being, and spurning at slavery.'

"During the remainder of the evening, my uncle's tenderness led him frequently to revert to the subject, and utter, with increasing warmth, sentiments to the same purport. At length it was necessary to say 'Farewell!'—and we parted—gracious God! to meet no more.

CHAPTER XI

A gentleman of large fortune and of polished manners, had lately visited very frequently at our house, and treated me, if possible, with more respect than Mr. Venables paid him; my pregnancy was not yet visible. His society was a great relief to me, as I had for some time past, to avoid expence, confined myself very much at home. I ever disdained unnecessary, perhaps even prudent concealments; and my husband with great ease, discovered the amount of my uncle's parting present. A copy of a writ was the stale pretext to exhort it from me; and I had soon reason to believe that it was fabricated for the purpose. I acknowledged my folly in thus suffering myself to be continually imposed on. I had adhered to my resolution not to apply to my uncle, on the part of my husband, any more; yet, when I had received a sum sufficient to supply my own wants, and to enable me to pursue a plan I had in view, to settle my younger brother in a respectable employment, I allowed myself to be duped by Mr. Venables' shallow pretences, and hypocritical professions.

"Thus did he pillage me and my family, thus frustrate all my plans of usefulness. Yet this was the man I was bound to respect and esteem: as if respect and esteem depended on an arbitrary will of our own! But a wife being as much a man's property as his horse, or his ass, she has nothing she can call her own. He may use any means to get at what the law considers as his, the moment his wife is in possession of it, even to the forcing of a lock, as Mr. Venables did, to search for notes in my writing-desk—and all this is done with a show of equity, because, forsooth, he is responsible for her maintenance.

"The tender mother cannot *lawfully* snatch from the gripe of the gambling spendthrift, or beastly drunkard, unmindful of his offspring, the fortune which falls to her by chance; or (so flagrant is the injustice) which she earns by her own exertions. No; he can rob her with impunity, even to waste publicly on a courtezan; and the laws of her country—if women have a country—afford her no protection or redress from the oppressor, unless she have the plea of bodily fear; yet how many ways are there of goading the soul almost to madness, equally unmanly, though not so mean? When such laws were framed, should not impartial lawgivers have first decreed, in the style of a great assembly, who recognized the existence of an *etre supreme*,[1] to fix the national belief, that the husband should always be wiser and more virtuous than his wife, in order to entitle him, with a show of justice, to keep this idiot, or perpetual minor, for ever in bondage. But I must have done—on this subject, my indignation continually runs away with me.

"The company of the gentleman I have already mentioned, who had a general acquaintance with literature and subjects of taste, was grateful to me; my countenance brightened up as he approached, and I unaffectedly expressed the pleasure I felt. The amusement his conversation afforded me, made it easy to comply with my husband's request, to endeavour to render our house agreeable to him.

"His attentions became more pointed; but, as I was not of the number of women, whose virtue, as it is termed, immediately takes alarm, I endeavoured, rather by raillery than serious expostulation, to give a different turn to his conversation. He assumed a new mode of attack, and I was, for a while, the dupe of his pretended friendship.

"I had, merely in the style of *badinage*,[2] boasted of my conquest, and repeated his lover-like compliments to my husband. But he begged me, for God's sake, not to affront his friend, or I should destroy all his projects, and be his ruin. Had I more

---

[1] Supreme Being. The reference is to the French Assembly and its declaration in May 1794 that the French people recognize the existence of a Supreme Being.
[2] Playful raillery, banter.

affection for my husband, I should have expressed my contempt of this time-serving politeness: now I imagined that I only felt pity; yet it would have puzzled a casuist to point out in what the exact difference consisted.

"This friend began now, in confidence, to discover to me the real state of my husband's affairs. 'Necessity,' said Mr. S——; why should I reveal his name? for he affected to palliate the conduct he could not excuse, 'had led him to take such steps, by accommodation bills, buying goods on credit, to sell them for ready money, and similar transactions, that his character in the commercial world was gone. He was considered,' he added, lowering his voice, 'on 'Change[3] as a swindler.'

"I felt at that moment the first maternal pang. Aware of the evils my sex have to struggle with, I still wished, for my own consolation, to be the mother of a daughter; and I could not bear to think, that the *sins* of her father's entailed disgrace, should be added to the ills to which woman is heir.

"So completely was I deceived by these shows of friendship (nay, I believe, according to his interpretation, Mr. S—— really was my friend) that I began to consult him respecting the best mode of retrieving my husband's character: it is the good name of a woman only that sets to rise no more. I knew not that he had been drawn into a whirlpool, out of which he had not the energy to attempt to escape. He seemed indeed destitute of the power of employing his faculties in any regular pursuit. His principles of action were so loose, and his mind so uncultivated, that every thing like order appeared to him in the shape of re-straint; and, like men in the savage state, he required the strong stimulus of hope or fear, produced by wild speculations, in which the interests of others went for nothing, to keep his spirits awake. He one time professed patriotism, but he knew not what it was to feel honest indignation; and pretended to be an advocate for

---

[3] The Exchange, or the area in London where financial transactions take place. The gentleman's comments indicate that George Venables' reputation is ruined among the financial set.

liberty, when, with as little affection for the human race as for individuals, he thought of nothing but his own gratification. He was just such a citizen, as a father. The sums he adroitly obtained by a violation of the laws of his country, as well as those of humanity, he would allow a mistress to squander; though she was, with the same *sang froid*, consigned, as were his children, to poverty, when another proved more attractive.

"On various pretences, his friend continued to visit me; and, observing my want of money, he tried to induce me to accept of pecuniary aid; but this offer I absolutely rejected, though it was made with such delicacy, I could not be displeased.

"One day he came, as I thought accidentally, to dinner. My husband was very much engaged in business, and quitted the room soon after the cloth[4] was removed. We conversed as usual, till confidential advice led again to love. I was extremely morti-fied. I had a sincere regard for him, and hoped that he had an equal friendship for me. I therefore began mildly to expostulate with him. This gentleness he mistook for coy encouragement; and he would not be diverted from the subject. Perceiving his mistake, I seriously asked him how, using such language to me, he could profess to be husband's friend? A significant sneer excited my curiosity, and he, supposing this to be my only scruple, took a letter deliberately out of his pocket, saying, 'Your husband's honour is not inflexible. How could you, with your discern-ment, think it so? Why, he left the room this very day on pur-pose to give me an opportunity to explain myself; *he* thought me too timid—too tardy.

"I snatched the letter with indescribable emotion. The pur-port of it was to invite him to dinner, and to ridicule his chival-rous respect for me. He assured him, 'that every woman had her price, and, with gross indecency, hinted, that he should be glad to have the duty of a husband taken off his hands. These he termed *liberal sentiments*. He advised him not to shock my ro-mantic notions, but to attack my credulous generosity, and weak

[4] Tablecloth.

pity; and concluded with requesting him to lend him five hundred pounds for a month or six weeks.' I read this letter twice over; and the firm purpose it inspired, calmed the rising tumult of my soul. I rose deliberately, requested Mr. S——to wait a moment, and instantly going into the counting-house, desired Mr. Venables to return with me to the dining-parlour.

"He laid down his pen, and entered with me, without observing any change in my countenance. I shut the door, and, giving him the letter, simply asked, 'whether he wrote it, or was it a forgery?'

"Nothing could equal his confusion. His friend's eye met his, and he muttered something about a joke—But I interrupted him—'It is sufficient—We part for ever.'

"I continued with solemnity, 'I have borne with your tyranny and infidelities. I disdain to utter what I have borne with. I thought you unprincipled, but not so, decidedly vicious. I formed a tie, in the sight of heaven—I have held it sacred; even when men, more conformable to my taste, have made me feel—I despise all subterfuge!—that I was not dead to love. Neglected by you, I have resolutely stifled the enticing emotions, and respected the plighted faith you outraged. And you dare now to insult me, by selling me to prostitution!—Yes—equally lost to delicacy and principle—you dared sacrilegiously to barter the honour of the mother of your child.'

"Then, turning to Mr. S——, I added, 'I call on you, Sir, to witness,' and I lifted my hands and eyes to heaven, 'that, as solemnly as I took his name, I now abjure it,' I pulled off my ring, and put it on the table; 'and that I mean immediately to quit his house, never to enter it more. I will provide for myself and child. I leave him as free as I am determined to be myself—he shall be answerable for no debts of mine.'

"Astonishment closed their lips, till Mr. Venables, gently pushing his friend, with a forced smile, out of the room, nature for a moment prevailed, and, appearing like himself, he turned round, burning with rage, to me: but there was no terror in the frown, excepting when contrasted with the malignant smile which preceded it. He bade me 'leave the house at my peril; told me he despised my threats; I had no resource; I could not swear the peace against him!—I was not afraid of my life!—he had never struck me!'

"He threw the letter in the fire, which I had incautiously left in his hands; and, quitting the room, locked the door on me.

"When left alone, I was a moment or two before I could recollect myself. One scene had succeeded another with such rapidity, I almost doubted whether I was reflecting on a real event. 'Was it possible? Was I, indeed, free?'—Yes; free I termed myself, when I decidedly perceived the conduct I ought to adopt. How had I panted for liberty—liberty, that I would have purchased at any price, but that of my own esteem! I rose, and shook myself; opened the window, and methought the air never smelled so sweet. The face of heaven grew fairer as I viewed it, and the clouds seemed to flit away obedient to my wishes, to give my soul room to expand. I was all soul, and (wild as it may appear) felt as if I could have dissolved in the soft balmy gale that kissed my cheek, or have glided below the horizon on the glowing, descending beams. A seraphic satisfaction animated, without agitating my spirits; and my imagination collected, in visions sublimely terrible, or soothingly beautiful, an immense variety of the endless images, which nature affords, and fancy combines, of the grand and fair. The luster of these bright picturesque sketches faded with the setting sun; but I was still alive to the calm delight they had diffused through my heart.

"There may be advocates for matrimonial obedience, who, making a distinction between the duty of a wife and of a human being, may blame my conduct.—To them I write not—my feelings are not for them to analyze; and may you, my child, never be able to ascertain, by heart-rending experience, what your mother felt before the present emancipation of her mind!

"I began to write a letter to my father, after closing one to my uncle; not to ask advice, but to signify my determination; when I was interrupted by the entrance of Mr. Venables. His manner was changed. His views on my uncle's fortune made him averse to my quitting his house, or he would, I am convinced, have been glad to have shaken off even the slight restraint my presence imposed on him; the restraint of showing me some respect. So far from having an affection for me, he really hated me, because he was convinced that I must despise him.

"He told me, that, 'As I now had had time to cool and reflect, he did not doubt but that my prudence, and nice sense of propriety, would lead me to overlook what was passed.'

"'Reflection,' I replied, 'had only confirmed my purpose, and no power on earth could divert me from it.'

"Endeavouring to assume a soothing voice and look, when he would willingly have tortured me, to force me to feel his power, his countenance had an infernal expression, when he desired me, 'Not to expose myself to the servants, by obliging him to confine me in my apartment; if then I would give my promise not to quit the house precipitately, I should be free—and—.' I declared, interrupting him, 'that I would promise nothing. I had no measures to keep with him—I was resolved, and would not condescend to subterfuge.'

"He muttered, 'that I should soon repent of these preposterous airs;' and, ordering tea to be carried into my little study, which had a communication with my bed-chamber, he once more locked the door upon me, and left me to my own meditations. I had passively followed him up stairs, not wishing to fatigue myself with unavailing exertion.

"Nothing calms the mind like a fixed purpose. I felt as if I had heaved a thousand weight from my heart; the atmosphere seemed lightened; and, if I execrated the institutions of society, which thus enable men to tyrannize over women, it was almost a disinterested sentiment. I disregarded present inconveniences, when my mind had done struggling with itself,—when reason and inclination had shaken hands and were at peace. I had no longer the cruel task before me, in endless perspective, aye, during the tedious for ever of life, of labouring to overcome my repugnance—of labouring to extinguish the hopes, the maybes of a lively imagination. Death I had hailed as my only chance for deliverance; but, while existence had still so many charms, and life promised happiness, I shrunk from the icy arms of an unknown tyrant, though far more inviting than those of the man, to whom I supposed myself bound without any other alternative; and was content to linger a little longer, waiting for I knew not what, rather than leave 'the warm precincts of the cheerful day,'[4] and all the unenjoyed affection of my nature.

"My present situation gave a new turn to my reflection; and I wondered (now the film seemed to be withdrawn, that obscured the piercing sight of reason) how I could, previously to the deciding outrage, have considered myself as everlastingly united to vice and folly! 'Had an evil genius cast a spell at my birth; or a demon stalked out of chaos, to perplex my understanding, and enchain my will, with delusive prejudices?'

"I pursued this train of thinking; it led me out of myself, to expatiate on the misery peculiar to my sex. 'Are not,' I thought, 'the despots for ever stigmatized, who, in the wantonness of power, commanded even the most atrocious criminals to be chained to dead bodies? though surely those laws are much more inhuman, which forge adamantine fetters to bind minds together, that never can mingle in social communion! What indeed can equal the wretchedness of that state, in which there is no alternative, but to extinguish the affections, or encounter infamy?'

[4] Thomas Gray, *Elegy Written in a Country Courtyard* (1751), l. 87: "For who to dumb Forgetfulness a prey,/This pleasing anxious being e'er resigned,/Left the warm precincts of the cheerful day,/Nor cast one longing look behind?"

Chapter XII

Towards midnight Mr. Venables entered my chamber; and, with calm audacity preparing to go to bed, he bade me make haste, 'for that was the best place for husbands and wives to end their differences.' He had been drinking plentifully to aid his courage.

"I did not at first deign to reply. But perceiving that he affected to take my silence for consent, I told him that, 'If he would not go to another bed, or allow me, I should sit up in my study all night.' He attempted to pull me into the chamber, half joking. But I resisted; and, as he had determined not to give me any reason for saying that he used violence, after a few more efforts, he retired, cursing my obstinacy, to bed.

"I sat musing some time longer; then, throwing my cloak around me, prepared for sleep on a sopha. And, so fortunate seemed my deliverance, so sacred the pleasure of being thus wrapped up in myself, that I slept profoundly, and woke with a mind composed to encounter the struggles of the day. Mr. Venables did not wake till some hours after; and then he came to me half-dressed, yawning and stretching, with haggard eyes, as if he scarcely recollected what had passed the preceding evening. He fixed his eyes on me for a moment, then, calling me a fool, asked 'How long I intended to continue this pretty farce? For his part, he was devilish sick of it; but this was the plague of marrying women who pretended to know something.'

"I made no other reply to this harangue, than to say, 'That he ought to be glad to get rid of a woman so unfit to be his companion—and that any change in my conduct would be mean dissimulation; for maturer reflection only gave the sacred seal of reason to my first resolution.'

"He looked as if we could have stamped with impatience, at

being obliged to stifle his rage; but, conquering his anger (for weak people, whose passions seem the most ungovernable, restrain them with the greatest ease, when they have sufficient motive), he exclaimed, 'Very pretty, upon my soul! very pretty, theatrical flourishes! Pray, fair Roxana,[1] stoop from your altitudes, and remember that you are acting a part in real life.'

"He uttered this speech with a self-satisfied air, and went down stairs to dress.

"In about an hour he came to me again; and in the same tone said, 'That he came as my gentleman-usher to hand me down to breakfast.'

"'Of the black rod?'[2] asked I.

"This question, and the tone in which I asked it, a little disconcerted him. To say the truth, I now felt no resentment; my firm resolution to free myself from my ignoble thraldom, had absorbed the various emotions which, during six years, had racked my soul. The duty pointed out by my principles seemed clear; and not one tender feeling intruded to make me swerve. The dislike which my husband had inspired was strong; but it only led me to wish to avoid, to wish to let him drop out of my memory; there was no misery, no torture that I would not deliberately have chosen, rather than renew my lease of servitude.

"During the breakfast, he attempted to reason with me on the folly of romantic sentiments; for this was the indiscriminate epithet he gave to every mode of conduct or thinking superior to his own. He asserted, 'that all the world were governed by their own interest; those who pretended to be actuated by different motives, were only deeper knaves, or fools crazed by books, who took for gospel all the rodomantade[3] nonsense written by men who knew nothing of the world. For his part, he thanked God, he was no hypocrite; and if he stretched a point sometimes, it

---

[1] The murderess in Nathaniel Lee's *The Rival Queens, or the Death of Alexander the Great* (1677).
[2] An officer of the House of Lords responsible for bringing defendants to trial.
[3] Bragging; boastful; ranting (*OED*).

was always with an intention of paying every man his own.'

"He then artfully insinuated, 'that he daily expected a vessel to arrive, a successful speculation, that would make him easy for present, and that he had other schemes actually depending, that could not fail. He had no doubt of becoming rich in a few years, though he had been thrown back by some unlucky adventures at the setting out.'

"I mildly replied, 'That I wished he might not involve himself still deeper.'

"He had no notion that I was governed by a decision of judgment, not to be compared with a mere spurt of resentment. He knew not what it was to feel indignation against vice, and often boasted of his placable temper, and readiness to forgive injuries. True; for he only considered the being deceived, as an effort of skill he had not guarded against; and then, with a cant of candour, would observe, 'that he did not know how he might himself have been tempted to act in the same circumstances.' And, as his heart never opened to friendship, it never was wounded by disappointment. Every new acquaintance he protested, it is true, was 'the cleverest fellow in the world;' and he really thought so; till the novelty of his conversation or manners ceased to have any effect on his sluggish spirits. His respect for rank or fortune was more permanent, though he chanced to have no design of availing himself of the influence of either to promote his own views.

"After a prefatory conversation,—my blood (I thought it had been cooler) flushed over my whole countenance as he spoke— he alluded to my situation. He desired me to reflect—'and act like a prudent woman, as the best proof of my superior understanding; for he must own I had sense, did I know how to use it. I was not,' he laid a stress on his words, 'without my passions; and a husband was a convenient cloke.—He was liberal in his way of thinking; and why might not we, like many other married people, who were above vulgar prejudices, tacitly consent to let each other follow their own inclination?—He meant nothing more, in the letter I made the ground of complaint; and the pleasure which I seemed to take in Mr. S.'s company, led him to conclude, that he was not disagreeable to me."

"A clerk brought in the letters of the day, and I, as I often did, while he was discussing subjects of business, went to the *piano forte*, and began to play a favourite air to restore myself, as it were, to nature, and drive the sophisticated sentiments I had just been obliged to listen to, out of my soul.

"They had excited sensations similar to those I have felt, in viewing the squalid inhabitants of some of the lanes and back streets of the metropolis, mortified at being compelled to consider them as my fellow-creatures, as if an ape had claimed kindred with me. Or, as when surrounded by a mephitical[4] fog, I have wished to have a volley of cannon fired, to clear the incumbered atmosphere, and give me room to breathe and move.

"My spirits were all in arms, and I played a kind of extemporary prelude. The cadence was probably wild and impassioned, while, lost in thought, I made the sounds a kind of echo to my train of thinking.

"Pausing for a moment, I met Mr. Venables' eyes. He was observing me with an air of conceited satisfaction, as much as to say—'My last insinuation has done the business—she begins to know her own interest.' Then gathering up his letters, he said, 'That he hoped he should hear no more romantic stuff, well enough in a miss just come from boarding-school;' and went, as was his custom, to the counting-house. I still continued playing; and, turning to a sprightly lesson, I executed it with uncommon vivacity. I heard footsteps approach the door, and was soon convinced that Mr. Venables was listening; the consciousness only gave more animation to my fingers. He went down into the kitchen, and the cook, probably by his desire, came to me, to know what I would please to order for dinner. Mr. Venables came into the parlour again, with apparent carelessness. I perceived that the cunning man was over-reaching himself; and I gave my directions as usual, and left the room.

[4] Offensive to the smell; pestilential, noxious, poisonous (*OED*).

"While I was making some alteration in my dress, Mr. Venables peeped in, and, begging my pardon for interrupting me, disappeared. I took up some work[5] (I could not read), and two or three messages were sent to me, probably for no other purpose, but to enable Mr. Venables to ascertain what I was about.

"I listened whenever I heard the street-door open; at last I imagined I could distinguish Mr. Venables' step, going out. I laid aside my work; my heart palpitated; still I was afraid hastily to enquire; and I waited a long half hour, before I ventured to ask the boy whether his master was in the counting-house?

"Being answered in the negative, I bade him call me a coach, and collecting a few necessaries hastily together, with a little parcel of letters and papers which I had collected the preceding evening. I hurried into it, desiring the coachman to drive to a distant part of the town.

"I almost feared that the coach would break down before I got out of the street; and, when I turned the corner, I seemed to breathe a freer air. I was ready to imagine that I was rising above the thick atmosphere of earth; or I felt, as wearied souls might be supposed to feel on entering another state of existence.

"I stopped at one or two stands of coaches to elude pursuit, and then drove round the skirts of the town to seek for an obscure lodging, where I wished to remain concealed, till I could avail myself of my uncle's protection. I had resolved to assume my own name immediately, and openly to avow my determination, without any formal vindication, the moment I had found a home, in which I could rest free from the daily alarm of expecting to see Mr. Venables enter.

"I looked at several lodgings; but finding that I could not, without a reference to some acquaintance, who might inform my tyrant, get admittance into a decent apartment—men have not all this trouble—I thought of a woman whom I had assisted to furnish a little haberdasher's[6] shop, and who I knew had a

---

[5] Needlework.
[6] A dealer in small articles appertaining to dress (*OED*).

first floor to let.

"I went to her, and though I could not persuade her, that the quarrel between me and Mr. Venables would never be made up, still she agreed to conceal me for the present; yet assuring me at the same time, shaking her head, that, when a woman was once married, she must bear every thing. Her pale face, on which appeared a thousand haggard lines and delving wrinkles, produced by what is emphatically termed fretting, inforced her remark; and I had afterwards an opportunity of observing the treatment she had to endure, which grizzled her into patience. She toiled from morning till night; yet her husband would rob the till, and take away the money reserved for paying bills; and, returning home drunk, he would beat her if she chanced to offend him, though she had a child at the breast.

"These scenes awoke me at night; and, in the morning, I heard her, as usual, talk to her dear Johnny—he, forsooth, was her master; no slave in the West Indies had one more despotic; but fortunately she was of the true Russian breed of wives.[7]

"My mind, during the few past days, seemed, as it were, disengaged from my body; but, now the struggle was over, I felt forcibly the effect which perturbation of spirits produces on a woman in my situation.

"The apprehension of a miscarriage, obliged me to confine myself to my apartment near a fortnight; but I wrote to my uncle's friend for money, promising 'to call on him, and explain my situation, when I was well enough to go out; mean time I earnestly intreated him, not to mention my place of abode to any one, lest my husband—such the law considered him—should disturb the mind he could not conquer. I mentioned my intention of setting out for Lisbon, to claim my uncle's protection, the moment my health would permit.'

"The tranquility however, which I was recovering, was soon interrupted. My landlady came up to me one day, with eyes

[7] I.e., loyal to her husband even when subjected to physical abuse, as believed true of Russian wives.

swollen with weeping, unable to utter what she was commanded to say. She declared, 'That she was never so miserable in her life; that she must appear an ungrateful monster; and that she would readily go down on her knees to me; to intreat me to forgive her, as she had done to her husband to spare her the cruel task.' Sobs prevented her from proceeding, or answering my impatient enquiries, to know what she meant.

"When she became a little more composed, she took a newspaper out of her pocket, declaring, 'that her heart smote her, but what could she do?—she must obey her husband.' I snatched the paper from her. An advertisement quickly met my eye, purporting that 'Maria Venables had, without any assignable cause, absconded from her husband; and any person harbouring her, was menaced with the utmost severity of the law.'

"Perfectly acquainted with Mr. Venables' meanness of soul, this step did not excite my surprise, and scarcely my contempt. Resentment in my breast, never survived love. I bade the poor woman, in a kind tone, wipe her eyes, and request her husband to come up, and to speak to me himself.

"My manner awed him. He respected a lady, though not a woman; and began to mutter out an apology.

"'Mr. Venables was a rich gentleman; he wished to oblige me, but he had suffered enough by the law already, to tremble at the thought; besides, for certain, we should come together again, and then even I should not thank him for being accessory to keeping us asunder.—A husband and wife were, God knows, just as one,—and all would come round at last.' He uttered a drawling 'Hem!' and then with an arch look, added—'Master might have had his little frolics—but—Lord bless your heart!— men would be men while the world stands.'

"To argue with this privileged first-born of reason, I perceived, would be vain. I therefore only requested him to let me remain another day at his house, while I sought for a lodging; and not to inform Mr. Venables that I had ever been sheltered there.

"He consented, because he had not the courage to refuse a

person for whom he had an habitual respect; but I heard the pent-up choler burst forth in curses, when he met his wife, who was waiting impatiently at the foot of the stairs, to know what effect my expostulations would have on him.

"Without wasting any time in the fruitless indulgence of vexation, I once more set out in search of an abode in which I could hide myself for a few weeks.

"Agreeing to pay an exorbitant price, I hired an apartment, without any reference being required relative to my character: indeed, a glance at my shape seemed to say, that my motive for concealment was sufficiently obvious. Thus was I obliged to shroud my head in infamy.

"To avoid all danger of detection—I use the appropriate word, my child, for I was hunted out like a felon—I determined to take possession of my new lodgings that very evening.

"I did not inform my landlady where I was going. I knew that she had a sincere affection for me, and would willingly have run any risk to show her gratitude; yet I was fully convinced, that a few kind words from Johnny would have found the woman in her, and her dear benefactress, as she termed me in an agony of tears, would have been sacrificed, to recompense her tyrant for condescending to treat her like an equal. He could be kind-hearted, as she expressed it, when he pleased. And this thawed sternness, contrasted with his habitual brutality, was the more acceptable, and could not be purchased at too dear a rate.

"The sight of the advertisement made me desirous of taking refuge with my uncle, let what would be the consequence; and I repaired in a hackney coach (afraid of meeting some person who might chance to know me, had I walked) to the chambers of my uncle's friend.

"He received me with great politeness (my uncle had already prepossessed him in my favour), and listened, with interest, to my explanation of the motives which had induced me to fly from home, and skulk in obscurity, with all the timidity of fear that ought only to be the companion of guilt. He lamented, with rather more gallantry than, in my situation, I thought delicate, that such a woman should be thrown away on a man insensible to the charms of beauty or grace. He seemed at a loss what to advise me to do, to evade my husband's search, without hastening to my uncle, whom, he hesitating said, I might not find alive. He uttered this intelligence with visible regret; requested me, at least, to wait for the arrival of the next packet;[8] offered me what money I wanted, and promised to visit me.

"He kept his word: still no letter arrived to put an end to my painful state of suspense. I procured some books and music, to beguile the tedious solitary days.

'Come, ever smiling Liberty,

'And with thee bring thy jocund train:'[9]

I sung—and sung till, saddened by the strain of joy, I bitterly lamented the fate that deprived me of all social pleasure. Comparative liberty indeed I had possessed myself of; but the jocund train lagged far behind!

[8] Mail boat.
[9] Handel, *Judas Maccabaeus* (1746).

CHAPTER XIII

By watching my only visitor, my uncle's friend, or by some other means, Mr. Venables discovered my residence, and came to enquire for me. The maid-servant assured him there was no such person in the house. A bustle ensued—I caught the alarm—listened—distinguished his voice, and immediately locked the door. They suddenly grew still; and I waited near a quarter of an hour, before I heard him open the parlour door, and mount the stairs with the mistress of the house, who obsequiously declared that she knew nothing of me.

"Finding my door locked, she requested me to 'open it, and prepare to go home with my husband, poor gentleman! to whom I had already occasioned sufficient vexation.' I made no reply. Mr. Venables then, in an assumed tone of softness, intreated me, 'to consider what he suffered, and my own reputation, and get the better of childish resentment.' He ran on in the same strain, pretending to address me, but evidently adapting his discourse to the capacity of the landlady; who, at every pause, uttered an exclamation of pity; or 'Yes, to be sure—Very true, sir.'

"Sick of the farce, and perceiving that I could not avoid the hated interview, I opened the door, and he entered. Advancing with easy assurance to take my hand, I shrunk from his touch, with an involuntary start, as I should have done from a noisome reptile, with more disgust than terror. His conductress was retiring, to give us, as she said, an opportunity to accommodate matters. But I bade her come in, or I would go out; and curiosity impelled her to obey me.

"Mr. Venables began to expostulate; and this woman, proud of his confidence, to second him. But I calmly silenced her, in the midst of a vulgar harangue, and turning to him, asked, 'Why he vainly tormented me? declaring that no power on earth should force me back to his house.'

"After a long altercation, the particulars of which, it would be to no purpose to repeat, he left the room. Some time was spent in loud conversation in the parlour below, and I discovered that he had brought his friend, an attorney, with him.

****

****

****

The tumult on the landing place, brought out a gentleman, who had recently taken apartments in the house; he enquired why I was thus assailed?* The voluble attorney instantly repeated the trite tale. The stranger turned to me, observing, with the most soothing politeness and manly interest, that 'my countenance told a very different story.' He added, 'that I should not be insulted, or forced out of the house, by any body.'

"'Not by her husband?' asked the attorney.

"'No, sir, not by her husband.' Mr. Venables advanced towards him—But there was a decision in his attitude, that so well seconded that of his voice,

****

****

They left the house: at the same time protesting, that any one that should dare protect me, should be prosecuted with the utmost rigour.

"They were scarcely out of the house, when my landlady came up to me again, and begged my pardon, in a very different tone. For, though Mr. Venables had bid her, at her peril, harbour me, he had not attended, I found, to her broad hints, to dis-

---

* The introduction of Darnford as the deliverer of Maria, in an early stage of the history, is already stated (Chap. III.) to have been an afterthought of the author. This has probably caused the imperfectness of the manuscript in the above passage; though, at the same time, it must be acknowledged to be somewhat uncertain, whether Darnford is the stranger intended in this place. It appears from Chap. XVII, that an interference of a more decisive nature was designed to be attributed to him. EDITOR. [Godwin's note].

charge the lodging. I instantly promised to pay her, and make her a present to compensate for my abrupt departure, if she would procure me another lodging, at a sufficient distance; and she, in return, repeating Mr. Venables' plausible tale, I raised her indignation, and excited her sympathy, by telling her briefly the truth.

"She expressed her commiseration with such honest warmth, that I felt soothed; for I have none of that fastidious sensitiveness, which a vulgar accent or gesture can alarm to the disregard of real kindness. I was ever glad to perceive in others the humane feelings I delighted to exercise; and the recollection of some ridiculous characteristic circumstances, which have occurred in a moment of emotion, has convulsed me with laughter, though at the instant I should have thought it sacrilegious to have smiled. Your improvement, my dearest girl, being ever present to me while I write, I note these feelings, because women, more accustomed to observe manners than actions, are too much alive to ridicule. So much so, that their boasted sensibility is often stifled by false delicacy. True sensibility, the sensibility which is the auxiliary of virtue, and the soul of genius, is in society so occupied with the feelings of others, as scarcely to regard its own sensations. With what reverence have I looked up at my uncle, the dear parent of my mind! when I have seen the sense of his own sufferings, of mind and body, absorbed in a desire to comfort those, whose misfortunes were comparatively trivial. He would have been ashamed of being as indulgent to himself, as he was to others. 'Genuine fortitude,' he would assert, 'consisted in governing our own emotions, and making allowance for the weaknesses in our friends, that we would not tolerate in ourselves.' But where is my fond regret leading me!

"'Women must be submissive,' said my landlady. 'Indeed what could most women do? Who had they to maintain them, but their husbands? Every woman, and especially a lady, could not go through rough and smooth, as she had done, to earn a little bread.'

"She was in a talking mood, and proceeded to inform me

how she had been used in the world. 'She knew what it was to have a bad husband, or she did not know who should.' I perceived that she would be very much mortified, were I not to attend to her tale, and I did not attempt to interrupt her, though I wished her, as soon as possible, to go out in search of a new abode for me, where I could once more hide my head.

"She began by telling me, 'That she had saved a little money in service; and was over-persuaded (we must all be in love once in our lives) to marry a likely man, a footman in the family, nor worth a groat. My plan,' she continued, 'was to take a house, and let out lodgings; and all went on well, till my husband got acquainted with an impudent slut, who chose to live on other people's means—and then all went to rack and ruin. He ran in debt to buy her fine clothes, such clothes as I never thought of wearing myself, and—would you believe it?—he signed an execution on my very goods, bought with the money I worked so hard to get; and they came and took my bed from under me, before I heard a word of the matter. Aye, madam, these are misfortunes that you gentlefolks know nothing of;—but sorrow is sorrow, let it come which way it will.

"'I sought for a service again—very hard, after having a house of my own!—but he used to follow me, and kick up such a riot when he was drunk, that I could not keep a place; nay, he even stole my clothes, and pawned them; and when I went to the pawnbroker's, and offered to take my oath that they were not bought with a farthing of his money, they said, 'It was all as one, my husband had a right to whatever I had.'

"'At last he listed for a soldier, and I took a house, making an agreement to pay for the furniture by degrees; and I almost starved myself, till I once more got before-hand in the world.

"'After an absence of six years (God forgive me! I thought he was dead) my husband returned; found me out, and came with such a penitent face, I forgave him, and clothed him from head to foot. But he had not been a week in the house, before some of his creditors arrested him; and, he selling my goods, I found myself once more reduced to beggary; for I was not as well able to work, go to bed late, and rise early, as when I quitted service; and then I thought it hard enough. He was soon tired of me, when there was nothing more to be had, and left me again.

"I will not tell you how I was buffeted about, till, hearing for certain that he had died in an hospital abroad, I once more returned to my old occupation; but have not yet been able to get my head above water; so, madam, you must not be angry if I am afraid to run any risk, when I know so well, that women have always the worst of it, when law is to decide.'

"After uttering a few more complaints, I prevailed on my landlady to go out in quest of a lodging; and, to be more secure, I condescended to the mean shift of changing my name.

"But why should I dwell on similar incidents!—I was hunted, like an infected beast, from three different apartments, and should not have been allowed to rest in any, had not Mr. Venables, informed of my uncle's dangerous state of health, been inspired with the fear of hurrying me out of the world as I advanced in my pregnancy, by thus tormenting and obliging me to take sudden journeys to avoid him; and then his speculations on my uncle's fortune must prove abortive.

"One day, when he had pursued me to an inn, I fainted, hurrying from him; and, falling down, the sight of my blood alarmed him, and obtained a respite for me. It is strange that he should have retained any hope, after observing my unwavering determination; but, from the mildness of my behaviour, when I found all my endeavours to change his disposition unavailing, he formed an erroneous opinion of my character, imagining that, were we once more together, I should part with the money he could not legally force from me, with the same facility as formerly. My forbearance and occasional sympathy he had mistaken for weakness of character; and, because he perceived that I disliked resistance, he thought my indulgence and compassion mere selfishness; and never discovered that the fear of being unjust, or of unnecessarily wounding the feelings of another, was much more painful to me, than any thing I could have to endure myself. Perhaps it was pride which made me imagine, that

I could bear what I dreaded to inflict; and that it was often easier to suffer, than to see the sufferings of others.

"I forgot to mention that, during this persecution, I received a letter from my uncle, informing me, 'that he only found relief from continual change of air; and that he intended to return when the spring was a little more advanced (it was now the middle of February), and then we would plan a journey to Italy, leaving the fogs and cares of England far behind.' He approved of my conduct, promised to adopt my child, and seemed to have no doubt of obliging Mr. Venables to hear reason. He wrote to his friend, by the same post, desiring him to call on Mr. Venables in his name; and, in consequence of the remonstrances he dictated, I was permitted to lie-in tranquilly.

"The two or three weeks previous, I had been allowed to rest in peace; but, so accustomed was I to pursuit and alarm, that I seldom closed my eyes without being haunted by Mr. Venables' image, who seemed to assume terrific or hateful forms to torment me, wherever I turned.—Sometimes a wild cat, a roaring bull, or hideous assassin, whom I vainly attempted to fly; at others he was a demon, hurrying me to the brink of a precipice, plunging me into dark waves, or horrid gulfs; and I woke, in violent fits of trembling anxiety, to assure myself that it was all a dream, and to endeavour to lure my waking thoughts to wander to the delightful Italian vales, I hoped soon to visit; or to picture some august ruins, where I reclined in fancy on a mouldering column, and escaped, in the contemplation of the heart-enlarging virtues of antiquity, from the turmoil of cares that had depressed all the daring purposes of my soul. But I was not long allowed to calm my mind by the exercise of my imagination; for the third day after your birth, my child, I was surprised by a visit from my elder brother; who came in the most abrupt manner, to inform me of the death of my uncle. He had left the greater part of his fortune to my child, appointing me its guardian; in short, every step was taken to enable me to be mistress of his fortune, without putting any part of it in Mr. Venables' power. My brother came to vent his rage on me, for having, as he expressed himself, 'deprived him, my uncle's eldest nephew, of his inheritance;' though my uncle's property, the fruit of his own exertion, being all in the funds, or on landed securities, there was not a shadow of justice in the charge.

"As I sincerely loved my uncle, this intelligence brought on a fever, which I struggled to conquer with all the energy of my mind; for, in my desolate state, I had it very much at heart to suckle you, my poor babe. You seemed my only tie to life, a cherub, to whom I wished to be a father, as well as a mother; and the double duty appeared to me to produce a proportionate increase of affection. But the pleasure I felt, while sustaining you, snatched from the wreck of hope, was cruelly damped by melancholy reflections on my widowed state—widowed by the death of my uncle. Of Mr. Venables I thought not, even when I thought of the felicity of loving your father, and how a mother's pleasure might be exalted, and her care softened by a husband's tenderness—'Ought to be!' I exclaimed: and I endeavoured to drive away the tenderness that suffocated me; but my spirits were weak, and the unbidden tears would flow. 'Why was I,' I would ask thee, but thou didst not heed me,—'cut off from the participation of the sweetest pleasure of life?' I imagined with what extacy, after the pains of child-bed, I should have presented my little stranger, whom I had so long wished to view, to a re-spectable father, and with what maternal fondness I should have pressed them both to my heart!—Now I kissed her with less delight, though with the most endearing compassion, poor help-less one! when I perceived a slight resemblance to him, to whom she owed her existence; or, if any gesture reminded me of him, even in his best days, my heart heaved, and I pressed the inno-cent to my bosom, as if to purify it—yes, I blushed to think that its purity had been sullied, by allowing such a man to be its father.

"After my recovery, I began to think of taking a house in the country, or of making an excursion on the continent, to avoid Mr. Venables; and to open my heart to new pleasures and affec-tion. The spring was melting into summer, and you, my little companion, began to smile—that smile made hope bud out afresh, assuring me the world was not a desert. Your gestures were ever present to my fancy; and I dwelt on the joy I should feel when you would begin to walk and lisp. Watching your wakening mind, and shielding from every rude blast my tender blossom, I recovered my spirits—I dreamed not of the frost— 'the killing frost,'[1] to which you were destined to be exposed.— But I lose all patience—and execrate the injustice of the world— folly! ignorance!—I should rather call it; but, shut up from a free circulation of thought, and always pondering on the same griefs, I writhe under the torturing apprehensions, which ought to excite only honest indignation, or active compassion; and would, could I view them as the natural consequence of things. But, born a woman—and born to suffer, in endeavouring to repress my own emotions, I feel more acutely the various ills my sex are fated to bear—I feel that the evils they are subject to endure, degrade them so far below their oppressors, as almost to justify their tyranny; leading at the same time superficial reasoners to term that weakness the cause, which is only the consequence of short-sighted despotism.

---

[1] *Henry VIII*, III.ii.355: "The third day comes a frost, a killing frost."

Chapter XIV

As my mind grew calmer, the visions of Italy again returned with their former glow of colouring; and I resolved on quitting the kingdom for a time, in search of the cheerfulness, that naturally results from a change of scene, unless we carry the barbed arrow with us, and only see what we feel.

"During the period necessary to prepare for a long absence, I sent a supply to pay my father's debts, and settled my brothers in eligible situations; but my attention was not wholly engrossed by my family, though I do not think it necessary to enumerate the common exertions of humanity. The manner in which my uncle's property was settled, prevented me from making the addition to the fortune of my surviving sister, that I could have wished; but I had prevailed on him to bequeath her two thousand pounds, and she determined to marry a lover, to whom she had been some time attached. Had it not been for this engagement, I should have invited her to accompany me in my tour; and I might have escaped the pit, so artfully dug in my path, when I was the least aware of danger.

"I had thought of remaining in England, till I weaned my child; but this state of freedom was too peaceful to last, and I had soon reason to wish to hasten my departure. A friend of Mr. Venables, the same attorney who had accompanied him in several excursions to hunt me from my hiding places, waited on me to propose a reconciliation. On my refusal, he indirectly advised me to make over to my husband—for husband he would term him—the greater part of the property I had at command, menacing me with continual persecution unless I complied; and that, as a last resort, he would claim the child. I did not, though intimidated by the last insinuation, scruple to declare, that I would not allow him to squander the money left to me for far different purposes, but offered him five hundred pounds, if he would sign a bond not to torment me any more. My maternal anxiety made me thus appear to waver from my first determination, and probably suggested to him, or his diabolical agent, the infernal plot, which has succeeded but too well.

"The bond was executed; still I was impatient to leave England. Mischief hung in the air when we breathed the same; I wanted seas to divide us, and waters to roll between, till he had forgotten that I had the means of helping him through a new scheme. Disturbed by the late occurrences, I instantly prepared for my departure. My only delay was waiting for a maid-servant, who spoke French fluently, and had been warmly recommended to me. A valet I was advised to hire, when I fixed on my place of residence for any time.

"My God, with what a light heart did I set out for Dover!—It was not my country, but my cares, that I was leaving behind. My heart seemed to bound with the wheels, or rather appeared the center on which they twirled. I clasped you to my bosom, exclaiming 'And you will be safe—quite safe—when—we are once on board the packet.—Would we were there!' I smiled at my idle fears, as the natural effect of continual alarm; and I scarcely owned to myself that I dreaded Mr. Venables's cunning, or was conscious of the horrid delight he would feel, at forming stratagem after stratagem to circumvent me. I was already in the snare—I never reached the packet—I never saw thee more.—I grow breathless. I have scarcely patience to write down the details. The maid—the plausible woman I had hired—put, doubtless, some stupifying potion in what I ate or drank, the morning I left town. All I know is, that she must have quitted the chaise, shameless wretch! and taken (from my breast) my babe with her. How could a creature in a female form see me caress thee, and steal thee from my arms! I must stop, stop to repress a mother's anguish; lest, in bitterness of soul, I imprecate the wrath of heaven on this tiger, who tore my only comfort from me.

"How long I slept I know not; certainly many hours, for I

woke at the close of day, in a strange confusion of thought. I was probably roused to a recollection by some one thundering at a huge, unwieldy gate. Attempting to ask where I was, my voice died away, and I tried to raise it in vain, as I have done in a dream. I looked for my babe with affright; feared that it had fallen out of my lap, while I had so strangely forgotten her; and, such was the vague intoxication, I can give it no other name, in which I was plunged, I could not recollect when or where I last saw you; but I sighed, as if my heart wanted room to clear my head.

"The gates opened heavily, and the sullen sound of many locks and bolts drawn back, grated on my very soul, before I was appalled by the creeking of the dismal hinges, as they closed after me. The gloomy pile[1] was before me, half in ruins; some of the aged trees of the avenue were cut down, and left to rot where they fell; and as we approached some mouldering steps, a monstrous dog darted forwards to the length of his chain, and barked and growled infernally.

"The door was opened slowly, and a murderous visage peeped out, with a lantern. 'Hush!' he uttered, in a threatning tone, and the affrighted animal stole back to his kennel. The door of the chaise flew back, the stranger put down the lantern, and clasped his dreadful arms around me. It was certainly the effect of the soporific draught, for, instead of exerting my strength, I sunk without motion, though not without sense, on his shoulder, my limbs refusing to obey my will. I was carried up the steps into a close-shut hall. A candle flaring in the socket, scarcely dispersed the darkness, though it displayed to me the ferocious countenance of the wretch who held me.

"He mounted a wide staircase. Large figures painted on the walls seemed to start on me, and glaring eyes to meet me at every turn. Entering a long gallery, a dismal shriek made me spring out of my conductor's arms, with I know not what mys-

---

[1] I.e., the estate that served as the private madhouse. As befits a gothic setting, the mansion is represented as being in a ruinous state.

terious emotion of terror; but I fell on the floor, unable to sustain myself.

"A strange-looking female started out of one of the recesses, and observed me with more curiosity than interest; till, sternly bid retire, she flitted back like a shadow. Other faces, strongly marked, or distorted, peeped through the half-opened doors, and I heard some incoherent sounds. I had no distinct idea where I could be—I looked on all sides, and almost doubted whether I was alive or dead.

"Thrown on a bed, I immediately sunk into insensibility again; and next day, gradually recovering the use of reason, I began, starting affrighted from the conviction, to discover where I was confined—I insisted on seeing the master of the mansion—I saw him—and perceived that I was buried alive.—

"Such, my child, are the events of thy mother's life to this dreadful moment—Should she ever escape from the fangs of her enemies, she will add the secrets of her prison-house—and—"

Some lines were here crossed out, and the memoirs broke off abruptly with the names of Jemima and Darnford.

Appendix

ADVERTISEMENT.[1]

The performance, with a fragment of which the reader has now been presented, was designed to consist of three parts. The preceding sheets were considered as constituting one of those parts. Those persons who in the perusal of the chapters, already written and in some degree finished by the author, have felt their hearts awakened, and their curiosity excited as to the sequel of the story, will, of course, gladly accept even of the broken paragraphs and half-finished sentences, which have been found committed to paper, as materials for the remainder. The fastidious and cold-hearted critic may perhaps feel himself repelled by the incoherent form in which they are presented. But an inquisitive temper willingly accepts the most imperfect and mutilated information, where better is not to be had: and readers, who in any degree resemble the author in her quick apprehension of sentiment, and of the pleasures and pains of imagination, will, I believe, find gratification, in contemplating sketches, which were designed in a short time to have received the finishing touches of her genius; but which must now for ever remain a mark to record the triumphs of mortality, over schemes of usefulness, and projects of public interest.

---

[1] Composed by Godwin.

CHAPTER XV

Darnford returned the memoirs to Maria, with a most affectionate letter, in which he reasoned on the "the absurdity of the laws respecting matrimony, which, till divorces could be more easily obtained, was," he declared, "the most insufferable bondage. Ties of this nature could not bind minds governed by superior principles; and such beings were privileged to act above the dictates of laws they had no voice in framing, if they had sufficient strength of mind to endure the natural consequence. In her case, to talk of duty, was a farce, excepting what was due to herself. Delicacy, as well as reason, forbade her ever to think of returning to her husband: was she then to restrain her charming sensibility through mere prejudice? These arguments were not absolutely impartial, for he disdained to conceal, that, when he appealed to her reason, he felt that he had some interest in her heart.—The conviction was not more transporting, than sacred—a thousand times a day, he asked himself how he had merited such happiness?—and as often he determined to purify the heart she deigned to inhabit—He intreated to be again admitted to her presence."

He was: and the tear which glistened in his eye, when he respectfully pressed her to his bosom, rendered him peculiarly dear to the unfortunate mother. Grief had stilled the transports of love, only to render their mutual tenderness more touching. In former interviews, Darnford had contrived, by a hundred little pretexts, to sit near her, to take her hand, or to meet her eyes—now it was all soothing affection, and esteem seemed to have rivalled love. He adverted to her narrative, and spoke with warmth of the oppression she had endured.—His eyes, glowing with a lambent flame, told her how much he wished to restore her to liberty and love; but he kissed her hand, as if it had been that of a saint; and spoke of the loss of her child, as if it had been his own.—What could have been more flattering to Maria?—Every instance of self-denial was registered in her heart, and she loved him, for loving her too well to give way to the transports of passion.

They met again and again; and Darnford declared, while passion suffused his cheeks, that he never before knew what it was to love.—

One morning Jemima informed Maria, that her master intended to wait on her, and speak to her without witnesses. He came, and brought a letter with him, pretending that he was ignorant of its contents, though he insisted on having it returned to him. It was from the attorney already mentioned, who informed her of the death of her child, and hinted, "that she could not now have a legitimate heir, and that, would she make over the half of her fortune during life, she should be conveyed to Dover, and permitted to pursue her plan of traveling."

Maria answered with warmth, "That she had no terms to make with the murderer of her babe, nor would she purchase liberty at the price of her own respect."

She began to expostulate with her jailor; but he sternly bade her "Be silent—he had not gone so far, not to go further."

Darnford came in the evening. Jemima was obliged to be absent, and she, as usual, locked the door on them, to prevent interruption or discovery.—The lovers were, at first, embarrassed; but fell insensibly into confidential discourse. Darnford represented, "that they might soon be parted," and wished her "to put it out of the power of fate to separate them."

As her husband she now received him, and he solemnly pledged himself as her protector—and eternal friend—

There was one peculiarity in Maria's mind: she was more anxious not to deceive, than to guard against deception; and had rather trust without sufficient reason, than be for ever the prey of doubt. Besides, what are we, when the mind has, from reflection, a certain kind of elevation, which exalts the contemplation above the little concerns of prudence! We see what we wish, and

describes Wolstonecraft

make a world of our own—and, though reality may sometimes open a door to misery, yet the moments of happiness procured by the imagination, may, without a paradox, be reckoned among the solid comforts of life. Maria now, imagining that she had found a being of celestial mould—was happy,—nor was she deceived.—He was then plastic in her impassioned hand—and reflected all the sentiments which animated and warmed her∗∗∗

∗∗∗

∗∗∗

Chapter XVI

One morning confusion seemed to reign in the house, and Jemima came in terror, to inform Maria, "that her master had left it, with a determination, she was assured (and too many circumstances corroborated the opinion, to leave a doubt of its truth) of never returning. "I am prepared then," said Jemima, "to accompany you in your flight."

Maria started up, her eyes darting towards the door, as if afraid that some one should fasten it on her for ever.

Jemima continued, "I have perhaps no right now to expect the performance of your promise; but on you it depends to reconcile me with the human race."

"But Darnford!"—exclaimed Maria, mournfully—sitting down again, and crossing her arms—" I have no child to go to, and liberty has lost its sweets."

"I am much mistaken, if Darnford is not the cause of my master's flight—his keepers assure me, that they have promised to confine him two days longer, and then he will be free—you cannot see him; but they will give a letter to him the moment he is free.—In that inform him where he may find you in London; fix on some hotel. Give me your clothes; I will send them out of the house with mine, and we will slip out at the garden-gate. Write your letter while I make these arrangements, but lose no time!"

In an agitation of spirit, not to be calmed, Maria began to write to Darnford. She called him by the sacred name of "husband," and bade him "hasten to her, to share her fortune, or she would return to him."—An hotel in the Adelphi was the place of rendezvous.

The letter was sealed and given in charge; and with light footsteps, yet terrified at the sound of them, she descended, scarcely breathing, and with an indistinct fear that she should never get out at the garden gate. Jemima went first.

A being, with a visage that would have suited one possessed by a devil, crossed the path, and seized Maria by the arm. Maria had no fear but of being detained—"Who are you? what are you?" for the form was scarcely human. "If you are made of flesh and blood," his ghastly eyes glared on her, "do not stop me!"

"Woman," interrupted a sepulchral voice, 'what have I to do with thee?"—Still he grasped her hand, muttering a curse.

"No, no; you have nothing to do with me," she exclaimed, "this is a moment of life and death!"—

With supernatural force she broke from him, and, throwing her arms round Jemima, cried, "Save me!" The being, from whose grasp she had loosed herself, took up a stone as they opened the door, and with a kind of hellish sport threw it after them. They were out of his reach.

When Maria arrived in town, she drove to the hotel already fixed on. But she could not sit still—her child was ever before her; and all that had passed during her confinement, appeared to be a dream. She went to the house in the suburbs, where, as she now discovered, her babe had been sent. The moment she entered, her heart grew sick; but she wondered not that it had proved its grave. She made the necessary enquiries, and the church-yard was pointed out, in which it rested under a turf. A little frock, which the nurse's child wore (Maria had made it herself) caught her eye. The nurse was glad to sell it for half-a-guinea, and Maria hastened away with the relic, and, reentering the hackney-coach which waited for her, gazed on it, till she reached her hotel.

She then waited on the attorney who had made her uncle's will, and explained to him her situation. He readily advanced her some the money which still remained in his hands, and promised to take the whole of the case into consideration. Maria only wished to be permitted to remain in quiet—She found that several bills, apparently with her signature, had been presented to her agent, nor was she for a moment at a loss to guess by whom they had been forged; yet, equally averse to threaten or intreat, she requested her friend [the solicitor] to call on Mr. Venables. He was not to be found at home; but at length his agent, the attorney, offered a conditional promise to Maria, to leave her in peace, as long as she behaved with propriety, if she would give up the notes. Maria inconsiderately consented—Darnford was arrived, and she wished to be only alive to love; she wished to forget the anguish she felt whenever she thought of her child.

They took a ready-furnished lodging together, for she was above disguise; Jemima insisting on being considered as her house-keeper, and to receive the customary stipend. On no other terms would she remain with her friend.

Darnford was indefatigable in tracing the mysterious circumstances of his confinement. The cause was simply, that a relation, a very distant one, to whom he was heir, had died intestate, leaving a considerable fortune. On the news of Darnford's arrival [in England, a person, intrusted with the management of the property, and who had the writings in his possession, determining, by one bold stroke, to strip Darnford of the succession,] had planned his confinement; and [as soon as he had taken the measures he judged most conducive to his object, this ruffian, together with his instrument,] the keeper of the private madhouse, left the kingdom. Darnford, who still pursued his enquiries, at last discovered that they had fixed their place of refuge at Paris.

Maria and he determined therefore, with the faithful Jemima, to visit that metropolis, and accordingly were preparing for the journey, when they were informed that Mr. Venables had commenced an action against Darnford for seduction and adultery. The indignation Maria felt cannot be explained; she repented of the forbearance she had exercised in giving up the notes. Darnford could not put off his journey, without risking the loss of his property: Maria therefore furnished him with money for his expedition; and determined to remain in London till the termination of this affair.

She visited some ladies with whom she had formerly been

intimate, but was refused admittance; and at the opera, or Ranelagh,[1] they could not recollect her. Among these ladies there were some, not her most intimate acquaintance, who were generally supposed to avail themselves of the cloke of marriage, to conceal a mode of conduct, that would for ever have damned their fame, had they been innocent, seduced girls. These particularly stood aloof.—Had she remained with her husband, practicing insincerity, and neglecting her child to manage an intrigue, she would still have been visited and respected. If, instead of openly living with her lover, she could have condescended to call into play a thousand arts, which, degrading her own mind, might have allowed the people who were not deceived, to pretend to be so, she would have been caressed and treated like an honourable woman. "And Brutus* is an honourable man!" said Mark Antony with equal sincerity.[2]

With Darnford she did not taste uninterrupted felicity; there was a volatility in his manner which often distressed her; but love gladdened the scene; besides, he was the most tender, sympathizing creature in the world. A fondness for the sex often gives an appearance of humanity to the behaviour of men, who have small pretensions to the reality; and they seem to love others, when they are only pursuing their own gratification. Darnford appeared ever willing to avail himself of her taste and acquirements, while she endeavoured to profit by his decision of character, and to eradicate some of the romantic notions, which had taken root in her mind, while in adversity she had brooded over visions of unattainable bliss.

The real affections of life, when they are allowed to burst forth, are buds pregnant with joy and all the sweet emotions of the soul; yet they branch out with wild ease, unlike the artificial forms of felicity, sketched by an imagination painful alive. The

[1] Public gardens much frequented by the London gentry; the site of numerous gatherings and masquerades.

*The name in the manuscript is by mistake written Caesar. EDITOR [Godwin's note].

[2] *Julius Caesar*, III.ii.82.

substantial happiness, which enlarges and civilizes the mind, may be compared to the pleasure experienced in roving through nature at large, inhaling the sweet gale natural to the clime; while the reveries of a feverish imagination continually sport themselves in gardens full of aromatic shrubs, which cloy while they delight, and weaken the sense of pleasure they gratify. The heaven of fancy, below or beyond the stars, in this life, or in those ever-smiling regions surrounded by the unmarked ocean of futurity, have an insipid uniformity which palls. Poets have imagined scenes of bliss; but, fencing out sorrow, all the extatic emotions of the soul, and even its grandeur, seem to be equally excluded. We dose over the unruffled lake, and long to scale the rocks which fence the happy valley of contentment, though serpents hiss in the pathless desert, and danger lurks in the unexplored wiles. Maria found herself more indulgent as she was happier, and discovered virtues, in characters she had before disregarded, while chasing the phantoms of elegance and excellence, which sported in the meteors that exhale in the marshes of misfortune. The heart is often shut by romance against social pleasure; and, fostering a sickly sensibility, grows callous to the soft touches of humanity.

To part with Darnford was indeed cruel.—It was to feel most painfully alone; but she rejoiced to think, that she should spare him the care and perplexity of the suit, and meet him again, all his own. Marriage, as at present constituted, she considered as leading to immorality—yet, as the odium of society impedes usefulness, she wished to avow her affection to Darnford, by becoming his wife according to established rules; not to be confounded with women who act from very different motives, though her conduct would be just the same without the ceremony as with it, and her expectations from him not less firm. The being summoned to defend herself from a charge which she was determined to plead guilty to, was still galling, as it roused bitter reflections on the situation of women in society.

Chapter XVII

Such was her state of mind when the dogs of law were let loose on her. Maria took the task of conducting Darnford's defence upon herself. She instructed his counsel to plead guilty to the charge of adultery; but to deny that of seduction.

The counsel for the plaintiff opened the cause, by observing, "that his client had ever been an indulgent husband, and had borne with several defects of temper, while he had nothing criminal to lay to the charge of his wife. But that she left his house without assigning any cause. He could not assert that she was then acquainted with the defendant; yet, when he was once endeavouring to bring her back to her home, this man put the peace-officers to flight, and took her he knew not whither. After the birth of her child, her conduct was so strange, and a melancholy malady having afflicted one of the family, which delicacy forbade the dwelling on, it was necessary to confine her. By some means the defendant enabled her to make her escape, and they had lived together, in despite of all sense of order and decorum. The adultery was allowed, it was not necessary to bring any witnesses to prove it; but the seduction, though highly probable from the circumstances which he had the honour to state, could not be so clearly proved.—It was of the most atrocious kind, as decency was set at defiance, and respect for reputation, which shows internal compunction, utterly disregarded."

A strong sense of injustice had silenced every emotion, which a mixture of true and false delicacy might otherwise have excited in Maria's bosom. She only felt in earnest to insist on the privilege of her nature. The sarcasms of society, and the condemnation of a mistaken world, were nothing to her, compared with acting contrary to those feelings which were the foundation of her principles. [She therefore eagerly put herself forward, instead of desiring to be absent, on this memorable occasion.]

Convinced that the subterfuges of the law were disgraceful, she wrote a paper, which she expressly desired might be read in court:

"Married when scarcely able to distinguish the nature of the engagement, I yet submitted to the rigid laws which enslave women, and obeyed the man whom I could no longer love. Whether the duties of the state are reciprocal, I mean not to discuss; but I can prove repeated infidelities which I overlooked or pardoned. Witnesses are not wanting to establish these facts. I at present maintain the child of a maid servant, sworn to him, and born after our marriage.[1] I am ready to allow, that education and circumstances lead men to think and act with less delicacy, than the preservation of order in society demands from women; but surely I may without assumption declare, that, though I could excuse the birth, I could not the desertion of this unfortunate babe:—and, while I despised the man, it was not easy to venerate the husband. With proper restrictions however, I revere the institution which fraternizes the world. I exclaim against the laws which throw the whole weight of the yoke on the weaker shoulders, and force women, when they claim protectorship as mothers, to sign a contract, which renders them dependent on the caprice of the tyrant, whom choice or necessity has appointed to reign over them. Various are the cases, in which a woman ought to separate herself from her husband; and mine, I may be allowed emphatically to insist, comes under the

---

[1] Although George Venables can divorce Maria on the grounds of adultery, the law did not operate in the reverse. She can only be granted a divorce on the basis of incest, bigamy, impotence, or physical abuse. Divorce itself was extremely rare and only recently available as a legal option. In the late seventeenth century, divorce became possible through a private Act of Parliament; yet as Lawrence Stone reports, "This was a very expensive procedure, and it was almost entirely confined … to those who had very large properties at stake to hand to a male heir by a second marriage. Between 1670 and 1799, there were only 131 such Acts, virtually all instituted by husbands, and only seventeen passed before 1750" (34). [Lawrence Stone, *The Family, Sex and Marriage in England 1500-1800* (New York: Harper & Row, 1977)].

description of the most aggravated.

"I will not enlarge on those provocations which only the individual can estimate; but will bring forward such charges only, the truth of which is an insult upon humanity. In order to promote certain destructive speculations, Mr. Venables prevailed on me to borrow certain sums of a wealthy relation; and, when I refused further compliance, he thought of bartering my person; and not only allowed opportunities to, but urged, a friend from whom he borrowed money, to seduce me. On the discovery of this act of atrocity, I determined to leave him, and in the most decided manner, for ever. I consider all obligation as made void by his conduct; and hold, that schisms which proceed from want of principles, can never be healed.

"He received a fortune with me to the amount of five thousand pounds. On the death of my uncle, convinced that I could provide for my child, I destroyed the settlement of that fortune. I required none of my property to be returned to me, nor shall enumerate the sums extorted from me during six years that we lived together.

"After leaving, what the law considers as my home, I was hunted like a criminal from place to place, though I contracted no debts, and demanded no maintenance—yet, as the laws sanction such proceeding, and make women the property of their husbands, I forbear to animadvert. After the birth of my daughter, and the death of my uncle, who left a very considerable property to myself and child, I was exposed to new persecution; and, because I had, before arriving at what is termed years of discretion, pledged my faith, I was treated by the world, as bound for ever to a man whose vices were notorious. Yet what are the vices generally known, to the various miseries that a woman may be subject to, which, though deeply felt, eating into the soul, elude description, and may be glossed over! A false morality is even established, which makes all the virtue of women consist in chastity, submission, and the forgiveness of injuries.

"I pardon my oppressor—bitterly as I lament the loss of my child, torn from me in the most violent manner. But nature revolts, and my soul sickens at the bare supposition, that it could ever be a duty to pretend affection, when a separation is necessary to prevent my feeling hourly aversion.

"To force me to give my fortune, I was imprisoned—yes; in a private madhouse.—There, in the heart of misery, I met the man charged with seducing me. We became attached—I deemed, and ever shall deem, myself free. The death of my babe dissolved the only tie which subsisted between me and my, what is termed, lawful husband.

"To this person, thus encountered, I voluntarily gave myself, never considering myself as any more bound to transgress the laws of moral purity, because the will of my husband might be pleaded in my excuse, than to transgress those laws to which [the policy of artificial society has] annexed [positive] punishments.—While no command of a husband can prevent a woman from suffering for certain crimes, she must be allowed to consult her conscience, and regulate her conduct, in some degree, by her own sense of right. The respect I owe to myself, demanded my strict adherence to my determination of never viewing Mr. Venables in the light of a husband, nor could it forbid me from encouraging another. If I am unfortunately united to an unprincipled man, am I for ever to be shut out from fulfilling the duties of a wife and mother?—I wish my country to approve of my conduct; but, if laws exist, made by the strong to oppress the weak, I appeal to my own sense of justice, and declare that I will not live with the individual, who has violated every moral obligation which binds man to man.

"I protest equally against any charge being brought to criminate the man, whom I consider as my husband. I was six-and-twenty when I left Mr. Venables' roof; if ever I am to be supposed to arrive at an age to direct my own actions, I must by that time have arrived at it.—I acted with deliberation.—Mr. Darnford found me a forlorn and oppressed woman, and promised the protection women in the present state of society want.— But the man who now claims me—was he deprived of my society by this conduct? The question is an insult to common sense, considering where Mr. Darnford met me.—Mr. Venables' door was indeed open to me—nay, threats and intreaties were used to induce me to return; but why? Was affection or honour the motive?—I cannot, it is true, dive into the recesses of the human heart—yet I presume to assert, [borne out as I am by a variety of circumstances,] that he was merely influenced by the most rapacious avarice.

"I claim then a divorce, and the liberty of enjoying, free from molestation, the fortune left to me by a relation, who was well aware of the character of the man with whom I had to contend.—I appeal to the justice and humanity of the jury—a body of men, whose private judgment must be allowed to modify laws, that must be unjust, because definite rules can never apply to indefinite circumstances—and I deprecate punishment [upon the man of my choice, freeing him, as I solemnly do, from the charge of seduction.]

"I did not put myself into a situation to justify a charge of adultery, till I had, from conviction, shaken off the fetters which bound me to Mr. Venables.—While I lived with him, I defy the voice of calumny to sully what is termed the fair fame of women.— Neglected by my husband, I never encouraged a lover; and preserved with scrupulous care, what is termed my honour, at the expence of my peace, till he, who should have been its guardian, laid traps to ensnare me. From that moment I believed myself, in the sight of heaven, free—and no power on earth shall force me to renounce my resolution."

The judge, in summing up the evidence, alluded to "the fallacy of letting women plead their feelings, as an excuse for the violation of the marriage-vow. For his part, he had always determined to oppose all innovation, and the new-fangled notions which incroached on the good old rules of conduct. We did not want French principles in public or private life—and, if women were allowed to plead their feelings, as an excuse or palliation of infidelity, it was opening a flood-gate for immorality. What virtuous woman thought of her feelings?—It was her duty to love and obey the man chosen by her parents and relations, who were qualified by their experience to judge better for her, than she could for herself. As to the charges brought against the husband, they were vague, supported by no witnesses, excepting that of imprisonment in a private madhouse. The proofs of an insanity in the family, might render that however a prudent measure; and indeed the conduct of the lady did not appear that of a person of sane mind. Still such a mode of proceeding could not be justified, and might perhaps entitle the lady [in another court] to a sentence of separation from bed and board, during the joint lives of the parties;[2] but he hoped that no Englishman would legalize adultery, by enabling the adulteress to enrich her seducer. Too many restrictions could not be thrown in the way of divorces, if we wished to maintain the sanctity of marriage; and, though they might bear a little hard on a few, very few individuals, it was evidently for the good of the whole."

---

[2] In a legal separation, a woman could be granted divorce from bed and board. She would then be provided alimony, but would not be allowed to remarry.

CONCLUSION,

BY THE EDITOR

Very few hints exist respecting the plan of the remainder of the work. I find only two detached sentences, and some scattered heads for the continuation of the story. I transcribe the whole.

I.

"Darnford's letters were affectionate; but circumstances occasioned delays, and the miscarriage of some letters rendered the reception of wished-for answers doubtful: his return was necessary to calm Maria's mind."

II.

"As Darnford had informed her that his business was settled, his delaying to return seemed extraordinary; but love to excess, excludes fear or suspicion."

The scattered heads for the continuation of the story, are as follow.*

I.

"Trial for adultery—Maria defends herself—A separation from bed and board is the consequence—Her fortune is thrown into chancery[1]—Darnford obtains a part of his property—Maria goes into the country."

---

* To understand these minutes, it is necessary the reader should consider each of them as setting out from the same point in the story, *viz*, the point to which it is brought down in the preceding chapter. [Godwin's note].

[1] Highest judicial court next to the House of Lords. As a court of equity, it could modify the rulings imposed through the rigors of common law and hence provide some process for reconsideration through an appeal to conscience. As Gillian

II.

"A prosecution for adultery commenced—Trial—Darnford sets out for France—Letters—Once more pregnant—He returns—Mysterious behaviour—Visit—Expectation—Discovery—Interview—Consequence."

III.

"Sued by her husband—Damages awarded to him—Separation from bed and board—Darnford goes abroad—Maria into the country—Provides for her father—Is shunned—Returns to London—Expects to see her lover—The rack of expectation—Finds herself again with child—Delighted—A discovery—A visit—A miscarriage—Conclusion."

IV.

"Divorced by her husband—Her lover unfaithful—Pregnancy—Miscarriage—Suicide."

[The following passage appears in some respects to deviate from the preceding hints. It is superscribed],

"THE END.

"She swallowed the laudanum;[2] her soul was calm—the tempest had subsided—and nothing remained but an eager longing to forget herself—to fly from the anguish she endured to escape from thought—from this hell of disappointment.

"Still her eyes closed not—one remembrance with frightful velocity followed another—All the incidents of her life were in arms, embodied to assail her, and prevent her sinking into the sleep of death.—Her murdered child again appeared to her,

Skinner notes, "Equity offered ways in which the feme-covert could look after her interests, allowing her to sue her husband … and treating her, at least with respect to her separate property as a feme sole" (94). ["Women's Status as Legal and Civic Subjects," *Women and Literature in Britain 1700-1800.* Edited by Vivien Jones. (Cambridge: Cambridge University Press, 2000).]

mourning for the babe of which she was the tomb.—'And could it have a nobler?—Surely it is better to die with me, than to enter on life without a mother's care!—I cannot live!—but could I have deserted my child the moment it was born?—thrown it on the troubled wave of life, without a hand to support it?'— She looked up: 'What have I not suffered!—may I find a father where I am going!'—Her head turned; a stupor ensued; a faintness—'Have a little patience,'[3] said Maria, holding her swimming head (she thought of her mother), 'this cannot last long; and what is a little bodily pain to the pangs I have endured?'

"A new vision swam before her. Jemima seemed to enter—leading a little creature, that, with tottering footsteps, approached the bed. The voice of Jemima sounding as at a distance, called her—she tried to listen, to speak, to look!

"'Behold your child!' exclaimed Jemima. Maria started off the bed, and fainted.—Violent vomiting followed.

"When she was restored to life, Jemima addressed her with great solemnity: '—led me to suspect, that your husband and brother had deceived you, and secreted the child. I would not torment you with doubtful hopes, and I left you (at a fatal moment) to search for the child!—I snatched her from misery—and (now she is alive again) would you leave her alone in the world, to endure what I have endured?'

"Maria gazed wildly at her, her whole frame was convulsed with emotion; when the child, whom Jemima had been tutoring all the journey, uttered the word 'Mamma!' She caught her to her bosom, and burst into a passion of tears—then, resting the child gently on the bed, as if afraid of killing it,—she put her hand to her eyes, to conceal as it were the agonizing struggle of her soul. She remained silent for five minutes, crossing her arms over her bosom, and reclining her head,—then exclaimed: 'The conflict is over!—I will live for my child!'"

---

[2] A preparation in which opium was the main ingredient (*OED*).

A few readers perhaps, in looking over these hints, will wonder how it could have been practicable, without tediousness, or remitting in any degree the interest of the story, to have filled, from these slight sketches, a number of pages, more considerable than those which have been already presented. But, in reality, these hints, simple as they are, are pregnant with passion and distress. It is the refuge of barren authors only, to crowd their fictions with so great a number of events, as to suffer no one of them to sink into the reader's mind. It is the province of true genius to develop events, to discover their capabilities, to ascertain the different passions and sentiments with which they are fraught, and to diversify them with incidents, that give reality to the picture, and take a hold upon the mind of a reader of taste, from which they can never be loosened. It was particularly the design of the author, in the present instance, to make her story subordinate to a great moral purpose, that "of exhibiting the misery and oppression, peculiar to women, that arise out of the partial laws and customs of society.—This view restrained her fancy*." It was necessary for her, to place in a striking point of view, evils that are too frequently overlooked, and to drag into light those details of oppression, of which the grosser and more insensible part of mankind make little account.

THE END.

---

³ See Chapter VIII, note #1.
* See author's preface. [Godwin's note].

Photo credit: Tate Gallery, London/Art Resource, NY

Portrait of William Godwin. By J. W. Chandler, 1798.

Mary Wollstonecraft Godwin.

London, Published Jan.ˤ 1798, by J.Johnson, S.ᵗ Pauls Church Yard.

Frontispiece of the first edition of *Memoirs of the Author of "A Vindication of the Rights of Woman."* Engraving after the portrait of Mary Wollstonecraft. By John Opie, 1797.

MEMOIRS

OF THE

AUTHOR

OF A

VINDICATION OF THE RIGHTS OF WOMAN.

By WILLIAM GODWIN.

LONDON:

PRINTED FOR J. JOHNSON, NO. 72, ST. PAUL'S
CHURCH-YARD; AND G. G. AND J. ROBINSON,
PATERNOSTER-ROW.

1798.

Title page of the first edition of *Memoirs of the Author of "A Vindication of the Rights of Woman."*

Memoirs of the Author of A Vindication of the Rights of Woman

She was a great woman and I want to honor her memory

MEMOIRS.[1]

CHAP. I

1759-1775

It has always appeared to me, that to give to the public some account of the life of a person of eminent merit deceased, is a duty incumbent on survivors. It seldom happens that such a person passes through life, without being the subject of thoughtless calumny, or malignant misrepresentation. It cannot happen that the public at large should be on a footing with their intimate acquaintance, and be the observer of those virtues which discover themselves principally in personal intercourse. Every benefactor of mankind is more or less influenced by a liberal passion for fame; and survivors only pay a debt due to these benefactors, when they assert and establish on their part, the honour they loved. The justice which is thus done to the illustrious dead, converts into the fairest source of animation and encouragement to those who would follow them in the same carreer. The human species at large is interested in this justice, as it teaches them to place their respect and affection, upon those qualities which best deserve to be esteemed and loved. I cannot easily prevail on myself to doubt, that the more fully we are presented with the picture and story of such persons as the subject of the following narrative, the more generally shall we feel in

[1] The text of *The Memoirs* reprinted here is that of the first edition, published in January 1798, five months after the death of Wollstonecraft. Godwin published a second edition very soon after the first, in the summer of that same year, after readers responded to the original text with widespread condemnation of Wollstonecraft herself and of Godwin's choice to publish the more controversial details of her life. That edition proved more select in its choice of details than the first.

ourselves an attachment to their fate, and a sympathy in their excellencies. There are not many individuals with whose character the public welfare and improvement are more intimately connected, than the author of A Vindication of the Rights of Woman.

The facts detailed in the following pages, are principally taken from the mouth of the person to whom they relate; and of the veracity and ingenuousness of her habits, perhaps no one that was ever acquainted with her, entertains a doubt. The writer of this narrative, when he has met with persons, that in any degree created to themselves an interest and attachment in his mind, has always felt a curiosity to be acquainted with the scenes through which they had passed, and the incidents that had contributed to form their understandings and character. Impelled by this sentiment, he repeatedly led the conversation of Mary to topics of this sort; and, once or twice, he made notes in her presence, of a few dates calculated to arrange the circumstances in his mind. To the materials thus collected, he has added an industrious enquiry among the persons most intimately acquainted with her at the different periods of her life.

Mary Wollstonecraft was born on the 27th of April 1759. Her father's name was Edward John, and the name of her mother Elizabeth, of the family of Dixons of Ballyshannon in the kingdom of Ireland: her paternal grandfather was a respectable manufacturer in Spitalfields,[2] and is supposed to have left to his son a property of about 10,000£.[3] Three of her brothers and two sisters are still living; their names, Edward, James, Charles, Eliza, and Everina. Of these, Edward only was older than herself: he resides in London. James is in Paris, and Charles in or near Philadelphia in America. Her sisters have for some years been engaged in the office of governesses in private families, and are both at present in Ireland.

I am doubtful whether the father of Mary was bred to any

---

[2] An area to the east of London, known for its cloth manufacturing.
[3] This would have been a sizeable inheritance.

profession; but, about the time of her birth, he resorted, rather perhaps as an amusement than a business, to the occupation of farming. He was of very active, and somewhat versatile disposition, and so frequently changed his abode, as to throw some ambiguity upon the place of her birth. She told me, that the doubt in her mind in that respect, lay between London, and a farm upon Epping Forest,[4] which was the principal scene of the five first years of her life.

Mary was distinguished in early youth, by some portion of that exquisite sensibility, soundness of understanding, and decision of character, which were the leading features of her mind through the whole course of her life. She experienced in the first period of her existence, but few of those indulgences and marks of affection, which are principally calculated to sooth the subjection and sorrows of our early years. She was not the favourite either of her father or mother. Her father was a man of a quick, impetuous disposition, subject to alternate fits of kindness and cruelty. In his family he was a despot, and his wife appears to have been the first, and most submissive of his subjects. The mother's partiality was fixed upon the eldest son, and her system of government relative to Mary, was characterized by considerable rigour. She, at length, became convinced of her mistake, and adopted a different plan with her younger daughters. When, in the Wrongs of Woman, Mary speaks of "the petty cares which obscured the morning of her heroine's life; continual restraint in the most trivial matters; unconditional submission to orders, which, as a mere child, she soon discovered to be unreasonable, because inconsistent and contradictory; and the being often obliged to sit, in the presence of her parents, for three or four hours together, without daring to utter a word;"[5] she is, I believe, to be considered as copying the outline of the first period of her own existence.

But it was in vain, that the blighting winds of unkindness or

---

[4] An agricultural area 15 miles north of London.
[5] See pp. 112-113.

indifference, seemed destined to counteract the superiority of Mary's mind. It surmounted every obstacle; and, by degrees, from a person little considered in the family, she became in some sort its director and umpire. The despotism of her education cost her many a heart-ache. She was not formed to be the contented and unresisting subject of a despot; but I have heard her remark more than once, that, when she felt she had done wrong, the reproof or chastisement of her mother, instead of being a terror to her, she found to be the only thing capable of reconciling her to herself. The blows of her father on the contrary, which were the mere ebullitions of a passionate temper, instead of humbling her, roused her indignation. Upon such occasions she felt her superiority, and was apt to betray marks of contempt. The quickness of her father's temper, led him sometimes to threaten similar violence towards his wife. When that was the case, Mary would often throw herself between the despot and his victim, with the purpose to receive upon her own person the blows that might be directed against her mother. She has even laid whole nights upon the landing-place near their chamber-door, when, mistakenly, or with reason, she apprehended that her father might break out into paroxysms of violence. The conduct he held towards the members of his family, was of the same kind as that he observed towards animals. He was for the most part extravagantly fond of them; but, when he was displeased, and this frequently happened, and for very trivial reasons, his anger was alarming. Mary was what Dr. Johnson would have called, "a very good hater."[6] In some instance of passion exercised by her father to one of his dogs, she was accustomed to speak of her emotions of abhorrence, as having risen to agony. In a word, her conduct during her girlish years, was such, as to extort some portion of affection from her mother, and to hold her father in considerable awe.

---

[6] Hester Piozzi, *Anecdotes of the late Dr. Johnson, LL.D.* (1786): *"I like a good hater. I like a man to be with me or against me, either to be hot or cold. Dr. Johnson called Bathhurst the physician a 'good hater,' because he hated a fool, and he hated a rogue, and he hated a Whig; 'he,' said the Doctor, 'was a very good hater.'"*

In one respect, the system of education of the mother appears to have had merit. All her children were vigorous and healthy. This seems very much to depend upon the management of our infant years. It is affirmed by some persons of the present day, most profoundly skilled in the sciences of health and disease, that there is no period of human life so little subject to mortality, as the period of infancy. Yet, from the mismanagement to which children are exposed, many of the diseases of childhood are rendered fatal, and more persons die in that, than in any other period of human life. Mary had projected a work upon this subject, which she had carefully considered, and well understood. She has indeed left a specimen of her skill in this respect in her eldest daughter, three years and a half old, who is a singular example of vigorous constitution and florid health.[7] Mr. Anthony Carlisle,[8] surgeon, of Soho-square, whom to name is sufficiently to honour, had promised to revise her production. This is but one out of numerous projects of activity and usefulness, which her untimely death has fatally terminated.

The rustic situation in which Mary spent her infancy, no doubt contributed to confirm the stamina of her constitution. She sported in the open air, and amidst the picturesque and refreshing scenes of nature, for which she always retained the most exquisite relish. Dolls and the other amusements usually appropriated to female children, she held in contempt; and felt a much greater propensity to join in the active and hardy sports of her brothers, than to confine herself to those of her own sex.

About the time that Mary completed the fifth year of her age, her father removed to a small distance from his former habitation, and took a farm near the Whalebone[9] upon Epping Forest, a little way out of the Chelmsford road. In Michaelmas 1765,[10]

---

[7] Fanny Imlay, daughter of Mary Wollstonecraft and Gilbert Imlay.

[8] Sir Anthony Carlisle (1768-1840), surgeon at Westminster Hospital 1793-1840. Carlisle tended to Wollstonecraft on her deathbed.

[9] Whale Bone Inn.

[10] The feast of St. Michael, 29 Sept., one of the four quarter-days of the English business year (*OED*).

he once more changed his residence, and occupied a convenient house behind the town of Barking in Essex, eight miles from London. In this situation some of their nearest neighbours were, Bamber Gascoyne, esquire, successively member of parliament for several boroughs, and his brother, Mr. Joseph Gascoyne.[11] Bamber Gascoyne resided but little on this spot; but his brother was almost a constant inhabitant, and his family in habits of the most frequent intercourse with the family of Mary. Here Mr. Wollstonecraft remained for three years. In September 1796, I accompanied my wife in a visit to this spot. No person reviewed with greater sensibility, the scenes of her childhood. We found the house uninhabited, and the garden in a wild and ruinous state. She renewed her acquaintance with the market-place, the streets, and the wharf, the latter of which we found crowded with barges, and full of activity.

In Michaelmas 1768, Mr. Wollstonecraft again removed to a farm near Beverley in Yorkshire.[12] Here the family remained for six years, and consequently, Mary did not quit this residence, till she had attained the age of fifteen years and five months. The principal part of her school-education passed during this period: but it was not to any advantage of infant literature, that she was indebted for her subsequent eminence; her education in this respect was merely such, as was afforded by the day-schools of the place, in which she resided. To her recollections Beverley appeared a very handsome town, surrounded by genteel families, and with a brilliant assembly. She was surprised, when she visited it in 1795, upon her voyage to Norway, to find the reality so very much below the picture in her imagination.

Hitherto Mr. Wollstonecraft had been a farmer; but the restlessness of his disposition would not suffer him to content him-

---

[11] Sons of the Lord Mayor of London and landowners of considerable holdings.
[12] At that time, Yorkshire referred to the largest of the northern counties of England. This move represents a more disruptive one for Wollstonecraft, the family relocating far from London and from family. "Each farm [Wollstonecraft's father] took was poorer and remoter than the last" [Janet Todd, *Mary Wollstonecraft: Revolutionary Life* (New York: Columbia University Press, 2000) 8].

self with the occupation in which for some years he had been engaged, and the temptation of a commercial speculation of some sort being held out to him, he removed to a house in Queen's-Row, in Hoxton near London, for the purpose of its execution. Here he remained for a year and a half; but, being frustrated in his expectations of profit, he, after that term, gave up the project in which he was engaged, and returned to his former pursuits. During this residence at Hoxton, the writer of these memoirs inhabited, as a student, at the dissenting college in that place.[13] It is perhaps a question of curious speculation to enquire, what would have been the amount of difference in the pursuits and enjoyments of each party, if they had met, and considered each other with the same distinguishing regard in 1776, as they were afterwards impressed with in the year 1796. The writer had then completed the twentieth, and Mary the seventeenth year of her age. Which would have been predominant; the disadvantages of obscurity, and the pressure of a family; or the gratifications and improvement that might have flowed from their intercourse?

One of the acquaintances Mary formed at this time was a Mr. Clare,[14] who inhabited the next house to that which was tenanted by her father, and to whom she was probably in some degree indebted for the early cultivation of her mind. Mr. Clare was a clergyman, and appears to have been a humourist of a very singular cast. In his person he was deformed and delicate; and his figure, I am told, bore a resemblance to that of the celebrated Pope.[15] He had a fondness for poetry, and was not destitute of

[13] William Godwin attended Hoxton College from 1773-1777. Dissenting refers to a religious group that differs from the established doctrines or modes of worship (*OED*). In England, the established church was Anglican.

[14] Reverend Claire. He and Mrs. Claire were responsible for introducing Wollstonecraft to Fanny Blood and probably of locating Wollstonecraft a position as a lady's companion. [See Janet Todd, *Mary Wollstonecraft: A Revolutionary Life* (New York: New York University Press), 22, 28].

[15] Alexander Pope (1688-1744), much admired poet and critic. Early in life, he contracted tuberculosis of the bone which stunted his growth and left him crippled and delicate in health.

taste. His manners were expressive of a tenderness and benevolence, the demonstrations of which appeared to have been somewhat too artificially cultivated. His habits were those of a perfect recluse. He seldom went out of his drawing-room,[16] and he
showed to a friend of Mary a pair of shoes, which had served
him, he said, for fourteen years. Mary frequently spent days and
weeks together, at the house of Mr. Clare.

[16] A private chamber attached to a public room (*OED*).

CHAP. II.

1775-1783

But a connection more memorable originated about this time, between Mary and a person of her own sex, for whom she contracted a friendship so fervent,[1] as for years to have constituted the ruling passion of her mind. The name of this person was Frances Blood; she was two years older than Mary. Her residence was at that time at Newington Butts, a village near the southern extremity of the metropolis; and the original instrument for bringing these two friends acquainted, was Mrs. Clare, wife of the gentleman already mentioned, who was on a footing of considerable intimacy with both parties. The acquaintance of Fanny, like that of Mr. Clare, contributed to ripen the immature talents of Mary.

The situation in which Mary was introduced to her, bore a resemblance to the first interview of Werter with Charlotte.[2] She was conducted to the door of a small house, but furnished with peculiar neatness and propriety. The first object that caught her sight, was a young woman of a slender and elegant form, and eighteen years of age, busily employed in feeding and managing some children, born of the same parents, but considerably inferior to her in age. The impression Mary received from this spectacle was indelible; and, before the interview was concluded, she had taken, in her heart, the vows of an eternal friendship.

Fanny was a young woman of extraordinary accomplishments.

---

[1] In the second edition of *The Memoirs*, "fervent" is replaced with "warm."

[2] Johann Wolfgang von Goethe, *The Sorrows of Young Werther* (1774). An immensely popular work, Godwin refers to the first scene in which young Werther spies Charlotte S. in the midst of a domestic scene, and falls fatally in love with a woman already promised to another man. This reference to *Werther* is omitted in the second edition.

She sung and played with taste. She drew with exquisite fidelity and neatness; and, by the employment of this talent, for some time maintained her father, mother, and family, but ultimately ruined her health by her extraordinary exertions. She read and wrote with considerable application; and the same ideas of minute and delicate propriety followed her in these, as in her other oc-cupations.

Mary, a wild, but animated and aspiring girl of sixteen, con-templated Fanny, in the first instance, with sentiments of inferi-ority and reverence. Though they were much together, yet, the distance of their habitation being considerable, they supplied the want of more frequent interviews by an assiduous correspon-dence. Mary found Fanny's letters better spelt and better in-dited than her own, and felt herself abashed. She had hitherto paid but a superficial attention to literature. She had read, to gratify the ardour of an inextinguishable thirst of knowledge; but she had not thought of writing as an art. Her ambition to excel was now awakened, and she applied herself with passion and earnestness. Fanny undertook to be her instructor; and, so far as related to accuracy and method, her lessons were given with considerable skill.

It has already been mentioned that, in the spring of the year 1776, Mr. Wollstonecraft quitted his situation at Hoxton, and returned to his former agricultural pursuits. The situation upon which he now fixed was in Wales,[3] a circumstance that was felt as a severe blow to Mary's darling spirit of friendship. The prin-cipal acquaintance of the Wollstonecrafts in this retirement, was the family of a Mr. Allen,[4] two of whose daughters are since married to the two elder sons of the celebrated English potter, Josiah Wedgwood.[5]

Wales however was Mr. Wollstonecraft's residence for little more than a year. He returned to the neighbourhood of Lon-

---

[3] Region in SW Great Britain.
[4] John Bartlett Allen of Cresselly, Whig landowner.
[5] Josiah Wedgwood (1730-95), famous potter.

don; and Mary, whose spirit of independence was unalterable, had influence enough to determine his choice in favour of the village of Walworth, that she might be near her chosen friend. It was probably before this, that she has once or twice started the idea of quitting her parental roof, and providing for herself. But she was prevailed upon to resign this idea, and conditions were stipulated with her, relative to her having an apartment in the house that should be exclusively her own, and her commanding the other requisites of study. She did not however think herself fairly treated in these instances, and either the conditions abovementioned, or some others, were not observed in the sequel, with the fidelity she expected. In one case, she had procured an eligible situation, and every thing was settled respecting her removal to it, when the intreaties and tears of her mother led her to surrender her own inclinations, and abandon the engagement.

These however were only temporary delays. Her propensities continued the same, and the motives by which she was instigated were unabated. In the year 1778, she being nineteen years of age, a proposal was made to her of living as a companion with a Mrs. Dawson[6] of Bath, a widow lady, with one son already adult. Upon enquiry she found that Mrs. Dawson was a woman of great peculiarity of temper, that she had had a variety of companions in succession, and that no one had found it practicable to continue with her. Mary was not discouraged by this information, and accepted the situation, with a resolution that she would effect in this respect, what none of her predecessors had been able to do. In the sequel she had reason to consider the account she had received as sufficiently accurate, but she did not relax in her endeavours. By method, constancy and firmness, she found the means of making her situation tolerable; and Mrs. Dawson would occasionally confess, that Mary was the only person that had lived with her in that situation, in her treatment of whom she had felt herself under any restraint.

---

[6] Sarah Dawson of Bath, wealthy widow.

With Mrs. Dawson she continued to reside for two years, and only left her, summoned by the melancholy circumstance of her mother's rapidly declining health. True to the calls of humanity, Mary felt in this intelligence an irresistible motive, and eagerly returned to the paternal roof, which she had before resolutely quitted. The residence of her father at this time, was at Enfield, near London. He had, I believe, given up agriculture from the time of his quitting Wales, it appearing that he now made it less a source of profit than loss, and being thought advisable that he should rather live upon the interest of his property already in possession.

The illness of Mrs. Wollstonecraft was lingering, but hopeless. Mary was assiduous in her attendance upon her mother. At first, every attention was received with acknowledgments and gratitude; but, as the attentions grew habitual, and the health of the mother more and more wretched, they were rather exacted, than received. Nothing would be taken by the unfortunate patient, but from the hands of Mary; rest was denied night or day, and by the time nature was exhausted in the parent, the daughter was qualified to assume her place, and become in turn herself a patient. The last words her mother ever uttered were, "A little patience, and all will be over!" and these words are repeatedly referred to by Mary in the course of her writings.[7]

Upon the death of Mrs. Wollstonecraft, Mary bid a final adieu to the roof of her father. According to my memorandums, I find her next the inmate of Fanny at Walham Green, near the village of Fulham. Upon what plan they now lived together I am unable to ascertain; certainly not that of Mary's becoming in any degree an additional burthen upon the industry of her friend. Thus situated, their intimacy ripened; they approached more nearly to a footing of equality; and their attachment became more rooted and active.

Mary was ever ready at the call of distress, and, in particular, during her whole life was eager and active to promote the wel-

[7] See p. 124 for an example.

fare of every member of her family. In 1780 she attended the death-bed of her mother; in 1782 she was summoned by a not less melancholy occasion, to attend her sister Eliza, married to a Mr. Bishop, who, subsequently to a dangerous lying-in, remained for some months in a very afflicting situation. Mary continued with her sister without intermission, to her perfect recovery.[8]

---

[8] After the birth of her daughter, Eliza experienced post-natal depression and Wollstonecraft attended her during this illness. Ultimately, Wollstonecraft arranged for the escape of her youngest sister from this unhappy marriage to a well-to-do but somewhat older man. She and Eliza fled the home, leaving the infant daughter behind. Eliza and her husband, Meridith Bishop never divorced, as the process would have proven not only financially costly, but also costly to both their reputations. Neither remarried, and Eliza's daughter died just prior to her first birthday and before Eliza could arrange a reunion. [Janet Todd, *Mary Wollstonecraft: A Revolutionary Life* (New York: New York University Press), 45-57].

CHAP. III.

1783-1785

Mary was now arrived at the twenty-fourth year of her age. Her project, five years before, had been personal independence; it was now usefulness. In the solitude of attendance on her sister's illness, and during the subsequent convalescence, she had had leisure to ruminate upon purposes of this sort. Her expanded mind led her to seek something more arduous than the mere removal of personal vexations; and the sensibility of her heart would not suffer her to rest in solitary gratifications. The derangement of her father's affairs daily became more and more glaring; and a small independent provision made for herself and her sisters, appears to have been sacrificed in the wreck. For ten years, from 1782 to 1792, she may be said to have been, in a great degree, the victim of a desire to promote the benefit of others. She did not foresee the severe disappointment with which an exclusive purpose of this sort is pregnant; she was inexperienced enough to lay a stress upon the consequent gratitude of those she benefited; and she did not sufficiently consider that, in proportion as we involve ourselves in the interests and society of others, we acquire a more exquisite sense of their defects, and are tormented with their untractableness and folly.

The project upon which she now determined, was no other than that of a day-school, to be superintended by Fanny Blood, herself, and her two sisters.

They accordingly opened one in the year 1783, at the village of Islington; but in the course of a few months removed it to Newington Green.[1] Here Mary formed some acquaintances who

---

[1] Both villages were located north of and only a few miles from London.

influenced the future events of her life. The first of these in her own estimation, was Dr. Richard Price, well known for his political and mathematical calculations, and universally esteemed by those who knew him, for the simplicity of his manners, and the ardour of his benevolence.[2] The regard conceived by these two persons for each other, was mutual, and partook of a spirit of purest attachment. Mary had been bred in the principles of the church of England, but her esteem for this venerable preacher led her occasionally to attend upon his public instructions. Her religion was, in reality, little allied to any system of forms; and, as she has often told me, was founded rather in taste, than in the niceties of polemical discussion. Her mind constitutionally attached itself to the sublime and the amiable. She found an inexpressible delight in the beauties of nature, and in the splendid reveries of the imagination. But nature itself, she thought, would be no better than a vast blank, if the mind of the observer did not supply it with an animating soul. When she walked amidst the wonders of nature, she was accustomed to converse with her God. To her mind he was pictured as not less amiable, generous and kind, than great, wise and exalted. In fact, she had received few lessons of religion in her youth, and her religion was almost entirely of her own creation. But she was not on that account the less attached to it, or the less scrupulous in discharging what she considered as its duties. She could not recollect the time when she had believed the doctrine of future punishments. The tenets of her system were the growth of her own moral taste, and her religion therefore had always been a gratification, never a terror, to her. She expected a future state; but she would not allow her ideas of that future state to be modified by the notions of judgment and retribution. From this sketch, it is sufficiently evident, that the pleasure she took in an occasional attendance upon the sermons of Dr. Price, was not accompanied

---

[2] Richard Price (1723-91), nonconformist minister at Newington Green and longtime friend of Wollstonecraft. See text box "Wollstonecraft and the Revolution Debate," p. 239.

with a superstitious adherence to his doctrines. The fact is, that, as far down as the year 1787, she regularly frequented public worship, for the most part according to the forms of the church of England. After that period her attendance became less constant, and in no long time was wholly discontinued. I believe it may be admitted as a maxim, that no person of a well furnished mind, that has shaken off the implicit subjection of youth, and is not the zealous partizan of a sect, can bring himself to conform to the public and regular routine of sermons and prayers.

Another of the friends she acquired at this period, was Mrs. Burgh, widow of the author of the Political Disquisitions, a woman universally well spoken of for the warmth and purity of her benevolence.[3] Mary, whenever she had the occasion to allude to her, to the last period of her life, paid the tribute due to her virtues. The only remaining friend necessary to be enumerated in this place, is the rev. John Hewlet,[4] now master of a boarding-school at Shacklewel near Hackney, whom I shall have occasion to mention hereafter.

I have already said that Fanny's health had been materially injured by her incessant labours for the maintenance of her family. She had also suffered a disappointment, which preyed upon her mind. To these different sources of ill health she became gradually a victim; and at length discovered all the systems of a pulmonary consumption.[5] By the medical men that attended her, she was advised to try the effects of a southern climate; and, about the beginning of the year 1785, sailed for Lisbon.[6]

The first feeling with which Mary had contemplated her friend, was a sentiment of inferiority and reverence; but that, from the operation of a ten years' acquaintance, was considerably changed. Fanny had originally been far before her in liter-

[3] Sarah Harding Burgh (d. 1788), married to James Burgh (1714-75), author of *Political Disquisitions* (1774-5).
[4] John Hewlett (1762-1844), Anglican clergyman, schoolteacher, and religious scholar.
[5] Tuberculosis of the lungs.
[6] Seaport capital of Portugal.

ary attainments; this disparity no longer existed. In whatever degree Mary might endeavour to free herself from the delusions of self-esteem, this period of observation upon her own mind and that of her friend, could not pass, without her perceiving that there were some essential characteristics of genius, which she possessed, and in which her friend was deficient. The principal of these was a firmness of mind, an unconquerable greatness of soul, by which, after a short internal struggle, she was accustomed to rise above difficulties and suffering. Whatever Mary undertook, she perhaps in all instances accomplished; and, to her lofty spirit, scarcely any thing she desired, appeared hard to perform. Fanny, on the contrary, was a woman of a timid and irresolute nature, accustomed to yield to difficulties, and probably priding herself in this morbid softness of her temper. One instance that I have heard Mary relate of this sort, was, that, at a certain time, Fanny, dissatisfied with her domestic situation, expressed an earnest desire to have a home of her own. Mary, who felt nothing more pressing than to relieve the inconveniences of her friend, determined to accomplish this object for her. It cost her infinite exertions; but at length she was able to announce to Fanny that a house was prepared, and that she was on the spot to receive her. The answer which Fanny returned to the letter of her friend, consisted almost wholly of an enumeration of objections to the quitting her family, which she had not thought of before, but which now appeared to her of considerable weight.

The judgment which experience had taught Mary to form of the mind of her friend, determined her in the advice she gave, at the period to which I have brought down the story. Fanny was recommended to seek a softer climate, but she had no funds to defray the expence of such an undertaking. At this time Mr. Hugh Skeys[7] of Dublin, but then resident in the kingdom of Portugal, paid his addresses to her. The state of her health Mary considered as such as scarcely to afford the shadow of a hope; it

---

[7] Hugh Skeys, Irish businessman.

was not therefore a time at which it was most obvious to think of marriage. She conceived however that nothing should be omitted, which might alleviate, if it could not cure; and accordingly urged her speedy acceptance of the proposal. Fanny accordingly made the voyage to Lisbon; and the marriage took place on the twenty-fourth of February 1785.

The change of climate and situation was productive of little benefit; and the life of Fanny was only prolonged by a period of pregnancy, which soon declared itself. Mary, in the mean time, was impressed with the idea that her friend would die in this distant country; and, shocked with the recollection of her separation from the circle of her friends, determined to pass over to Lisbon to attend her. This resolution was treated by her acquaintance as in the utmost degree visionary; but she was not to be diverted from her point. She had not money to defray her expences: she must quit for a long time the school, the very existence of which probably depended upon her exertions.

No person was ever better formed for the business of education; if it be not a sort of absurdity to speak of a person as formed for an inferior object, who is in possession of talents, in the fullest degree adequate to something on a more important and comprehensive scale. Mary had a quickness of temper, not apt to take offence with inadvertencies, but which led her to imagine that she saw the mind of the person with whom she had any transaction, and to refer the principle of her approbation or displeasure to the cordiality or injustice of their sentiments. She was occasionally severe and imperious in her resentments; and, when she strongly disapproved, was apt to express her censure in terms that gave a very humiliating sensation to the person against whom it was directed. Her displeasure however never assumed its severest form, but when it was barbed by disappointment. Where she expected little, she was not very rigid in her censure of error.

But, to whatever the defects of her temper might amount, they were never exercised upon her inferiors in station or age. She scorned to make use of an ungenerous advantage, or to wound the defenceless. To her servants there never was a mistress more considerate or more kind. With children she was the mirror of patience. Perhaps, in all her extensive experience upon the subject of education, she never betrayed one symptom of irascibility. Her heart was the seat of every benevolent feeling; and accordingly, in all her intercourse with children, it was kindness and sympathy alone that prompted her conduct. Sympathy, when it mounts to a certain height, inevitably begets affection in the person towards whom it is exercised; and I have heard her say, that she never was concerned in the education of one child, who was not personally attached to her, and earnestly concerned not to incur her displeasure. Another eminent advantage she possessed in the business of education, was that she was little troubled with scepticism and uncertainty. She saw, as it were by intuition, the path which her mind determined to pursue, and had a firm confidence in her own power to effect what she desired. Yet, with all this, she had scarcely a tincture of obstinacy. She carefully watched symptoms as they rose, and the success of her experiments; and governed herself accordingly. While I thus enumerate her more than maternal qualities, it is impossible not to feel a pang at the recollection of her orphan children!

Though her friends earnestly dissuaded her from the journey to Lisbon, she found among them a willingness to facilitate the execution of her project, when it was once fixed. Mrs. Burgh in particular, supplied her with money, which however she always conceived came from Dr. Price. This loan, I have reason to believe, was faithfully repaid.

It was during her residence at Newington Green, that she was introduced to the acquaintance of Dr. Johnson,[8] who was at that time considered as in some sort the father of English literature. The doctor treated her with particular kindness and atten-

---

[8] Samuel Johnson (1709-84), best known for having compiled *The Dictionary of the English Language* and for being remarkably prolific and proficient in many literary forms (including the essay, verse satire, and criticism). A favorable reception from Johnson would have carried much weight.

tion, had a long conversation with her, and desired her to repeat her visit often. This she firmly purposed to do; but the news of his last illness, and then of his death, intervened to prevent her making a second visit.

Her residence in Lisbon was not long. She arrived but a short time before her friend was prematurely delivered, and the event was fatal to both mother and child. Frances Blood, hitherto the chosen object of Mary's attachment, died on the twenty-ninth of November 1785.

It is thus that she speaks of her in her Letters from Norway,[9] written ten years after her decease. "When a warm heart has received strong impressions, they are not to be effaced. Emotions become sentiments; and the imagination renders even transient sensations permanent, by fondly retracing them. I cannot, without a thrill of delight, recollect views I have seen, which are not to be forgotten, nor looks I have felt in every nerve, which I shall never more meet. The grave has closed over a dear friend, the friend of my youth; still she is present with me, and I hear her soft voice warbling as I stray over the heath."

Sensibility

---

[9] *Letters Written During a Short Residence in Sweden, Norway, and Denmark* (1796), letter 6. See text box "She Speaks of Her Sorrows," p. 266.

CHAP. IV.
1785-1787

No doubt the voyage to Lisbon tended considerably to enlarge the understanding of Mary. She was admitted into the best company the England factory[1] afforded. She made many profound observations on the character of the natives, and the baleful effects of superstition.[2] The obsequies of Fanny, which it was necessary to perform by stealth and in darkness, tended to invigorate these observations in her mind.

She sailed upon her voyage home about the twentieth of December. On this occasion a circumstance occurred, that deserves to be recorded. While they were on their passage, they fell in with a French vessel, in great distress, and in daily expectation of foundering at sea, at the same time that it was almost destitute of provisions. The Frenchman hailed them, and intreated the English captain, in consideration of his melancholy situation, to take him and his crew on board. The Englishman represented in reply, that his stock of provisions was by no means adequate to such an additional number of mouths, and absolutely refused compliance. Mary, shocked at his apparent insensibility, took up the cause of the sufferers, and threatened the captain to have him called to a severe account, when he arrived in England. She finally prevailed, and had the satisfaction to reflect, that the persons in question possibly owed their lives to her interposition.

When she arrived in England, she found that her school had suffered considerably in her absence. It can be little reproach to any one, to say that they were found incapable of supplying her

---

[1] Area inhabited by merchants.
[2] This term would have been read as referring to Roman Catholicism.

place. She not only excelled in the management of children, but had also the talent of being attentive and obliging to the parents, without degrading herself.

The period at which I am now arrived is important, as conducting to the first step of her literary carreer. Mr. Hewlet had frequently mentioned literature to Mary as a certain source of pecuniary produce, and had urged her to make trial of the truth of his judgment. At this time she was desirous of assisting the father and mother of Fanny in an object they had in view, the transporting themselves to Ireland; and, as usual, what she desired in a pecuniary view, she was ready to take on herself to effect. For this purpose she wrote a duodecimo pamphlet of one hundred and sixty pages, entitled, Thoughts on the Education of Daughters.[3] Mr. Hewlet obtained from the bookseller, Mr. Johnson[4] in St. Paul's Church Yard, ten guineas for the copyright of this manuscript, which she immediately applied to the object of the sake of which the pamphlet was written.

Every thing urged Mary to put an end to the affair of the school. She was dissatisfied with the different appearance it presented upon her return, from the state in which she left it. Experience impressed upon her a rooted aversion to that sort of cohabitation with her sisters, which the project of the school imposed. Cohabitation is a point of delicate experiment, and is, in a majority of instances, pregnant with ill-humour and unhappiness.[5] The activity and ardent spirit of adventure which characterized Mary, were not felt in an equal degree by her sisters, so that a disproportionate share of every burthen attendant upon the situation, fell to her lot. On the other hand, they could scarcely perhaps be perfectly easy, in observing the superior degree of

[3] *Thoughts on the Education of Daughters: with Reflections on Female Conduct, in the More Important Duties of Life* (1787).

[4] Joseph Johnson (1738-1809), bookseller and publisher. Johnson becomes a long-term friend and employer of Wollstonecraft, publishing all her major works and hiring her as a staff writer for *The Analytical Review*.

[5] See text box "On Co-habitation, Love, and Fidelity" (p. 279) for a discussion of Godwin's attitude toward cohabitation.

deference and courtship, which her merit extorted from almost every one that knew her. Her kindness for them was not diminished, but she resolved that the mode of its exertion in future should be different, tending to their benefit, without intrenching upon her own liberty.

Thus circumstanced, a proposal was made her, such as, regarding only the situations through which she had lately passed, is usually termed advantageous. This was, to accept the office of governess to the daughters of lord viscount Kingsborough,[6] eldest son to the earl of Kingston of the kingdom of Ireland.[7] The terms held out to her was such as she determined to accept, at the same time resolving to retain the situation only for a short time. Independence was the object after which she thirsted, and she was fixed to try whether it might not be found in literary occupation. She was desirous however first to accumulate a small sum of money, which should enable her to consider at leisure the different literary engagements that might offer, and provide in some degree for the eventual deficiency of her earliest attempts.

The situation in the family of lord Kingsborough, was offered to her through the medium of the rev. Mr. Prior, at that time one of the under masters of Eton school.[8] She spent some time at the house of this gentleman, immediately after her giving up the school at Newington Green. Here she had an opportunity of making an accurate observation upon the manners of and conduct of that celebrated seminary, and the ideas she retained of it were by no means favourable. By all that she saw, she was confirmed in a very favourite opinion of her's, in behalf of day-schools, where, as she expressed it, "children have the opportunity of conversing with children, without interfering with domestic affections, the foundation of virtue."

---

[6] Robert King, Viscount Kingsborough (1754-99).
[7] See text box "A Something Betwixt and Between" in *Wrongs of Woman* (p. 134) for a discussion of Wollstonecraft's attitude toward being a governess.
[8] Eton College, elite boys' school.

Though her residence in the family of lord Kingsborough continued scarcely more than twelve months, she left behind her, with them and their connections, a very advantageous impression. The governesses the young ladies had hitherto had, were only a species of upper servants, controlled in every thing by the mother; Mary insisted upon the unbounded exercise of her own discretion. When the young ladies heard of their governess coming from England, they heard in imagination of a new enemy, and declared their resolution to guard themselves accordingly. Mary however speedily succeeded in gaining their confidence, and the friendship that soon grew up between her and Margaret King, now countess Mount Cashel, the eldest daughter, was in an uncommon degree cordial and affectionate. Mary always spoke of this young lady in terms of the truest applause, both in relation to the eminence of her intellectual powers, and the ingenuous amiableness of her disposition. Lady Kingsborough, from the best motives, had imposed upon her daughters a variety of prohibitions, both as to the books they should read, and in many other respects. These prohibitions had their usual effects; inordinate desire for the things forbidden, and clandestine indulgence. Mary immediately restored the children to their liberty, and undertook to govern them by their affections only. The consequence was, that their indulgences were moderate, and they were uneasy under any indulgence that had not the sanction of their governess. The salutary effects of the new system of education were speedily visible; and lady Kingsborough soon felt no other uneasiness, than lest the children should love their governess better than their mother.

Mary made many friends in Ireland, among the persons who visited lord Kingsborough's house, for she always appeared there with the air of an equal, and not of a dependent. I have heard her mention the ludicrous distress of a woman of quality, whose name I have forgotten, that, in a large company, singled out Mary, and entered into a long conversation with her. After the conversation was over, she enquired whom she had been talking with, and found, to her utter mortification and dismay, that it was Miss King's governess.

One of the persons among her Irish acquaintance, whom Mary was accustomed to speak of with the highest respect, was Mr. George Ogle, member of parliament for the county of Wexford. She held his talents in very high estimation; she was strongly prepossessed in favour of the goodness of his heart; and she always spoke of him as the most perfect gentleman she had ever known. She felt the regret of a disappointed friend, at the part he has lately taken in the politics of Ireland.[9]

Lord Kingsborough's family passed the summer of the year 1787 at Bristol Hot-Wells,[10] and had formed the project of proceeding from thence to the continent, a tour in which Mary purposed to accompany them. The plan however was ultimately given up, and Mary in consequence closed her connection with them, earlier than she otherwise had purposed to do.

At Bristol Hot-Wells she composed the little book which bears the title Mary, a Fiction.[11] A considerable part of this story consists, with certain modifications, of the incidents of her own friendship with Fanny. All the events that do not relate to that subject are fictitious.

This little work, if Mary had never produced any thing else, would serve, with persons of true taste and sensibility, to establish the eminence of her genius. The story is nothing. He that looks into the book only for incident, will probably lay it down with disgust. But the feelings are of the truest and most exquisite class; every circumstance is adorned with that species of imagination, which enlists itself under the banners of delicacy and sentiment. A work of sentiment, as it is called, is too often another name for a work of affectation. He that should imagine that the sentiments of this book are affected, would indeed be entitled to our profoundest commiseration.

---

[9] George Ogle (1742-1814), writer of sentimental verse and conservative Irish politician. Mary was much charmed by him; later he opposed proposals allowing the Irish greater political autonomy.
[10] A spa resort near Bath.
[11] *Mary, A Fiction* (1788).

An "Exercise in Sensibility":
From *Mary, A Fiction*

"The story is nothing," writes Godwin of Wollstonecraft's first novel, and in large part he is right. *Mary, A Fiction* is driven not by plot, but by character, in particular the highly sensitive nature of its heroine. Yet in many ways that story parallels Wollstonecraft's own and, obviously, the plot of her other semi-autobiographical work, *The Wrongs of Woman; or Maria*. Both novels focus on the plight of a strong, but neglected daughter raised by a weak mother and abusive father, details that proved formative in Wollstonecraft's own life story. In both novels, the heroines end up in a loveless marriage and, by consequence, emotional intimacy takes the form of female friendship and an ill-fated relationship with another man. In *Mary*, the description of the female friendship clearly recounts that of Wollstonecraft's own intense relationship with the recently deceased Fanny Blood. Her relationship with the male suitor ends no more happily— although as Godwin points out, he is a purely fictional character—as he dies before they can act upon their mutual sympathy for one another. The novel concludes with the heroine still married but wishing for "a world *where there is neither marrying*, nor giving in marriage" (73).

But whereas *Maria* is interested in the broader social context that occasions these misfortunes, *Mary* remains focused on the inner life of its heroine. In this novel, "a mother's illness, [a] friend's misfortunes" take on almost a positive cast, as through the contemplation of them the heroine's "sensibility [is] called forth and exercised." In this respect, this novel is very much in line with the "cult of sensibility" that flourished in the mid to late eighteenth century. "Sensibility," according to Janet Todd, "came to denote the faculty of feeling, the capacity for extremely refined emotion and a quickness to display compassion for suffering," and fiction became one of its primary mediums (7). Hence, Godwin's praise for this work is in many ways quite generic—

his emphasis on her delicacy of feeling, for example—yet he also clearly distinguishes this "little work" from other more standard texts in this genre. By contrast with many, he notes, it is not a work of affectation, evoking emotion for emotion's sake. A comparison of the following passage with excerpts from William Cowper's quintessential poem of sentiment "The Castaway" (1799) lends weight to his assessment and suggests that it derives from more than his love for her:

From *Mary, A Fiction*

The wind still continued contrary; a week, a dismal week, had she struggled with her sorrows; and the struggle brought on a slow fever, which sometimes gave her false spirits.

The winds then became very tempestuous, the Great Deep was troubled, and all the passengers appalled. Mary then left her bed, and went on deck, to survey the contending elements: the scene accorded with the present state of her soul; she thought in a few hours I may go home; the prisoner may be released. The vessel rose on a wave and descended into a yawning gulph—Not slower did her mounting soul return to earth, for—Ah! Her treasure and her heart were there. The squalls rattled amongst the sails, which were quickly taken down; the wind would then die away, and the wild undirected waves rushed on every side with a tremendous roar. In a little vessel in the midst of such a storm she was not dismayed: she felt herself independent.

Just then one of the crew perceived a signal of distress; by the help of a glass he could plainly discover a small vessel dismasted, drifted about, for the rudder had been broken by the violence of the storm. Mary's thoughts were now all engrossed by the crew on the brink of destruction. They bore down to the wreck; they reached it, and hailed the trembling wretches: at the sound of the friendly greeting, loud cries of tumultuous joy were mixed with the roaring of the waves, and with ecstatic transport they leaped on the shattered deck, launched their boat in a moment, and committed themselves to the mercy of the sea. Stowed between two casks, and leaning on a sail, she watched the boat, and when a wave intercepted it from her view—she ceased to breathe, or rather held her breath until it rose again.

At last the boat arrived safe along-side the ship, and Mary caught the poor trembling wretches as they stumbled into it, and joined them in thanking that gracious Being, who though He had not thought fit to still the raging of the sea, had afforded them unexpected succour.

Amongst the wretched crew was one poor woman, who fainted when she was hauled on board: Mary undressed her, and when she had recovered, and soothed her, left her to enjoy the rest she required to recruit her strength, which fear had quite exhausted. She returned again to view the angry deep, and when she gazed on its perturbed state, she thought of the Being who rode on the wings of the wind, and stilled the noise of the sea; and the madness of the people—He only could speak peace to the troubled spirit! she grew more calm; the late transaction had gratified her benevolence. And stole her out of herself. (50-51)

> "The Castaway"
> Obscurest night involved the sky,
>   Th' Atlantic billows roared,
> When such a destined wretch as I,
>   Washed headlong from on board,
> Of friends, of hope, of all bereft,
> His floating home forever left.

***

He shouted; nor his friends had failed
    To check the vessel's course,
But so the furious blast prevailed,
    That, pitiless perforce,
They left their outcast mate behind,
And scudded still before the wind.

Some succour yet they could afford;
    And, such as storms allow,
The cask, the coop, the floated cord,
    Delayed not to bestow.
But he (they knew) nor ship, nor shore,
Whate'er they gave, should visit more.

Nor, cruel as it seemed, could he
    Their haste himself condemn,
Aware that flight, in such a sea,
    Alone could rescue them;
Yet bitter felt it still to die
Deserted, and his friends so nigh.

            ***

At length, his transient respite past,
    His comrades, who before
Had heard his voice in ev'ry blast,
    Could catch the sound no more.
For then, by toil subdued, he drank
The stifling wave, and then he sank.

No poet wept him; but the page
    Of narrative sincere,
That tells his name, his worth, his age,
    Is wet with Anson's tear.
And tears by bards or heroes shed
Alike immortalize the dead.

I therefore purpose not or dream,
    Descanting on his fate,

To give the melancholy theme
A more enduring date:
But misery still delights to trace
Its semblance in another's case.

No voice divine the storm allayed,
No light propitious shone,
When, snatched from all effectual aid,
We perished, each alone;
But I beneath a rougher sea,
And whelmed in deeper gulfs than he. (616)

Whereas the witnessing of this harrowing scene by the speaker of Cowper's poem draws him further and helplessly into himself, Mary's draws her outside of herself and into a kind of active compassion and emotion of almost heroic nature. Indeed, from details mentioned earlier in this chapter of *The Memoirs*, it is clear that she is even more the hero in this scene than she lets on. On her trip home from Lisbon, Wollstonecraft did in fact experience such a storm and witness such a shipwreck, but it was only upon her active intervention that the passengers of that ship were saved. Little wonder then that Godwin, upon the onset of Wollstonecraft's labor with their child, took down *Mary* to reread yet again, that it was *this* Mary he wanted to be reminded of (Todd 449).

Sources

William Cowper. *The Poems of William Cowper*. Vol. 3. Edited by John D. Baird and Charles Ryskamp. Oxford: Clarendon Press, 1980.

Janet Todd. *Mary Wollstonecraft; A Revolutionary Life*. New York: Columbia University Press, 2000.

———. *Sensibility: An Introduction*. London: Methuen, 1986.

Mary Wollstonecraft. *Mary, A Fiction*. In *The Works of Mary Wollstonecraft*. Vol.1. Edited by Janet Todd and Marilyn Butler. New York: New York University Press, 1989.

Chap. V.
1787-1790

Being now determined to enter upon her literary plan, Mary came immediately from Bristol to the metropolis. Her conduct under this circumstance was such as to do credit both to her own heart, and that of Mr. Johnson, her publisher, between whom and herself there now commenced an intimate friendship. She had seen him upon occasion of publishing her Thoughts on the Education of Daughters, and she addressed two or three letters to him during her residence in Ireland. Upon her arrival in London in August 1787, she went immediately to his house, and frankly explained to him her purpose, at the same time requesting his advice and assistance as to its execution. After a short conversation, Mr. Johnson invited her to make his house her home, till she should have suited herself with a fixed residence. She accordingly resided at this time two or three weeks under his roof. At the same period she paid a visit or two of similar duration to some friends, at no great distance from the metropolis.

At Michaelmas 1787,[1] she entered upon a house in George Street, on the Surry side of Black Friar's Bridge, which Mr. Johnson had provided for her during her excursion into the country. The three years immediately ensuing, may be said, in the ordinary acceptance of the term, to have been the most active period of her life. She brought with her to this habitation, the novel of Mary, which had not yet been sent to the press, and the commencement of a sort of oriental tale, entitled the Cave of Fancy,[2] which she thought afterwards to lay aside unfinished. I am told

---

[1] September 29. See Chapter I, p. 206.
[2] Godwin prints this unfinished tale in *The Posthumous Works of Mary Wollstonecraft* in which *The Wrongs of Woman* (1798) is included.

that at this period she appeared under great dejection of spirits, and filled with melancholy regret for the loss of her youthful friend. A period of two years had elapsed since the death of that friend; but it was possibly the composition of the fiction of Mary, that renewed her sorrows in their original force. Soon after entering upon her new habitation, she produced a little work, entitled, Original Stories from Real Life, intended for the use of children.[3] At the commencement of her literary carreer, she is said to have conceived a vehement aversion to the being regarded, by her ordinary acquaintance, in the character of an author, and to have employed some precautions to prevent its occurrence.

The employment which the bookseller suggested to her, as the easiest and most certain source of pecuniary income, of course, was translation. With this view she improved herself in her French, with which she had previously but a slight acquaintance, and acquired the Italian and German languages. The greater part of her literary engagements at this time, were such as were presented to her by Mr. Johnson. She new-modelled and abridged a work, translated from the Dutch, entitled, Young Grandison: she began a translation from the French, of a book, called, the New Robinson; but in this undertaking, she was, I believe, anticipated by another translator: and she compiled a series of extracts in verse and prose, upon the model of Dr. Enfield's Speaker, which bears the title of the Female Reader;[4] but which, from a cause not worth mentioning, has hitherto been printed with a different name in the title-page.

About the middle of the year 1788, Mr. Johnson instituted the Analytical Review,[5] in which Mary took a considerable share.

---

[3] *Original Stories from Real Life* (1788), with illustrations by William Blake.

[4] *The Female Reader* (1789). The name that appeared on the title page was Mr. Cresswick, Teacher of Elocution. William Enfield's *The Speaker* was a collection of pieces from "the Best English Writers" and was a popular elocutionary book. *The Female Reader* was also such a reader, but explicitly directed toward "the Improvement of Young Women."

[5] *The Analytical Review* (1788-1799), published by Joseph Johnson and Thomas Christie. Mostly reviews, the magazine was "aimed at a general educated public of liberal persuasion" (14). Wollstonecraft wrote for the journal from its inception

She also translated Necker on the Importance of Religious Opinions; made an abridgement of Lavater's Physiognomy, from the French, which has never been published; and compressed Salzmann's Elements of Morality, a German production, into a publication in three volumes duodecimo. The translation of Salzmann produced a correspondence between Mary and the author; and he afterwards repaid the obligation to her in kind, by a German translation of the Rights of Woman. Such were her principal literary occupations, from the autumn of 1787, to the autumn of 1790.

It perhaps deserves to be remarked that this sort of miscellaneous literary employment, seems, for the time at least, rather to damp and contract, than to enlarge and invigorate, the genius. The writer is accustomed to see his performances answer the mere mercantile purpose of the day, and confounded with those of persons to whom he is secretly conscious of a superiority. No neighbour mind serves as a mirror to reflect the generous confidence he felt within himself; and perhaps the man never yet existed, who could maintain his enthusiasm to its full vigour, in the midst of this kind of solitariness. He is touched with the torpedo[6] of mediocrity. I believe that nothing which Mary produced during this period, is marked with those daring flights, which exhibit themselves in the little fiction she composed just before its commencement. Among effusions of a nobler cast, I find occasionally interspersed some of that homily-language, which, to speak from my own feelings, is calculated to damp the moral courage, it was intended to awaken. This is probably to be assigned to the causes above described.

I have already said that one of the purposes which Mary had conceived, a few years before, as necessary to give a relish to the otherwise insipid, or embittered, draught of human life, was

---

and periodically throughout her life; she also served as editorial assistant to Johnson. [Janet Todd and Marilyn Butler, "Prefatory Note," *The Works of Mary Wollstonecraft*, Vol. 7 (New York: New York University Press, 1989].
[6] "That which has a benumbing influence" (*OED*).

usefulness. On this side, the period of her existence of which I am now treating, is more brilliant, than in a literary view. She determined to apply as great a part as possible of the produce of her present employments, to the assistance of her friends and of the distressed; and, for this purpose, laid down to herself rules of the most rigid economy. She began with endeavouring to promote the interest of her sisters. She conceived that there was no situation in which she could place them, at once so respectable and agreeable, as that of governesses in private families. She determined therefore in the first place, to endeavour to qualify them for such an undertaking. Her younger sister she sent to Paris,[7] where she remained near two years. The elder she placed in a school near London, first as a parlour-border,[8] and afterwards as a teacher. Her brother James, who had already been at sea, she first took into her house, and next sent to Woolwich for instruction, to qualify him for a respectable situation in the royal navy, where he was shortly after made a lieutenant. Charles, who was her favourite brother, had been articled to the eldest, an attorney in the Minories;[9] but, not being satisfied with his situation, she removed him; and in some time after, having first placed him with a farmer for instruction, she fitted him out for America, where his speculations, founded upon the basis she had provided, are said to have been extremely prosperous. The reason so much of this parental sort of care fell upon her, was, that her father had by this time considerably embarrassed his circumstances. His affairs having grown too complex for himself to disentangle, he had intrusted them to the management of a near relation; but Mary, not being satisfied with the conduct of the business, took them into her own hands. The exertions she made, and the struggle into which she entered however, in this instance, were ultimately fruitless. To the day of her death her

[7] Wollstonecraft locates lodging for Everina in Paris. A decent governess position required proficiency in French.
[8] A boarding-school pupil who lives in the family of the principal and has privileges not shared by the ordinary boarders (*OED*).
[9] A street in the commercial district of London.

father was almost wholly supported by funds which she supplied to him. In addition to her exertions for her own family, she took a young girl of about seven years of age under her protection and care, the niece of Mrs. John Hunter, and the present Mrs. Skeys, for whose mother, then lately dead, she had entertained a sincere friendship.

The period, from the end of the year 1787 to the end of the year 1790, though consumed in labours of little eclat, served still further to establish her in a friendly connection from which she derived many pleasures. Mr. Johnson, the bookseller, contracted a great personal regard for her, which resembled in many respects that of a parent. As she frequented his house, she of course became acquainted with his guests. Among those may be mentioned as persons possessing her esteem, Mr. Bonnycastle,[10] the mathematician, the late Mr. George Anderson,[11] accountant to the board of control, Dr. George Fordyce,[12] and Mr. Fuseli,[13] the celebrated painter. Between both of the two latter and herself, there existed sentiments of genuine affection and friendship.

[10] John Bonnycastle (1750-1821), mathematician and author.
[11] George Anderson (1760-96), once a lower-class mathematician "discovered" by Bonnycastle.
[12] George Fordyce F.R.S. (1736-1802), physician at St. Thomas Hospital, one of the first doctors consulted after Wollstonecraft experiences complications arising from childbirth.
[13] Henry Fuseli (1741-1825), gifted yet eccentric Swiss painter best known for his painting "The Nightmare."

CHAP. VI.
1790-1792

H itherto the literary carreer of Mary, had for the most part, been silent; and had been productive of income to herself, without apparently leading to the wreath of fame. From this time she was destined to attract the notice of the public, and perhaps no female writer ever obtained so great a degree of celebrity throughout Europe.

It cannot be doubted that, while, for three years of literary employment, she "held the noiseless tenor of her way,"[1] her mind was insensibly advancing towards a vigorous maturity. The uninterrupted habit of composition gave a freedom and firmness to the expression of her sentiments. The society she frequented, nourished her understanding, and enlarged her mind. The French revolution,[2] while it gave a fundamental shock to the human intellect through every region of the globe, did not fail to produce a conspicuous effect in the progress of Mary's reflections. The prejudices of her early years suffered a vehement concussion. Her respect for establishments was undermined. At this period occurred a misunderstanding upon public grounds, with one of her early friends, whose attachment to musty creeds and exploded absurdities, had been increased, by the operation of those very circumstances, by which her mind had been rapidly advanced in the race of independence.

The event, immediately introductory to the rank which from

[1] Thomas Gray, *Elegy Written in a Country Churchyard* (1751), l. 76: "They kept the noiseless tenor of the way" (adapted).
[2] In 1789, the French Revolution commences with the meeting of the National Assembly and the storming of the French political prison, the Bastille. In that same year, the French King Louis XVI and his Queen, Marie Antoinette, are imprisoned and the Declaration of the Rights of Man issued.

this time she held in the lists of literature, was the publication of Burke's Reflections on the Revolution in France.[3] This book, after having been long promised to the world, finally made its appearance on the first of November 1790; and Mary, full of sentiments of liberty, and impressed with a warm interest in the struggle that was now going on, seized her pen in the first burst of indignation, an emotion of which she was strongly susceptible. She was in the habit of composing with rapidity, and her answer, which was the first of the numerous ones that appeared, obtained extraordinary notice. Marked as it is with the vehemence and impetuousness of its eloquence, it is certainly chargeable with a too contemptuous and intemperate treatment of the great man against whom its attack is directed. But this circumstance was not injurious to the success of the publication. Burke had been warmly loved by the most liberal and enlightened friends of freedom, and they were proportionably inflamed and disgusted by the fury of his assault, upon what they deemed to be its sacred cause.

Short as was the time in which Mary composed her Answer to Burke's Reflections,[4] there was one anecdote she told me concerning it, which seems worth recording in this place. It was sent to the press, as is the general practice when the early publication of a piece is deemed a matter of importance, before the composition was finished. When Mary had arrived at about the middle of her work, she was seized with a temporary fit of torpor and indolence, and began to repent of her undertaking. In this state of mind, she called, one evening, as she was in the practice of doing, upon her publisher, for the purpose of relieving herself by an hour or two's conversation. Here, the habitual ingenuousness of her nature, led her to describe what had just past in her thoughts. Mr. Johnson immediately, in a kind and friendly way, intreated her not to put any constraint upon her inclination,

---

[3] See text box on "Wollstonecraft and the Revolution Debate," p. 239.
[4] *A Vindication of the Rights of Man, in a Letter to the Right Honorable Edmund Burke* (1790).

and to give herself no uneasiness about the sheets already printed, which he would cheerfully throw aside, if it would contribute to her happiness. Mary had wanted stimulus. She not expected to be encouraged, in what she well knew to be an unreasonable access of idleness. Her friend's so readily falling in with her ill-humour, and seeming to expect that she would lay aside her undertaking, piqued her pride. She immediately went home; and proceeded to the end of her work, with no other interruptions but what were absolutely indispensable.

WOLLSTONECRAFT AND THE REVOLUTION DEBATE:
FROM *A VINDICATION OF THE RIGHTS OF MAN*

By the time of the publication of *A Vindication of the Rights of Man*, Wollstonecraft had published an educational tract for young women, a novel of sensibility, and a collection of stories for children. Any literary output by a woman was still a risky venture in the late eighteenth century, but these early works still fell within what would have been deemed women's "proper sphere"—the domestic. *A Vindication of the Rights of Man* represented her entry into the more public and "masculine" world of political writing and ultimately led to the publication of her highly influential and definitive work *A Vindication of the Rights of Woman*. Her willingness to enter into this new arena may in part have grown out of the more public role she had recently assumed as a reviewer for Joseph Johnson's *Analytical Review*. It certainly grew more broadly out of her sympathies with the French Revolution and more particularly from loyalty to her friend Dr. Richard Price. A dissenting minister, Price published a sermon equating the rights gained by the French Revolution with those secured by the English Glorious Revolution in 1688, which had prompted Edmund Burke's vehement disagreement and the publication of his highly popular and controversial *Reflections on the Revolution in France* (1790).

Burke's *Reflections* inspired many responses, forty-five in all with Tom Paine's *The Rights of Man* proving by far the most influential and best-selling. (By some estimates it sold two hundred thousand copies between 1791 and 1793.) Wollstonecraft's was the first and although quickly written, proved "moderately successful." Burke's *Reflections* came out on November 1, 1790; Wollstonecraft's *A Vindication of the Rights of Man*, published anonymously, appeared only 28 days later on November 29. The second edition was published only 20 days after the first and this time with Wollstonecraft's name on the title page. From that point on, Wollstonecraft became firmly associated with England's radical circle, and her life assumed a public dimension.

Burke, a "long-established critic of the power of the monarchy" and "an opponent of the American war" had angered many in this radical circle with his critique of the French Revolution (Butler 33). Burke, although a consistent advocate for governmental restraint, objected to the notion of inherent human rights predicated upon the exercise of individual reason. For Burke, tradition would check governmental excess; human rights evolved from human institutions. This was the lesson, according to Burke, of the Glorious Revolution. For Wollstonecraft, in what would have been a conventional argument for her political circle, *tradition* was suspect, serving to formalize the caprices of feeling and to romanticize inequity, and individual *reason*, by contrast, provided the best guide for human happiness:

I perceive, from the whole tenor of your Reflections, that you have a mortal antipathy to reason; but, if there is any thing like argument, or first principles, in your wild declamation, behold the result:— that we are to reverence the rust of antiquity, and term the unnatural customs, which ignorance and mistaken self-interest have consolidated, the sage fruit of experience; nay, that, if we do discover some errors, our *feelings* should lead us to excuse, with blind love, or unprincipled filial affection, the venerable vestiges of ancient days. These are gothic notions of beauty—the ivy is beautiful, but, when it insidiously destroys the trunk from which it receives support, who would not grub it up?

***

The civilization which has taken place in Europe has been very partial, and, like every custom that an arbitrary point of honour has established, refines the manners at the expence of morals, by making sentiments and opinions current in conversation that have no root in the heart, or weight in the cooler resolves of the mind.—And what has stopped its progress?—hereditary property—hereditary honours. The man has been changed into an artificial monster by the station in which he was born, and the consequent homage that benumbed his faculties like the torpedo's touch; —or a being, with a capacity or reasoning, would not have failed to discover, as his faculties unfolded, that true happiness arose from the friendship and intimacy which can only be enjoyed by equals; and that charity is not a condescending distribution of alms, but an intercourse of good offices and mutual benefits, founded on respect for justice and humanity. (10-11)

What most distinguished Wollstonecraft's argument was her direct engagement with the *gendered* terms of Burke's argument. For Burke, it was the lack of gallantry toward Marie Antoinette, the Queen of France, that best illustrated the wrongs of the French Revolution and the dangers of the individual exercise of reason. Speaking of her imprisonment, he exclaims in *Reflections*:

Little did I dream that I should have lived to see such disasters fallen upon her in a nation of gallant men, in a nation of men of honor and of cavaliers. I thought ten thousand swords must have leaped from their scabbards to avenge even a look that threatened her with insult. But the age of chivalry is gone.

That of sophisters, economists, and calculators, has succeeded; and the glory of Europe is extinguished forever. Never, never more shall we behold that generous loyalty to rank and sex, that proud submission, that dignified obedience, that subordination of the heart which kept alive, even in servitude itself, the spirit of an exalted freedom. That unbought grace of life, the cheap defense of nations, the nurse of manly sentiment and heroic enterprise, is gone! It is gone—that sensibility of principle, that charity of honor which felt a stain like a wound, which inspired courage whilst it mitigated ferocity, which enobled whatever it touched, and under which vice itself lost half its evil, by losing all its grossness.

***

On this scheme of things, a king is but a man; a queen is but a woman; a woman is but an animal; and an animal not of the highest order. All homage paid to the sex in general as such, and without distinct views, is to be regarded as romance and folly. (86-87)

Wollstonecraft, in her response, does not so much disagree with Burke's observations, but reinterprets their significance:

'On this scheme of things a king *is* but a man; a queen *is* but a woman; a women *is but* an animal, and an animal not of the highest order.' —All true, Sir: if she is not more attentive to the duties of humanity than queens and fashionable ladies in general are. I will still further accede to the opinion you have so justly conceived of the spirit which begins to animate this age.—'All homage paid to the sex in general, as such, and without distinct views, is to be regarded as *romance* and folly.' Undoubtedly; because such homage vitiates them, prevents their endeavouring to obtain solid personal merit; and, in short makes those beings vain inconsiderate dolls, who ought to be prudent mothers and useful members of society. (25)

And whereas Burke reserves his passion for the loss of gallantry, Wollstonecraft saves her sense of outrage for the miseries of the poor and enslaved. Near the conclusion of *A Vindication of the Rights of Man*, she offers this moving counter-image to that of Burke's embattled queen:

> What were the outrages of a day to these continual miseries? Let those sorrows hide their diminished head before the tremendous mountain of woe that thus defaces our globe! Man preys on man; and you mourn for the idle tapestry that decorated a gothic pile, and the dronish bell that summoned the fat priest to prayer. You mourn for the empty pageant of a name, when slavery flaps her wing, and the sick heart retires to die in lonely wilds, far from the abodes of men. Did the pangs you felt for insulted nobility, the anguish that rent your heart when the gorgeous robes were torn off the idol human weakness had set up, deserve to be compared with the long-drawn sigh of melancholy reflection, when misery and vice are thus seen to haunt our steps, and swim on the top of very cheering prospect? Why is our fancy to be appalled by terrific perspectives of a hell beyond the grave? –Hell stalks abroad; —the lash resounds on the slave's naked sides; and the sick wretch, who can no longer earn the sour bread of unremitting labour, steals to a ditch to bid the world a long good night – or, neglected in some ostentatious hospital, breathes his last amidst the laugh of mercenary attendants.
>
> Such misery demands more than tears – I pause to recollect myself; and smother the contempt I feel rising for your rhetorical flourishes and infantine sensibility. (58)

Wollstonecraft's silence on these issues will indeed be short lived, for with *A Vindication of the Rights of Man*, she finds her political voice, and only six months later she completes *A Vindication of the Rights of Woman.*

SOURCES

Burke, Edmund. *Reflections of the Revolution in France.* Edited by Thomas Mahoney. Indianapolis and New York: Liberal Arts Press, 1955.

Butler, Marilyn. Ed. *Burke, Paine, Godwin, and the Revolution Controversy.* Cambridge: Cambridge University Press, 1984.

Gaull, Marilyn *English Romanticism: The Human Context.* New York: Norton, 1988.

Wollstonecraft, Mary. *The Works of Mary Wollstonecraft.* Vol. 5, Edited by Janet Todd and Marilyn Butler. New York: New York University Press, 1989.

It is probable that the applause which attended her Answer to Burke, elevated the tone of her mind. She had always felt much confidence in her own powers; but it cannot be doubted, that the actual perception of a similar feeling respecting us in a multitude of others, must increase the confidence, and stimulate the adventure of any human being. Mary accordingly proceeded, in a short time after, to the composition of her most celebrated production, the Vindication of the Rights of Woman.[5]

Never did any author enter into a cause, with a more ardent desire to be found, not a flourishing and empty declaimer, but an effectual champion. She considered herself as standing forth in defence of one half of the human species, labouring under a yoke which, through all the records of time, had degraded them from the station of rational beings, and almost sunk them to the level of the brutes. She saw indeed, that they were often at-

---

[5] *A Vindication of the Rights of Woman* (1792). See text boxes 'On Reason, Madness, and Folly" (p. 54) and "On Love and Sensibility" (p. 77) in *Wrongs of Woman* for excerpts from this work.

tempted to be held in silken fetters, and bribed into the love of slavery; but the disguise and the treachery served only the more fully to confirm her opposition. She regarded her sex, in the language of Calista, as

"In every state of life the slaves of men:"[6]

the rich as alternately under the despotism of a father, a brother, and a husband; and the middling and the poorer classes shut out from the acquisition of bread with independence, when they are not shut out from the very means of an industrious subsistence. Such were the views she entertained of the subject; and such the feelings with which she warmed her mind.

The work is certainly a very bold and original production. The strength and firmness with which the author repels the opinions of Rousseau,[7] Dr. Gregory, and Dr. James Fordyce,[8] respecting the condition of women, cannot but make a strong impression upon every ingenuous reader. The public at large formed very different opinions respecting the character of the performance. Many of the sentiments are undoubtedly of a rather masculine description. The spirited and decisive way in which the author explodes the system of gallantry, and the species of homage with which the sex is usually treated, shocked the majority. Novelty produced a sentiment in their mind, which they mistook for a sense of injustice. The pretty, soft creatures that

---

[6] Nicolas Rowe, *The Fair Penitent* (1703), III, ii, l. 41: "Through ev'ry state of life the slaves of man." Calista, the tragic heroine of this popular play, is married against her will and ultimately commits suicide. Wollstonecraft also refers to Calista in *The Wrongs of Woman*. See Chapter IX, p. 129.

[7] Jean Jacques Rousseau (1712-78), French philosopher. His works, often questioning society and praising nature, were highly influential and contributed to the intellectual and cultural climate which resulted in the French Revolution. Maria in *The Wrongs of Woman* refers to Rousseau's novel *Julie, or The New Heloise* (1761) and Wollstonecraft dedicates central chapters of *A Vindication of the Rights of Woman* to refuting explicitly his ideas on the natural weakness of women as expressed in his novel *Emile* (1762).

[8] Both John Gregory (1724-73) and James Fordyce (1720-96) wrote conduct books directed at young women, penning respectively *A Father's Legacy to his Daughters* (1774) and *Sermons to Young Women* (1765). Wollstonecraft explicitly addresses both of these works in *A Vindication of the Rights of Woman*.

are so often to be found in the female sex, and that class of men who believe they could not exist without such pretty, soft creatures to resort to, were in arms against the author of so heretical and blasphemous a doctrine. There are also, it must be confessed, occasional passages of a stern and rugged feature, incompatible with the true stamina of the writer's character. But, if they did not belong to her fixed and permanent character, they belonged to her character *pro tempore*;[9] and what she thought, she scorned to qualify.

Yet, along with this rigid, and somewhat amazonian[10] temper, which characterized some parts of the book, it is impossible not to remark a luxuriance of imagination, and a trembling delicacy of sentiment, which would have done honour to a poet, bursting with all the visions of an Armida[11] and a Dido.[12]

The contradiction, to the public apprehension, was equally great, as to the person of the author, as it was when they considered the temper of the book. In the champion of her sex, who was described as endeavouring to invest them with all the rights of man, those whom curiosity prompted to seek the occasion of beholding her, expected to find a sturdy, muscular, raw-boned virago; and they were not a little surprised, when, instead of all this, they found a woman, lovely in her person, and, in the best and most engaging sense, feminine in her manners.

The Vindication of the Rights of Woman is undoubtedly a very unequal performance, and eminently deficient in method and arrangement. When tried by the hoary and long-established laws of literary composition, it can scarcely maintain its claim to be placed in the first class of human productions. But

---

[9] Temporarily.

[10] Pertaining to the Amazons, warlike, or masculine, as a woman (*OED*).

[11] A beautiful sorceress in Torquato Tasso's *Jerusalem Delivered* (1581) associated with the enchantments of a garden where men are overcome with indolence. Wollstonecraft also refers to Armida in *The Wrongs of Woman*. See Chapter IV, p. 82.

[12] Although loved and abandoned by Aeneas in Virgil's *Aeneid*, Dido, Queen of Carthage, remains strong and eloquent.

when we consider the importance of its doctrines, and the eminence of genius it displays, it seems not very improbable that it will be read as long as the English language endures. The publication of this book forms an epocha in the subject to which it belongs; and Mary Wollstonecraft will perhaps hereafter be found to have performed more substantial service for the cause of her sex, than all the other writers, male or female, that ever felt themselves animated in the behalf of oppressed and injured beauty.

The censure of the liberal critic as to the defects of this performance, will be changed into astonishment, when I tell him, that a work of this inestimable moment, was begun, carried on, and finished in the state in which it now appears, in a period of no more than six weeks.

It is necessary here that I should resume the subject of the friendship that subsisted between Mary and Mr. Fuseli, which proved the source of the most memorable events in her subsequent history. He is a native of the republic of Switzerland, but has spent the principal part of his life in the island of Great-Britain. The eminence of his genius can scarcely be disputed; it has indeed received the testimony which is the least to be suspected, that of some of the most considerable of his contemporary artists. He has one of the most striking characteristics of genius, a daring, as well as persevering, spirit of adventure. The work in which he is at present engaged, a series of pictures for the illustration of Milton, upon a very large scale, and produced solely upon the incitement of his own mind, is a proof of this, if indeed his whole life had not sufficiently proved it.[13]

Mr. Fuseli is one of Mr. Johnson's oldest friends, and was at this time in the habit of visiting him two or three times a week. Mary, one of whose strongest characteristics was the exquisite sensations of pleasure she felt from the associations of visible objects, had hitherto never been acquainted, or never intimately acquainted, with an eminent painter. The being thus intro-

[13] His exhibit of Milton illustrations did not prove successful. Fuseli resided in England from 1763.

duced therefore to the society of Mr. Fuseli, was a high gratification to her; while he found in Mary, a person perhaps more susceptible of the emotions painting is calculated to excite, than any other with whom he ever conversed. Painting, and subjects closely connected with painting, were their almost constant topics of conversation; and they found them inexhaustible. It cannot be doubted, but that this was a species of exercise very conducive to the improvement of Mary's mind.

Nothing human however is unmixed. If Mary derived improvement from Mr. Fuseli, she may also be suspected of having caught the infection of some of his faults. In early life Mr. Fuseli was ardently attached to literature; but the demands of his profession have prevented him from keeping up that extensive and indiscriminate acquaintance with it, that belles-lettres scholars frequently possess. Of consequence, the favourites of his boyish years remain his only favourites. Homer is with Mr. Fuseli the abstract and deposit of every human perfection. Milton, Shakespear, and Richardson, have also engaged much of his attention. The nearest rival of Homer, I believe, if Homer can have a rival, is Jean Jacques Rousseau.[14] A young man embraces entire the opinions of a favourite writer, and Mr. Fuseli has not had leisure to bring the opinions of his youth to a revision. Smitten with Rousseau's conception of the perfectness of the savage state, and the essential abortiveness of all civilization, Mr. Fuseli looks at all our little attempts at improvement, with a spirit that borders perhaps too much upon contempt and indifference. One of his favourite positions is the divinity of genius. This a power that comes complete at once from the hands of the Creator of all things, and the first essays of a man of real genius

---

[14] Godwin's list includes both writers that would have been considered part of any standard education (Homer, Shakespeare, and Milton) and two that only recently would have come into vogue: Samuel Richardson (1689-1761), author of the domestic novels, *Pamela* (1740-1) and *Clarissa* (1747-8) and Jean Jacques Rousseau, author of *Emile* (1762) and *Julie or the New Heloise* (1761). With the exception of Homer, Wollstonecraft makes either direct or indirect reference to the work of all these writers in *The Wrongs of Woman*.

are such, in all their grand and most important features, as no subsequent assiduity can amend. Add to this, that Mr. Fuseli is somewhat of a caustic turn of mind, with much wit, and a disposition to search, in every thing new or modern, for occasions of censure. I believe Mary came something more a cynic out of the school of Mr. Fuseli, than she went into it.

But the principal circumstance that relates to the intercourse of Mary, and this celebrated artist, remains to be told. She saw Mr. Fuseli frequently; he amused, delighted and instructed her. As a painter, it was impossible she should not wish to see his works, and consequently to frequent his house. She visited him; her visits were returned. Notwithstanding the inequality of their years, Mary was not of a temper to live upon terms of so much intimacy with a man of merit and genius, without loving him. The delight she enjoyed in his society, she transferred by association to his person.[15] What she experienced in this respect, was no doubt heightened, by the state of celibacy and restraint in which she had hitherto lived, and to which the rules of polished society condemn an unmarried woman. She conceived a personal and ardent affection for him. Mr. Fuseli was a married man, and his wife the acquaintance of Mary. She readily perceived the restrictions which this circumstance seemed to impose upon her; but she made light of any difficulty that might arise out of them. Not that she was insensible to the value of domestic endearments between persons of an opposite sex, but that she scorned to suppose, that she could feel a struggle, in conforming to the laws she should lay down to her conduct.

There cannot perhaps be a properer place than the present, to state her principles upon this subject, such at least as they were when I knew her best. She set a great value on a mutual affection between persons of an opposite sex. She regarded it as the principal solace of human life. It was her maxim, "that the imagination should awaken the senses, and not the senses the

[15] I.e., his body.

imagination."[16] In other words, that whatever related to the gratification of the senses, ought to arise, in a human being of a pure mind, only as the consequence of an individual affection. She regarded the manners and habits of the majority of our sex in that respect, with strong disapprobation. She conceived that true virtue would prescribe the most entire celibacy, exclusively of affection, and the most perfect fidelity to that affection when it existed.—There is no reason to doubt that, if Mr. Fuseli had been disengaged at the period of their acquaintance, he would have been the man of her choice. As it was, she conceived it both practicable and eligible, to cultivate a distinguishing affection for him, and to foster it by the endearment of personal intercourse and a reciprocation of kindness, without departing in the smallest degree from the rules she prescribed to herself.

In September 1791, she removed from the house she occupied in George-street, to a large and commodious apartment in Store street, Bedford-square. She began to think that she had been too rigid, in the laws of frugality and self-denial with which she set out in her literary career; and now added to the neatness and cleanliness which she had always scrupulously observed a certain degree of elegance, and those temperate indulgences in furniture and accommodation, from which a sound and uncorrupted taste never fails to derive pleasure.

It was in the month of November in the same year (1791), that the writer of this narrative was first in company with the person to whom it relates. He dined with her at a friend's, together with Mr. Thomas Paine and one or two other persons. The invitation was of his own seeking, his object being to see the author of the Rights of Man, with whom he had never conversed.[17]

---

[16] *Letters Written During a Short Residence in Sweden, Norway and Denmark* (1796), letter 2.

[17] Thomas Paine (1737-1809), author of *The Rights of Man; being an answer to Mr. Burke's attack on the French Revolution* (1791-2). Paine's response to Burke far eclipsed Wollstonecraft's own, selling an estimated 200,000 copies and serving as a political touchstone for many years to come for English radicalism.

The interview was not fortunate. Mary and myself parted, mutually displeased with each other. I had not read her Rights of Woman. I had barely looked into her Answer to Burke, and been displeased, as literary men are apt to be, with a few offences, against grammar and other minute points of composition. I had therefore little curiosity to see Mrs. Wollstonecraft,[18] and a very great curiosity to see Thomas Paine. Paine, in his general habits, is no great talker; and, though he threw in occasionally some shrewd and striking remarks; the conversation lay principally between me and Mary. I, of consequence, heard her, very frequently when I wished to hear Paine.

We touched on a considerable variety of topics, and particularly on the characters and habits of certain eminent men. Mary, as has already been observed, had acquired, in a very blameable degree, the practice of seeing every thing on the gloomy side, and bestowing censure with a plentiful hand, where circumstances were in any respect doubtful. I, on the contrary, had a strong propensity, to favourable construction, and particularly, where I found unequivocal marks of genius, strongly to incline to the supposition of generous and manly virtue. We ventilated in this way the characters of Voltaire[19] and others, who have obtained from some individuals an ardent admiration, while the greater number have treated them with extreme moral severity. Mary was at last provoked to tell me, that praise lavished in the way that I lavished it, could do no credit either to the commended or the commender. We discussed some questions on the subject of religion, in which her opinions approached much nearer to the received ones, than mine. As the conversation proceeded, I became dissatisfied with the tone of my own share in it. We touched upon all topics, without treating forcibly and connectedly upon any. Meanwhile, I did her the justice, in giving an account of the conversation to a party in which I supped, though I was not sparing of my blame, to yield her the

---

[18] Polite term of address for women (married and unmarried).
[19] Francois-Marie Arouet de Voltaire (1694-1778), French philosopher.

praise of a person of active and independent thinking. On her side, she did me no part of what perhaps I considered as justice.

We met two or three times in the course of the following year, but made a very small degree of progress towards a cordial acquaintance.

In the close of the year 1792, Mary went over to France, where she continued to reside for upwards of two years. One of her principal inducements to this step, related, I believe, to Mr. Fuseli. She had, at first, considered it as reasonable and judicious, to cultivate what I may be permitted to call, a Platonic affection for him; but she did not, in the sequel, find all the satisfaction in this plan, which she had originally expected from it. It was in vain that she enjoyed much pleasure in his society, and that she enjoyed it frequently. Her ardent imagination was continually conjuring up pictures of the happiness she should have found, if fortune had favoured their more intimate union. She felt herself formed for domestic affection, and all those tender charities, which men of sensibility have constantly treated as the dearest band of human society. General conversation and society could not satisfy her. She felt herself alone, as it were, in the great mass of her species; and she repined when she reflected, that the best years of her life were spent in this comfortless solitude. These ideas made the cordial intercourse of Mr. Fuseli, which had at first been one of her greatest pleasures, a source of perpetual torment to her. She conceived it necessary to snap the chain of this association in her mind; and, for that purpose, determined to seek a new climate, and mingle in different scenes.

It is singular, that during her residence in Store street, which lasted more than twelve months, she produced nothing, except a few articles in the Analytical Review. Her literary meditations were chiefly employed upon the Sequel to the Rights of Woman; but she has scarcely left behind her a single paper, that can, with any certainty, be assigned to have had this destination.

Chap. VII.
1792-1795

The original plan of Mary, respecting her residence in France, had no precise limits in the article of duration; the single purpose she had in view being that of an endeavour to heal her distempered mind. She did not proceed so far as even to discharge her lodging in London; and, to some friends who saw her immediately before her departure, she spoke merely of an absence of six weeks.

It is not to be wondered at, that her excursion did not originally seem to produce the effects she had expected from it. She was in a land of strangers; she had no acquaintance; she had even to acquire the power of receiving and communicating ideas with facility in the language of the country. Her first residence was in a spacious mansion to which she had been invited, but the master of which (monsieur Fillietaz) was absent at the time of her arrival.[1] At first therefore she found herself surrounded only with servants. The gloominess of her mind communicated its own colour to the objects she saw; and in this temper she began a series of Letters on the Present Character of the French Nation, one of which she forwarded to her publisher, and which appears in the collection of her posthumous works.[2] This performance she soon after discontinued; and it is, as she justly remarks, tinged with the saturnine temper which at that time pervaded her mind.

Mary carried with her introductions to several agreeable families in Paris. She renewed her acquaintance with Paine. There

---

[1] Wollstonecraft took advantage of family connections to find lodging in Paris, residing with Aline Fillietaz, the daughter of her sister Eliza's old headmistress. The daughter had since married a well-to-do French man.

[2] "Letter on the Character of the French Nation," *Posthumous Works* (1798), Vol. 4. This is the same collection in which *The Wrongs of Woman* appears.

also subsisted a very sincere friendship between her and Helen Maria Williams, author of a collection of poems of uncommon merit, who at that time resided in Paris.[3] Another person, whom Mary always spoke of in terms of ardent commendation, both for the excellence of his disposition, and the force of his genius, was a count Slabrendorf, by birth, I believe, a Swede. It is almost unnecessary to mention, that she was personally acquainted with the majority of the leaders in the French revolution.

But the house that, I believe, she principally frequented at the time, was that of Mr. Thomas Christie, a person whose pursuits were mercantile, and who had written a volume on the French revolution.[4] With Mrs. Christie her acquaintance was more intimate than with the husband.

It was about four months after her arrival in Paris in December 1792, that she entered into that species of connection, for which her heart secretly panted, and which had the effect of diffusing an immediate tranquility and cheerfulness over her manners. The person with whom it was formed (for it would be an idle piece of delicacy, to attempt to suppress a name, which is known to every one whom the reputation of Mary has reached, was Mr. Gilbert Imlay, native of the United States of North America.[5]

The place at which she first saw Mr. Imlay was at the house of Mr. Christie; and it perhaps deserves to be noticed, that the

---

[3] Helen Maria Williams (1762-1827) was known for her unflagging support of the French Revolution and for her celebrated parties, full of the intellectual and political elite of the period. She was also a novelist, poet, and letter writer, revising Rousseau's *Julie or the New Heloise* in her novel *Julia* (1790). Her controversial letters describing the French Revolution emphasize the role of women; Williams herself was briefly imprisoned during the Reign of Terror.

[4] *Letters on the Revolution in France and the New Constitution established by the National Assembly* (1791). Like Wollstonecraft's *A Vindication of the Rights of Man*, this work took issue with Burke's *Reflections on the Revolution in France* (1790). Christie was also co-publisher with Joseph Johnson of *The Analytical Review*.

[5] Gilbert Imlay (1754?-1828), author of *A Description of the Western Territory of North America* (1792) and *The Emigrants* (1793). See text box "'The American': Gilbert Imlay" in *Wrongs of Woman,* p. 71.

emotions he then excited in her mind, were, I am told, those of dislike, and that, for some time, she shunned all occasions of meeting him. This sentiment however speedily gave place to one of greater kindness.

Previous to the partiality she conceived for him, she had determined upon a journey to Switzerland, induced chiefly by motives of economy. But she had some difficulty in procuring a passport; and it was probably the intercourse that now originated between her and Mr. Imlay, that changed her purpose, and led her to prefer a lodging at Neuilly, a village three miles from Paris. Her habitation here was a solitary house in the midst of a garden, with no other inhabitants than herself and the gardener, an old man, who performed for her many of the offices of a domestic, and would sometimes contend for the honour of making her bed. The gardener had a great veneration for his guest, and would set before her, when alone, some grapes of a particularly fine sort, which she could not without the greatest difficulty obtain, when she had any person with her as a visitor. Here it was that she conceived, and for the most part executed, her Historical and Moral View of the French Revolution,*⁶ into which, as she observes, are incorporated most of the observations she had collected for her Letters, and which was written with more sobriety and cheerfulness than the tone in which they had been commenced. In the evening she was accustomed to refresh herself by a walk in the neighbouring wood, from which her old host in vain endeavoured to dissuade her, by recounting divers horrible robberies and murders than had been committed there.

The commencement of the attachment Mary now formed, had neither confident nor adviser. She always conceived it to be a gross breach of delicacy to have any confidant in a matter of this sacred nature, an affair of the heart. The origin of the con-

---

* No part of the proposed continuation of this work, has been found among the papers of the author. [Godwin's note].

⁶ *An Historical and Moral View of the Origin and Progress of the French Revolution; and the effect it has produced in Europe* (1794). One volume of this work was published (See Godwin's note.).

nection was about the middle of April 1793, and it was carried on in a private manner for four months. At the expiration of that period a circumstance occurred that induced her to declare it. The French convention, exasperated at the conduct of the British government, particularly in the affair of Toulon,[7] formed a decree against the citizens of this country, by one article of which the English, resident in France, were ordered into prison till the period of a general peace. Mary had objected to a marriage with Mr. Imlay, who, at the time their connection was formed had at no property whatever; because she would not involve him in certain family embarrassments to which she conceived herself exposed, or make him answerable for the pecuniary demands that existed against her. She however considered their engagement of the most sacred nature; and they had mutually formed the plan of emigrating to America, as soon as they should have realized a sum, enabling them to do it in the mode they desired. The decree however that I have just mentioned, made it necessary, not that a marriage should actually take place, but that Mary should take the name of Imlay, which, from the nature of their connection, she conceived herself entitled to do, and obtain a certificate from the American ambassador, as the wife of a native of that country.

Their engagement being thus avowed, they thought proper to reside under the same roof, and for that purpose moved to Paris.

Mary was now arrived at the situation, which, for two or three preceding years, her reason had pointed out to her as affording the most substantial prospect of happiness. She had been tossed and agitated by the waves of misfortunes. Her childhood, as she often said, had known few of the endearments, which constitute the principal happiness of childhood. The temper of her father had early given to her mind a severe cast of thought, and substituted the inflexibility of resistance to the confidence of affection. The cheerfulness of her entrance upon

[7] British defeat of the French garrison at Toulon.

womanhood, had been darkened, by an attendance upon the death-bed of her mother, and the still more affecting calamity of her eldest sister. Her exertions to create a joint independence for her sisters and herself, had been attended, neither with the success, nor the pleasure, she had hoped for them. Her first youthful passion, her friendship with Fanny, had encountered many disappointments, and, in fine, a melancholy and premature catastrophe. Soon after these accumulated mortifications, she was engaged in a contest with a near relation, whom she regarded as unprincipled, respecting the wreck of her father's fortune. In this affair she suffered the double pain, which arises from moral indignation, and disappointed benevolence. Her exertions to assist almost every member of her family, were great and unremitted. Finally, when she indulged a romantic affection for Mr. Fuseli, and fondly imagined that she should find in it the solace of her cares, she perceived too late, that, by continually impressing on her mind fruitless images of unreserved affection and domestic felicity, it only served to give pungency to the sensibility that was destroying her.

Some persons may be inclined to observe, that the evils here enumerated, are not among the heaviest in the catalogue of human calamities. But evils take their rank, more from the temper of the mind that suffers them, than from their abstract nature. Upon a man of a hard and insensible disposition, the shafts of misfortune often fall pointless and impotent. There are persons, by no means hard and insensible, who, from an elastic and sanguine turn of mind, are continually prompted to look on the fair side of things, and, having suffered one fall, immediately rise again, to pursue their course, with the same eagerness, the same hope, and the same gaiety, as before. On the other hand, we not infrequently meet with persons, endowed with the most exquisite and delicious sensibility, whose minds seem almost of too fine a texture to encounter the vicissitudes of human affairs, to whom pleasure is transport, and disappointment is agony indescribable. This character is finely pourtrayed by the author of the Sorrows of Werter. Mary was in this respect a female Werter.[8]

  She brought then, in the present instance, a wounded and sick heart, to take refuge in the bosom of a chosen friend. Let it not however be imagined, that she brought a heart, querulous, and ruined in its taste for pleasure. No; her whole character seemed to change with a change of fortune. Her sorrows, the depression of her spirits, were forgotten, and she assumed all the simplicity and the vivacity of a youthful mind. She was like a serpent upon a rock, that casts its slough, and appears again with the brilliancy, the sleekness, and the elastic activity of its happiest age.[9] She was playful, full of confidence, kindness and sympathy. Her eyes assumed new luster, and her cheeks new colour and smoothness. Her voice became chearful; her temper overflowing with universal kindness; and that smile of bewitching tenderness from day to day illuminated her countenance, which all who knew her will so well recollect, and which won, both heart and soul, the affection of almost every one that beheld it.

  Mary now reposed herself upon a person, of whose honour and principles she had the most exalted idea. She nourished an individual affection, which she saw no necessity of subjecting to restraint; and a heart like her's was not formed to nourish affection by halves. Her conception of Mr. Imlay's "tenderness and worth, had twisted him closely round her heart;" and she "indulged the thought, that she had thrown out some tendrils, to cling to the elm by which she wished to be supported." This was "talking a new language to her:" but, "conscious that she was not a parasite-plant," she was willing to encourage and foster the luxuriancies of affection.[10] Her confidence was entire; her love

---

[8] This is the second occasion in which Godwin compares Wollstonecraft to Werter. See Chapter II, p. 210. This novel concludes with the suicide of its highly impressionable and sentimental protagonist.

[9] In the second edition, Godwin removes this sentence, now sensitive to its sexual imagery.

[10] "Letters to Imlay," *Posthumous Works*, Vol. 3., Letter XVI reads, " You have, by your tenderness and worth, twisted yourself more artfully round my heart, than I

was unbounded. Now, for the first time in her life she gave loose to all the sensibilities of her nature.

Soon after the time I am now speaking of, her attachment to Mr. Imlay gained a new link, by finding reason to suppose herself with child.

Their establishment at Paris, was however broken up almost as soon as formed, by the circumstance of Mr. Imlay's entering into business, urged, as he said, by the prospect of a family, and this being a favourable crisis in French affairs for commercial speculation. The pursuits in which he was engaged, led him in the month of September to Havre de Grace, then called Havre Marat,[11] probably to superintend the shipping of goods, in which he was jointly engaged with some other person or persons. Mary remained in the capital.

The solitude in which she was now left, proved an unexpected trial. Domestic affections constituted the object upon which her heart was fixed; and she early felt, with an inward grief, that Mr. Imlay "did not attach those tender emotions round the idea of home,"[12] which, every time they recurred, dimmed her eyes with moisture. She had expected his return from week to week, and from month to month; but a succession of business still continued to detain him at Havre. At the same time the sanguinary character which the government of France began ev-

supposed possible.—Let me indulge the thought, that I have thrown out some tendrils to cling to the elm by which I wish to be supported.—This is talking a new language for me!—But, knowing that I am not a parasite-plant, I am willing to receive the proofs of affection, that every pulse replies to, when I think of being once more in the same house with you" (382), in *The Works of Mary Wollstonecraft*, Vol. 6, (New York: New York University Press, 1989). The "Letters to Imlay" were also included in *The Posthumous Works*; Godwin omits these lines in the second edition.

[11] Havre de Grace was renamed (Havre Marat) after Jean-Paul Marat, one of the revolutionary leaders.

[12] "Letters to Imlay." This portion of Letter XLII reads, "How can you love to fly about continually—dropping down, as it were, in a new world—cold and strange!—every other day? Why do you not attach those tender emotions round the idea of home, which even now dim my eyes?—This alone is affection—every thing else is only humanity, electrified by sympathy" (407), in *Works of Mary Wollstonecraft*, Vol. 6.

ery day more decisively to assume, contributed to banish tranquility from the first months of her pregnancy. Before she left Neuilly, she happened one day to enter Paris on foot (I believe, by the *Place de Louis Quinze*), when an execution, attended with some peculiar aggravations, had just taken place, and the blood of the guillotine appeared fresh upon the pavement. The emotions of her soul burst forth in indignant exclamations, while a prudent bystander warned her of her danger, and intreated her to hasten and hide her discontents. She described to me, more than once, the anguish she felt at hearing of the death of Brissot, Vergniaud, and the twenty deputies,[13] as one of the most intolerable sensations she had ever experienced.

Finding the return of Mr. Imlay continually postponed, she determined, in January 1794, to join him at Havre. One motive that influenced her, though, I believe, by no means the principal, was the growing cruelties of Robespierre,[14] and the desire she felt to be in any other place, rather than the devoted city, in the midst of which they were perpetuated.

From January to September, Mr. Imlay and Mary lived together, with great harmony, at Havre, where the child, with which she was pregnant, was born, on the fourteenth of May, and named Frances, in remembrances of the dear friend of her youth, whose image could never be erased from her memory.

In September, Mr. Imlay took his departure from Havre for the port of London. As this step was said to be necessary in the way of business, he endeavoured to prevail upon Mary to quit Havre, and once more take up her abode at Paris. Robespierre was now no more, and, of consequence, the only objection she had to residing in the capital, was removed. Mr. Imlay was

---

[13] Jean Pierre Brissot (1754-93) and Pierre-Victurien Vergniaud (1753-93), both leaders of the Girondins, considered the more moderate faction of the revolutionaries. In October 1793, these two leaders as well as 22 other Girondin deputies were expelled from the National Assembly and executed for "royalism."

[14] Maximiliem Francois Isidore de Robespierre (1758-94), leader of the more extremist faction of the revolutionaries, known for leading the purges against the more moderate opposition. He is himself executed once driven from power.

already in London, before she undertook her journey, and it proved the most fatiguing journey she ever made; the carriage, in which she traveled, being overturned no less than four times between Havre and Paris.

This absence, like that of the preceding year in which Mr. Imlay had removed to Havre, was represented as an absence that was to have a short duration. In two months he was once again to join her in Paris. It proved however the prelude to an eternal separation. The agonies of such a separation, or rather desertion, great as Mary would have found them upon every supposition, was vastly increased, by the lingering method in which it was effected, and the ambiguity that, for a long time, hung upon it. This circumstance produced the effect, of holding her mind, by force, as it were, to the most painful of all subjects, and not suffering her to derive the just advantage from the energy and elasticity of her character.

The procrastination of which I am speaking was however productive of one advantage. It put off the evil day. She did not suspect the calamities that awaited her, till the close of the year. She gained an additional three months of happiness. But she purchased it at a very dear rate. Perhaps no human creature ever suffered greater misery, than dyed the whole year 1795, in the life of this incomparable woman. It was wasted in that sort of despair, to the sense of which the mind is continually awakened, by a glimmering of fondly cherished, expiring hope.

Why did she thus obstinately cling to an ill-starred, unhappy passion? Because it is of the every essence of affection, to seek to perpetuate itself. He does not love, who can resign this cherished sentiment, without suffering some of the sharpest struggles that our nature is capable of enduring. Add to this, Mary had fixed her heart upon this chosen friend; and one of the last impressions a worthy mind can submit to receive, is that of the worthlessness of the person upon whom it has fixed its esteem. Mary had struggled to entertain a favourable opinion of human nature; she had unweariedly sought for a kindred mind, in whose integrity and fidelity to take up her rest. Mr. Imlay undertook to prove, in his letters written immediately after their complete separation, that his conduct towards her was reconcilable to the strictest rectitude; but undoubtedly Mary was of a different opinion. Whatever the reader may decide in this respect, there is one sentiment that, I believe, he will unhesitatingly admit: that of pity for the mistake of man, who, being in possession of such a friendship and attachment as those of Mary, could hold them at a trivial price, and, "like the base Indian, throw a pearl away, richer than all his tribe.*"[15]

---

* A person, from whose society at this time Mary derived particular gratification, was Archibald Hamilton Rowan,who had lately become a fugitive from Ireland, in consequence of a political persecution, and in whom she found those qualities which were always eminently engaging to her, great integrity of disposition, and great kindness of heart. [Godwin's note].

[15] *Othello,* V.ii.347-8: "Like the base Indian, threw a pearl away/ Richer than all his tribe."

CHAP. VIII.
1795, 1796

In April 1795, Mary returned once more to London, being requested to do so by Mr. Imlay, who even sent a servant to Paris to wait upon her in the journey, before she could complete the necessary arrangements for her departure. But, notwithstanding these favourable appearances, she came to England with a heavy heart, not daring, after all the uncertainties and anguish she had endured, to trust the suggestions of hope.

The gloomy forebodings of her mind, were but too faithfully verified. Mr. Imlay had already formed another connection; as it is said, with a young actress from a strolling company of players. His attentions therefore to Mary were formal and constrained, and she probably had but little of his society. This alteration could not escape her penetrating glance. He ascribed it to pressure of business, and some pecuniary embarrassments which, at that time, occurred to him; it was of little consequence to Mary what was the cause. She saw, but too well, though she strove not to see, that his affections were lost to her for ever.

It is impossible to imagine a period of greater pain and mortification than Mary passed, for about seven weeks, from the sixteenth of April to the sixth of June, in a furnished house that Mr. Imlay had provided for her. She had come over to England, a country for which she, at this time, expressed "a repugnance, that almost amounted to horror," in search of happiness.[1] She

---

[1] "Letters to Imlay." This portion of Letter XXXVII reads, " What sacrifices have you not made for a woman you did not respect!—But I will not go over this ground.—I want to tell you that I do not understand you. You say that you have not given up all thoughts of returning here —and I know that it will be necessary—nay, is. I cannot explain myself; but if you have not lost your memory, you will easily divine my meaning. What! is our life then only to be made up of

feared that that happiness had altogether escaped her; but she was encouraged by the eagerness and impatience which Mr. Imlay at length seemed to manifest for her arrival. When she saw him, all her fears were confirmed. What a picture was she capable of forming to herself, of the overflowing kindness of a meeting, after an interval of so much anguish and apprehension! A thousand images of this sort were present to her burning imagination. It is in vain, on such occasions, for reserve and reproach to endeavour to curb in the emotions of an affectionate heart. But the hopes she nourished were speedily blasted. Her reception by Mr. Imlay, was cold and embarrassed. Discussions ("explanations" they were called) followed; cruel explanations, that only added to the anguish of a heart already overwhelmed in grief! They had small pretensions indeed to explicitness; but they sufficiently told, that the case admitted not of remedy.

Mary was incapable of sustaining her equanimity in this pressing emergency. "Love, dear, delusive love!" as she expressed herself to a friend some time afterwards, "rigorous reason had forced her to resign; and now her rational prospects were blasted, just as she had learned to be contented with rational enjoyments." Thus situated, life became an intolerable burthen. While she was absent from Mr. Imlay, she could talk of purposes of separation and independence. But, now that they were in the same house, she could not withhold herself from endeavours to revive their mutual cordiality; and unsuccessful endeavours continually added fuel to the fire that destroyed her. She formed a desperate purpose to die.

This part of the story of Mary is involved in considerable obscurity. I only know, that Mr. Imlay became acquainted with her purpose, at a moment when he was uncertain whether or no it were already executed, and that his feelings were roused by the intelligence. It was perhaps owing to his activity and representations, that her life was, at this time, saved. She determined

---

separations? and am I only to return to a country, that has not merely lost all charms for me, but for which I feel a repugnance that almost amounts to horror, only to be left there a prey to it!" (403), in *Works of Mary Wollstonecraft*, Vol. 6.

to continue to exist. Actuated by this purpose, she took a resolution, worthy both of the strength and affectionateness of her mind. Mr. Imlay was involved in a question of considerable difficulty, respecting a mercantile adventure in Norway. It seemed to require the presence of some very judicious agent, to conduct the business to its desired termination. Mary determined to make the voyage, and take the business into her own hands. Such a voyage seemed the most desirable thing to recruit her health, and if possible, her spirits, in the present crisis. It was also gratifying to her feelings, to be employed in promoting the interest of a man, from whom she had experienced such severe unkindness, but to whom she ardently desired to be reconciled. The moment of desperation I have mentioned, occurred in the close of May, and, in about a week after, she set out upon this new expedition.

The narrative of this voyage is before the world, and perhaps a book of travels that so irresistibly seizes on the heart, never, in any other instance, found its way from the press.[2] The occasional harshness and ruggedness of character, that diversify her Vindication of the Rights of Woman, here totally disappear. If ever there was a book calculated to make a man in love with its author, this appears to me to be the book. She speaks of her sorrows, in a way that fills us with melancholy, and dissolves us in tenderness, at the same time that she displays a genius which commands all our admiration. Affliction had tempered her heart to a softness almost more than human; and the gentleness of her spirit seems precisely to accord with all the romance of unbounded attachment.

Thus softened and improved, thus fraught with imagination and sensibility, with all, and more than all, "that youthful poets fancy, when they love,"[3] she returned to England, and, if

---

[2] *Letters Written During A Short Residence in Sweden, Norway, and Denmark* (1796).
[3] Nicholas Rowe, *The Fair Penitent* (1703), III.i.257: "Is she not more than painting can express,/ Or youthful poets fancy when they love?" This play is also referenced in *Wrongs of Woman*. See Chapter IX, p. 129.

"She Speaks of Her Sorrows":
From *Letters Written During A Short Residence*

Godwin was not alone in his appreciation for this work. It was the best received of Wollstonecraft's writings, with even the conservative journal *The British Critic* finding it uncharacteristically feminine and her style much "improved" (606). In general, responses tended to be more effusive, prompting not only Godwin's proclamation of love, but that of several of his noted contemporaries as well and inspiring at least one marriage proposal. Romantic poet Robert Southey's remark captures some of the intensity of that response: "She has made me in love with a cold climate, and frost and snow with a northern moonlight" (qtd. in Wardle 256).

The irony was the work had this effect on seemingly everyone but its intended audience, her former lover the American, Gilbert Imlay (who is possibly the model for Henry Darnford of *The Wrongs of Woman*). Ostensibly, the book is a series of letters to Imlay composed while she conducted business for him in Norway, Sweden and Denmark and traveled with their young daughter, Fanny Imlay. For Wollstonecraft, the journey was a final attempt to join their futures and to save their relationship; for him, it was a convenient mechanism for ridding him of a lover who had already attempted suicide once and who was complicating his current affair with an actress.

The work was emotionally powerful, but not entirely spontaneous. Wollstonecraft revised the letters for publication after she had finally accepted the end of her relationship with Imlay and when in financial need; in many ways, it represents her most controlled and mature text. In the following passage, also "quote[d] with commendation"(606) in *The British Critic*, Wollstonecraft "speaks of her sorrows" in the voice that Godwin found so appealing and which came to characterize her later work. She weds a deeply personal and maternal sensibility with a broader, clear-eyed social perspective. As her journey nears completion, and as Imlay's disinterest becomes increasingly apparent with each unreciprocated letter, she reflects on a "familiar" pastoral scene and the fate of her own daughter:

My impatience, however, did not prevent my enjoying the journey. I had six weeks before passed over the same ground, still it had sufficient novelty to attract my attention, and beguile, if not banish, the sorrow that had taken up its abode in my heart. How interesting are the varied beauties of nature; and what peculiar charms characterize each season! The purple hue which the heath now assumed, gave it a degree of richness, that almost exceeded the lustre of the young green of spring—and harmonized exquisitely with the rays of the ripening corn. The weather was uninterruptedly fine, and the people busy in the fields cutting down the corn, or binding up the sheaves, continually varied the prospect. The rocks, it is true, were unusually rugged and dreary, yet as the road runs for a considerable way by the side of a fine river, with extended pastures on the other side, the image of sterility was not the predominant object, though the cottages looked still more miserable, after having seen the norwegian farms. The trees, likewise, appeared of the growth of yesterday, compared with those Nestors of the forest I have frequently mentioned. The women and children were cutting off branches from the beech, birch, oak, etc., and leaving them to dry—This way of helping out their fodder, injures the trees. But the winters are so long, that the poor cannot afford to lay in a sufficient stock of hay. By such means they just keep life in the poor cows, for little milk can be expected when they are so miserably fed.

It was saturday, and the evening was uncommonly serene. In the villages I every where saw preparations for sunday; and I passed by a little car loaded with rye, that presented, for the pencil and heart, the sweetest picture of a harvest home I had ever beheld. A little girl was mounted a straddle on a shaggy horse, brandishing a stick over its head; the father was walking at the side of the car with a child in his arms, who must have come to meet him with tottering steps, the little creature was stretching out its arms to cling round his neck; and a boy, just above petticoats, was labouring hard, with a fork, behind, to keep the sheaves from falling.

My eyes followed them to the cottage, and an involuntary sigh whispered to my heart, that I envied the mother, much as I dislike cooking, who was preparing their pottage. I was returning to my babe, who may never experience a father's care or tenderness. The bosom that nurtured her, heaved with a pang at the thought which only an unhappy mother could feel. (315)

SOURCES

The British Critic, VII (1796): 602-610.

Ralph Wardle. *Mary Wollstonecraft: A Critical Biography*. Lincoln: University of Nebraska Press, 1951.

Mary Wollstonecraft. *Letters Written During A Short Residence in Sweden, Norway, and Denmark*. In *The Works of Mary Wollstonecraft*. Vol. 6. Edited by Janet Todd and Marilyn Butler. New York: New York University Press, 1989.

he had so pleased, to the arms of her former lover. Her return was hastened by the ambiguity, to her apprehension, of Mr. Imlay's conduct. He had promised to meet her upon her return from Norway, probably at Hamburgh; and they were then to pass some time in Switzerland. The style however of his letters to her during her tour, was not such as to inspire confidence; and she wrote to him very urgently, to explain himself, relative to the footing upon which they were hereafter to stand to each other. In his answer, which reached her at Hamburgh; he treated her questions as "extraordinary and unnecessary," and desired her to be at the pains to decide for herself.[4] Feeling herself unable to accept this as an explanation, she instantly determined to sail for London by the very first opportunity, that she might thus bring to a termination the suspense that preyed upon her soul.

It was not long after her arrival in London in the commencement of October, that she attained the certainty she sought. Mr. Imlay procured her a lodging. But the neglect she experienced from him after she entered it, flashed conviction upon her, in spite of his asseverations. She made further enquiries, and at length was informed by a servant, of the real state of the case. Under the immediate shock which the painful certainty gave her, her first impulse was to repair to him at the ready-furnished house he had provided for his new mistress. What was the particular nature of their conference I am unable to relate. It is sufficient to say that the wretchedness of the night which succeeded this fatal discovery, impressed her with the feeling, that she would sooner suffer a thousand deaths, than pass another of equal misery.

The agony of her mind determined her; and that determination gave her a sort of desperate serenity. She resolved to plunge herself in the Thames; and, not being satisfied with any spot nearer to London, she took a boat, and rowed to Putney. Her first thought had led her to Battersea-bridge, but she found it too public. It was night when she arrived at Putney, and by that time had begun to rain with great violence. The rain suggested to her the idea of walking up and down the bridge, till her clothes were thoroughly drenched and heavy with the wet, which she did for half an hour without meeting a human being. She then leaped from the top of the bridge, but still seemed to find a difficulty in sinking, which she endeavoured to counteract by

---

[4] Godwin's text suggests that he is quoting from Imlay's letters; these letters have not been found.

pressing her clothes closely round her. After some time she became insensible; but she always spoke of the pain she underwent, as such, that, though she could afterwards have determined upon almost any other species of voluntary death, it would have been impossible for her to resolve upon encountering the same sensations again. I am doubtful, whether this is to be ascribed to the mere nature of suffocation, or was not rather owing to the preternatural action of a desperate spirit.

After having been for a considerable time insensible, she was recovered by the exertions of those by whom the body was found. She had sought, with cool and deliberate firmness, to put a period to her existence, and yet she lived to have every prospect of a long possession of enjoyment and happiness. It is perhaps not an unfrequent case with suicides, that we find reason to suppose, if they had survived their gloomy purpose, that they would, at a subsequent period, have been considerably happy. It arises indeed, in some measure, out of the very nature of a spirit of self-destruction; which implies a degree of anguish, that the constitution of the human mind will not suffer to remain long undiminished. This is a serious reflection. Probably no man would destroy himself from an impatience of present pain, if he felt a moral certainty that there were years of enjoyment still in reserve for him. It is perhaps a futile attempt, to think of reasoning with a man in that state of mind which precedes suicide. Moral reasoning is nothing but the awakening of certain feelings; and the feeling by which he is actuated, is too strong to leave us much chance of impressing him with other feelings, that should have force enough to counterbalance it. But, if the prospect of future tranquility and pleasure cannot be expected to have much weight with a man under an immediate purpose of suicide, it is so much the more to be wished, that men would impress their minds, in their sober moments, with a conception, which, being rendered habitual, seems to promise to act as a successful antidote in a paroxysm of desperation.

The present situation of Mary, of necessity produced some further intercourse between her and Mr. Imlay. He sent a physician to her; and Mrs. Christie, at his desire, prevailed on her to remove to her house in Finsbury-square. In the mean time, Mr. Imlay assured her that his present was merely a casual, sensual connection; and, of course, fostered in her mind the idea that it would be once more in her choice to live with him. With whatever intention the idea was suggested, it was certainly calculated to increase the agitation of her mind. In one respect however it produced an effect unlike that which might most obviously have been looked for. It roused within her the characteristic energy of mind, which she seemed partially to have forgotten. She saw the necessity of bringing the affair to a point, and not suffering months and years to roll on in uncertainty and suspence. This idea inspired her with an extraordinary resolution. The language she employed, was, in effect, as follows: "If we are ever to live together again, it must be now. We meet now, or we part for ever. You say, You cannot abruptly break off the connection you have formed. It is unworthy of my courage and character, to wait the uncertain issue of that connection. I am determined to come to a decision. I consent then, for the present, to live with you, and the woman to whom you have associated yourself. I think it is important that you should learn habitually to feel for your child the affection of a father. But, if you reject this proposal, here we end. You are now free. We will correspond no more. We will have no intercourse of any kind. I will be to you as a person that is dead."

The proposal she made, extraordinary and injudicious as it was, was at first accepted; and Mr. Imlay took her accordingly, to look at a house he was upon the point of hiring, that she might judge whether it was calculated to please her. Upon second thoughts however he retracted his concession.

In the following month, Mr. Imlay, and the woman with whom he was at present connected, went to Paris, where they remained three months. Mary had, previously to this, fixed herself in a lodging in Finsbury-place, where, for some time, she saw scarcely any one but Mrs. Christie, for the sake of whose neighbourhood she had chosen this situation; "existing," as she expressed it, "in a living tomb, and her life but an exercise of fortitude, continually on the stretch."[5]

Thus circumstanced, it was unavoidable for her thoughts to brood upon a passion, which all that she had suffered had not yet been able to extinguish. Accordingly, as soon as Mr. Imlay returned to England, she could not restrain herself from making another effort, and desiring to see him once more. "During his absence, affection had led her to make numberless excuses for his conduct," and she probably wished to believe that his present connection was, as he represented it, purely of a casual nature. To this application, she observes, that "he returned no other answer, except declaring, with unjustifiable passion, that he would not see her."

That answer, though, at the moment, highly irritating to Mary, was not the ultimate close of the affair. Mr. Christie was connected in business with Mr. Imlay, at the same time that the house of Mr. Christie was the only one at which Mary habitually visited. The consequence of this was, that, when Mr. Imlay had been already more than a fortnight in town, Mary called at Mr. Christie's one evening, at a time when Mr. Imlay was in the parlour. The room was full of company. Mrs. Christie heard Mary's voice in the passage, and hastened to her, to intreat her not to make an appearance. Mary however was not to be controlled. She thought, as she afterwards told me, that it was not consistent with conscious rectitude, that she should shrink, as if abashed, from the presence of one by whom she deemed herself injured. Her child was with her. She entered; and, in a firm manner, immediately led up the child, now near two years of age, to the knees of its father. He retired with Mary into another apartment, and promised to dine with her at her lodging, I believe, the next day.

In the interview which took place in consequence of this

---

[5] "Letters to Imlay." Letter LXXV reads, "My life therefore is but an exercise of fortitude, continually on the stretch—and hope never gleams in this tomb, where I am buried alive," (434) in *Works of Mary Wollstonecraft*, Vol. 6.

appointment, he expressed himself to her in friendly terms, and in a manner calculated to sooth her despair. Though he could conduct himself, when absent from her, in a way which she censured as unfeeling; this species of sternness constantly expired when he came into her presence. Mary was prepared at this moment to catch at every phantom of happiness; and the gentleness of his carriage, was to her as a sun-beam, awakening the hope of returning day. For an instant she gave herself up to delusive visions; and, even after the period of delirium expired, she still dwelt, with an aching eye, upon the air-built and unsubstantial prospect of a reconciliation.

At his particular request, she retained the name of Imlay, which, a short time before, he had seemed to dispute with her. "It was not," as she expresses herself in a letter to a friend, "for the world that she did so—not in the least—but she was unwilling to cut the Gordian knot, or tear herself away in appearance, when she could not in reality."[6]

The day after this interview, she set out upon a visit to the country, where she spent nearly the whole of the month of March. It was, I believe, while she was upon this visit, that some epistolary communication with Mr. Imlay, induced her resolutely to expel from her mind, all remaining doubt as to the issue of the affair.

Mary was now aware that every demand of forbearance towards him, of duty to her child, and even of indulgence to her own deep-rooted predilection, was discharged. She determined to rouse herself, and cast off for ever an attachment, which to her had been a spring of inexhaustible bitterness. Her present residence among the scenes of nature, was favourable to this purpose. She was at the house of an old and intimate friend, a lady of the name of Cotton,[7] whose partiality for her was strong and sincere. Mrs. Cotton's nearest neighbour was Sir William East,[8]

---

[6] See *Wrongs of Woman*, p. 127 for reference to the Gordian knot.
[7] Mrs. Cotton of Berkshire.
[8] Sir William East of Burchetts Green, Hurley.

baronet; and, from the joint effect of this kindness of her friend, and the hospitable and distinguishing attentions of this respectable family, she derived considerable benefit. She had been amused and interested in her journey to Norway; but with this difference, that, at that time, her mind perpetually returned with trembling anxiety to conjectures respecting Mr. Imlay's future conduct, whereas now, with a lofty and undaunted spirit, she threw aside every thought that recurred to him, while she felt herself called upon to make one more effort for life and happiness.

Once after this, to my knowledge, she saw Mr. Imlay; probably, not long after her return to town. They met by accident upon the New Road; he alighted from his horse, and walked with her for some time; and the rencounter passed, as she assured me, without producing in her any oppressive emotion.

Be it observed, by the way, and I may be supposed best to have known the real state of the case, she never spoke of Mr. Imlay with acrimony, and was displeased when any person, in her hearing, expressed contempt of him. She was characterized by a strong sense of indignation; but her emotions of this sort were short-lived, and in no long time subsided into a dignified sereneness and equanimity.

The question of her connection with Mr. Imlay, as we have seen, was not completely dismissed, till March 1796. But it is worthy to be observed, that she did not, like ordinary persons under extreme anguish of mind, suffer her understanding, in the mean time, to sink into littleness and debility. The most inapprehensive reader may conceive what was the mental torture she endured, when he considers, that she was twice, with an interval of four months, from the end of May to the beginning of October, prompted by it to purposes of suicide. Yet in this period she wrote her Letters from Norway. Shortly after its expiration she prepared them for the press, and they were published in the close of that year. In January 1796, she finished the sketch of a comedy, which turns, in the serious scenes, upon the incidents of her own story. It was offered to both the winter-managers, and remained among her papers at the period of her decease; but it appeared to me to be in so crude and imperfect a state, that I judged it most respectful to her memory to commit it to the flames. To understand this extraordinary degree of activity, we must recollect however the entire solitude, in which most of her hours were at that time consumed.

Chap. IX.
1796, 1797

I am now led, by the progress of the story, to the last branch of her history, the connection between Mary and myself. And this I shall relate with the same simplicity that has pervaded every other part of my narrative. If there ever were any motives of prudence or delicacy, that could impose a qualification upon the story, they are now over. They could have no relation but to factitious rules of decorum. There are no circumstances of her life, that, in the judgment of honour and reason, could brand her with disgrace. Never did there exist a human being, that needed, with less fear, expose all their actions, and call upon the universe to judge them. An event of the most deplorable sort, has awfully imposed silence upon the gabble of frivolity.

We renewed our acquaintance in January 1796, but with no particular effect, except so far as sympathy in her anguish, added to my mind in the respect I had always entertained for her talents. It was in the close of that month that I read her Letters from Norway; and the impression that book produced upon me has been already related.[1]

It was on the fourteenth of April that I first saw her after her excursion into Berkshire. On that day she called upon me in Somers Town, she having, since her return, taken a lodging in Cumming-street, Pentonville,[2] at no great distance from the place of my habitation. From that time our intimacy increased, by regular, but almost imperceptible degrees.

The partiality we conceived for each, was in that mode, which

---

[1] See p. 265.
[2] Formerly a suburb of London.

I have always regarded as the purest and most refined style of love. It grew with equal advances in the mind of each. It would have been impossible for the most minute observer to have said who was before, and who was after. One sex did not take the priority which long-established custom has awarded it, nor the other overstep that delicacy which is so severely imposed. I am not conscious that either party can assume to have been the agent or the patient, the toil-spreader or the prey, in the affair. When, in the course of things, the disclosure came, there was nothing, in a manner, for either party to disclose for the other.

In July 1796 I made an excursion into the county of Norfolk, which occupied nearly the whole of that month. During this period Mary removed, from Cumming-street, Pentonville, to Judd place West, which may be considered as the extremity of Somers Town. In the former situation, she had occupied a furnished lodging. She had meditated a tour to Italy or Switzerland, and knew not how soon she should set out with that view. Now however she felt herself reconciled to a longer abode in England, probably without exactly knowing why this change had taken place in her mind. She had a quantity of furniture locked up at a broker's ever since her residence in Store-street, and she now found it adviseable to bring it to use. This circumstance occasioned her present removal.

The temporary separation attendant on my little journey, had its effect on the mind of both parties. It gave a space for the maturing of inclination. I believe that, during this interval, each furnished to the other the principal topic of solitary and daily contemplation. Absence bestows a refined and aerial delicacy upon affection, which it with difficulty acquires in any other way. It seems to resemble the communication of spirits, without the medium, or the impediment, of this earthly frame.

When we met again, we met with new pleasure, and, I may add, with a more decisive preference for each other. It was however three weeks longer, before the sentiment which trembled upon the tongue, burst from the lips of either. There was, as I have already said, no period of throes and resolute explanation attendant on the tale. It was friendship melting into love. Previously to our mutual declaration, each felt half-assured, yet each felt a certain trembling anxiety to have assurance complete.

Mary rested her head upon the shoulder of her lover, hoping to find a heart with which she might safely treasure her world of affection; fearing to commit a mistake, yet, in spite of her melancholy existence, fraught with that generous confidence, which, in a great soul, is never extinguished. I had never loved till now; or, at least, had never nourished a passion to the same growth, or met with an object so consummately worthy.

We did not marry. It is difficult to recommend any thing to indiscriminate adoption, contrary to the established rules and prejudices of mankind; but certainly nothing can be so ridiculous upon the face of it, or so contrary to the genuine march of sentiment, as to require the overflowing of the soul to wait upon a ceremony, and that which, wherever delicacy and imagination exist, is of all things most sacredly private, to blow a trumpet before it, and to record the moment when it has arrived at its climax.

There were however other reasons why we did not immediately marry. Mary felt an entire conviction of the propriety of her conduct. It would be absurd to suppose that, with a heart withered by desertion, she was not right to give way to the emotions of kindness which our intimacy produced, and to seek for that support in friendship and affection, which could alone give pleasure to her heart, and peace to her meditations. It was only about six months since she had resolutely banished every thought of Mr. Imlay; but it was at least eighteen that he ought to have been banished, and would have been banished, had it not been for her scrupulous pertinacity in determining to leave no measure untried to regain him. Add to this, that the laws of etiquette ordinarily laid down in these cases, are essentially absurd, and that the sentiments of the heart cannot submit to be directed by the rule and the square. But Mary had an extreme aversion to be made the topic of vulgar discussion; and, if there be any weakness in this, the dreadful trials through which she had recently passed, may well plead in its excuse. She felt that she had been too much, and too rudely spoken of, in the former instance; and she could not resolve to do any thing that should immediately revive that painful topic.

For myself, it is certain that I had for many years regarded marriage with so well-grounded an apprehension, that, notwithstanding the partiality for Mary that had taken possession of my soul, I should have felt it very difficult, at least in the present stage of our intercourse, to have resolved on such a measure. Thus, partly from similar, and partly from different motives, we felt alike in this, as we did perhaps in every other circumstance that related to our intercourse.

I have nothing further that I find it necessary to record, till the commencement of April 1797. We then judged it proper to declare our marriage, which had taken place a little before. The principal motive for complying with this ceremony, was the circumstance of Mary's being in a state of pregnancy. She was unwilling, and perhaps with reason, to incur that exclusion from the society of many invaluable and excellent individuals, which custom awards in cases of this sort. I should have felt an extreme repugnance to the having caused her such an inconvenience. And, after the experiment of seven months of as intimate an intercourse as our respective modes of living would admit, there was certainly less hazard to either, in the subjecting ourselves to those consequences which the laws of England annex to the relations of husband and wife. On the sixth of April we entered into possession of a house, which had been taken by us in concert.

ON CO-HABITATION, LOVE, AND FIDELITY:
FROM *AN ENQUIRY CONCERNING POLITICAL JUSTICE*

William Godwin has every reason to sound defensive in his description of both his relationship with Wollstonecraft and their eventual marriage. His pronouncements on love and marriage had proved some of his most controversial in his two-volume philosophical treatise *An Enquiry Concerning Political Justice* (1793), a work that earned him the "reputation of being the most radical mind ever produced in England" (Smith 32). In this work, Godwin argued for the primacy of private judgment over institutional control. Through the exercise of individual reason, man was ultimately perfectible. Institutions, by contrast, were obstacles to man's happiness, limiting his ability to make free and non-prejudicial judgments. Marriage was one such institutional obstacle, and in *Political Justice* Godwin calls for its abolition and, even more scandalously, offered only lukewarm support for the concept of fidelity. From a practical point of view, he argues, individuals are likely to choose only one partner, as "it is the nature of the human mind, to persist, for a certain length of time, in its opinion or choice." Yet affections can change and to avoid "fraud and concerted hypocrisy" one must be free to act according to one's judgment. Marriage, he further argued, legislated against such independence of thought and, indeed, actively promoted fraud, dependency, and possessiveness, three impediments to man's perfectibility.

Hence, Godwin could not discuss the details of his relationship with Wollstonecraft and the reasons for their marriage without bringing under scrutiny his own political principles. In disclosing these particulars, Godwin was least vulnerable to the charge of fraud, as he had argued that this "evil of marriage" was largely a function of the youth of the typical couple, and neither he nor Wollstonecraft were young or without some romantic experience when they met:

> But the evil of marriage, as it is practised in European countries lies deeper than this. The habit is, for a thoughtless and romantic youth of each sex to come together, to see each other for a few times and under circumstances full of delusion, and then to vow to each other eternal attachment. What is the consequence of this? In almost every instance they find themselves deceived. They are reduced to make

the best of an irretrievable mistake. They are presented with the strongest imaginable temptation to
become the dupes of falshood. They are led to conceive it their wisest policy to shut their eyes upon
realities, happy if by any perversion of intellect they
can persuade themselves that they were right in their
first crude opinion of their companion. The institution of marriage is a system of fraud; and men who
carefully mislead their judgments in the daily affair
of their life, must always have a crippled judgment
in every other concern. (453)

Their relationship was somewhat more vulnerable to the
charge of dependency, as this condition was engendered
largely through co-habitation. Godwin is careful to point
out that he retained his separate workplace even after their
marriage, but clearly the pregnancy made desirable a common abode. Godwin had written dismissively of the kinds
of "interruptions" such shared accommodations occasioned
and the negative effect it could have on one's moral independence:

All attachments to individuals, except in proportion to their merits, are plainly unjust. It is therefore desirable, that we should be the friends of man
rather than of particular men, and that we should
pursue the chain of our own reflexions, with no other
interruption than information or philanthropy re-
quires. (453)

Godwin's attachment to Wollstonecraft is obvious
throughout *The Memoirs*, and especially in his description
of their courtship, and it is on this point that he proves most
vulnerable. Such personal preferences, Godwin argues in
Political Justice, represent real dangers and, even in the best
of circumstances, work against the kind of universal benevolence so central to a just society:

Add to this, that marriage is an affair of property,
and the worst of all properties. So long as two human beings are forbidden by positive institution to

follow the dictates of their own mind, prejudice is
alive and vigorous. So long as I seek to engross one
woman to myself, and to prohibit my neighbour
from proving his superior desert and reaping the
fruits of it, I am guilty of the most odious of all
monopolies. Over this imaginary prize men watch
with perpetual jealousy, and one man will find his
desires and his capacity to circumvent as much excited, as the other is excited to traverse his projects
and frustrate his hopes. As long as this state of society continues, philanthropy will be crossed and
checked in a thousand ways, and the still augment-
ing stream of abuse will continue to flow. (453-54)
Given this previous injunction against private affection, his
acknowledgement of love and commitment to Wollstonecraft
becomes one of his most charged political statements.

Sources

Godwin, William. *An Enquiry Concerning Political Justice*.
In *Political and Philosophical Writings of William Godwin*,
Vol 3. Edited by Mark Philp. London: Pickering &
Chatto, 1993.

Smith, Elton and Esther Greenwell Smith. *William
Godwin*. New York: Twayne Publishers, 1965.

In this place I have a very curious circumstance to notice,
which I am happy to have occasion to mention, as it tends to
expose certain regulations of polished society, of which the absurdity vies with the odiousness. Mary had long possessed the
advantage of an acquaintance with many persons of genius, and
with others whom the effects of an intercourse with elegant society, combined with a certain portion of information and good
sense, sufficed to render amusing companions. She had lately
extended the circle of her acquaintance in this respect; and her
mind, trembling between the opposite impressions of past an-

guish and renovating tranquility, found ease in this species of recreation. Wherever Mary appeared, admiration attended upon her. She had always displayed talents for conversation; but maturity of understanding, her travels, her long residence in France, the discipline of affliction, and the smiling, new-born peace which awaked a corresponding smile in her animate countenance, inexpressibly increased them. The way in which the story of Mr. Imlay was treated in these polite circles, was probably the result of the partiality she excited. These elegant personages were divided between their cautious adherence to forms, and the desire to seek their own gratification. Mary made no secret of the nature of her connection with Mr. Imlay; and in one instance, I well know, she put herself to the trouble of explaining it to a person totally indifferent to her, because he never failed to publish every thing he knew, and, she was sure, would repeat her explanation to his numerous acquaintance. She was of too proud and generous a spirit to stoop to hypocrisy. These persons however, in spite of all that could be said, persisted in shutting their eyes, and pretending they took her for a married woman.

Observe the consequence of this! While she was, and constantly professed to be, an unmarried mother; she was fit society for the squeamish and the formal. The moment she acknowledged herself a wife, and that by a marriage perhaps unexceptional, the case was altered. Mary and myself, ignorant as we were of these elevated refinements, supposed that our marriage would place her upon a surer footing in the calendar of polished society, than ever. But it forced these people to see the truth, and to confess their belief of what they had carefully been told; and this they could not forgive. Be it remarked, that the date of our marriage had nothing to do with this, that question being never once mentioned during this period. Mary indeed had, till now, retained the name of Imlay which had first been assumed from necessity in France; but its being retained thus long, was purely from the awkwardness that attends the introduction of a change, and not from an apprehension of consequences of this sort. Her scrupulous explicitness as to the nature of her situation, surely sufficed to make the name she bore perfectly immaterial.

It is impossible to relate the particulars of such a story, but in the language of contempt and ridicule. A serious reflection however upon the whole, ought to awaken emotions of a different sort. Mary retained the most numerous portion of her acquaintance, and the majority of those whom she principally valued. It was only the supporters and the subjects of the unprincipled manners of a court, that she lost. This however is immaterial. The tendency of the proceeding, strictly considered, and uniformly acted upon, would have been to proscribe her from all valuable society. And who was the person proscribed? The firmest champion, and, as I strongly suspect, the greatest ornament her sex ever had to boast! A woman, with sentiments as pure, as refined, and as delicate, as ever inhabited a human heart! It is fit that such persons should stand by, that we may have room enough for the dull and insolent dictators, the gamblers and demireps[3] of polished society!

Two of the persons, the loss of whose acquaintance Mary principally regretted upon this occasion, were Mrs. Inchbald and Mrs. Siddons.[4] Their acquaintance, it is perhaps fair to observe, is to be ranked among her recent acquisitions. Mrs. Siddons, I am sure, regretted the necessity, which she conceived to be imposed on her by the peculiarity of her situation, to conform to the rules I have described. She is endowed with that rich and generous sensibility, which should best enable its possessor completely to feel the merits of her deceased friend. She very truly observes, in a letter now before me, that the Travels in Norway were read by no one, who was in possession of "more

---

[3] I.e., disreputable persons.
[4] Elizabeth Inchbald (1753-1821), actress, playwright, and novelist. Inchbald maintained a reputation for virtue in spite of her association with the stage. In addition to numerous plays, she penned *A Simple Story* (1791) and *Nature and Art* (1796). At one time, she was a suitor of Godwin's. Sarah Siddons (1775-1831). Like Inchbald, she was an actress who had managed to maintain a respectable status. Wollstonecraft praises her performance of Calista in *Wrongs of Woman*. See Chapter IX, p. 129.

reciprocity of feeling, or more deeply impressed with admiration of the writer's extraordinary powers."

Mary felt a transitory pang, when the conviction reached her of so unexpected a circumstance, that was rather exquisite. But she disdained to sink under the injustice (as this ultimately was) of the supercilious and the foolish, and presently shook off the impression of the first surprize. That once subsided, I well know that the event was thought of, with no emotions, but those of superiority to the injustice she sustained; and was not of force enough, to diminish a happiness, which seemed hourly to become more vigorous and firm.

I think I may venture to say, that no two persons ever found in each other's society, a satisfaction more pure and refined. What it was in itself, can now only be known, in its full extent, to the survivor. But, I believe, the serenity of her countenance, the increasing sweetness of her manners, and that consciousness of enjoyment that seemed ambitious that every one she saw would be happy as well as herself, were matters of general observation to all her acquaintance. She had always possessed, in an unparalleled degree, the art of communicating happiness, and she was now in the constant and unlimited exercise of it. She seemed to have attained that situation, which her disposition and character imperiously demanded, but which she had never before attained; and her understanding and her heart felt the benefit of it.

While we lived as near neighbours only, and before our last removal, her mind had attained considerable tranquility, and was visited but seldom with those emotions of anguish, which had been but too familiar to her. But the improvement in this respect, which accrued upon our removal and establishment, was extremely obvious. She was a worshipper of domestic life. She loved to observe the growth of affection between me and her daughter, then three years of age, as well as my anxiety respecting the child not yet born. Pregnancy itself, unequal as the decree of nature seems to be in this respect, is the source of a thousand endearments. No one knew better than Mary how to extract sentiments of exquisite delight, from trifles, which a suspicious and formal wisdom would scarcely deign to remark. A little ride into the country with myself and the child, had sometimes produced a sort of opening of the heart, a general expression of confidence and affectionate soul, a sort of infantine, yet dignified endearment, which those who have felt may understand, but which I should in vain attempt to pourtray.

In addition to our domestic pleasures, I was fortunate enough to introduce her to some of my acquaintances of both sexes, to whom she attached herself with all the ardour of approbation and friendship.

Ours was not an idle happiness, a paradise of selfish and transitory pleasures. It is perhaps scarcely necessary to mention, that, influenced by the ideas I had long entertained upon the subject of cohabitation, I engaged an apartment, about twenty doors from our house in the Polygon, Somers Town, which I designed for the purpose of study and literary occupations. Trifles however will be interesting to some readers, when they relate to the last period of the life of such a person as Mary. I will add therefore, that we were both of us of opinion, that it was possible for two persons to be too uniformly in each other's company. Influenced by that opinion, it was my practice to repair to the apartment I have mentioned as soon as I rose, and frequently not to make an appearance in the Polygon, till the hour of dinner.[5] We agreed in condemning the notion, prevalent in many situations in life, that a man and his wife cannot visit in mixed society, but in company with each other; and we rather sought occasions of deviating from, than complying with, this rule. By these means, though, for the most part, we spent the latter half of each day in one another's society, yet we were in no danger of satiety. We seemed to combine, in a considerable degree, the novelty and lively sensation of a visit, with the more delicious and heart-felt pleasures of domestic life.

Whatever may be thought, in other respects, of the plan laid down to ourselves, we probably derived real advantage from it,

[5] I.e., lunchtime.

as to the constancy and uninterruptedness of our literary pursuits. Mary had a variety of projects of this sort, for the exercise of her talents, and the benefit of society; and, if she had lived, I believe the world would have had very little reason to complain of any remission of her industry. One of her projects, which has been already mentioned, was a series of Letters on the Management of Infants. Though she had been for some time digesting her ideas on this subject with a view to the press, I have found comparatively nothing that she had committed to paper respecting it. Another project, of longer standing, was of a series of books for the instruction of children. A fragment she left in execution of this project, is inserted in her Posthumous Works.[6]

But the principal work, in which she was engaged for more that twelve months before her decease, was a novel, entitled, The Wrongs of Woman.[7] I shall not stop here to explain the nature of the work, as so much of it as was already written, is now given to the public. I shall only observe that, impressed, as she could not fail to be, with the consciousness of her talents, she was desirous, in this instance, that they should effect what they were capable of effecting. She was sensible how arduous a task it is to produce a truly excellent novel; and she roused her faculties to grapple with it. All her other works were produced with a rapidity, that did not give her powers time fully to expand. But this was written slowly and with mature consideration. She began it in several forms, which she successively rejected, after they were considerable advanced. She wrote many parts of the work again and again, and, when she had finished what she intended for the first part, she felt herself more urgently stimulated to revise and improve what she had written, than to proceed, with constancy of application, in the parts that were to follow.

---

[6] "Lessons," *Posthumous Works*. Vol. 2 (1798).
[7] *The Wrongs of Woman; or Maria, A Fragment* in *Posthumous Works*, Vols. 1 & 2 (1798).

CHAP. X.

I am now led, by the course of my narrative, to the last fatal
scene of her life. She was taken in labour on Wednesday, the
thirtieth of August. She had been somewhat indisposed on
the preceding Friday, the consequence, I believe, of a sudden
alarm. But from that time she was in perfect health. She was so
far from being under any apprehension as to the difficulties of
child-birth, as frequently to ridicule the fashion of ladies in England, who keep their chamber for one full month after delivery.
For herself, she proposed coming down to dinner on the day
immediately following. She had already had some experience on
the subject in the case of Fanny; and I cheerfully submitted in
every point to her judgment and her wisdom. She hired no
nurse. Influenced by ideas of decorum, which certainly ought to
have no place, at least in cases of danger, she determined to have
a woman to attend her in the capacity of midwife. She was sensible that the proper business of a midwife, in the instance of a
natural labour, is to sit by and wait for the operations of nature,
which seldom, in these affairs, demand the interposition of art.

At five o'clock in the morning of the day of delivery, she felt
what she conceived to be some notices of the approaching labour.
Mrs. Blenkinsop, matron and midwife to the Westminster Lying in Hospital,[1] who had seen Mary several times previous to
her delivery, was soon after sent for, and arrived about nine.
During the whole day Mary was perfectly cheerful. Her pains
came on slowly; and, in the morning, she wrote several notes,
three addressed to me, who had gone, as usual, to my apartments, for the purpose of study. About two o'clock in the afternoon, she went up to her chamber—never more to descend.

---

[1] A maternity hospital, principally designed to minister to the poor.

The child was born at twenty minutes after eleven at night. Mary had requested that I would not come into the chamber till all was over, and signified her intention of then performing the interesting object of presenting the new-born child to its father. I was sitting in a parlour; and it was not till after two o'clock on Thursday morning, that I received the alarming intelligence, that the placenta was not yet removed, and that the midwife dared not proceed further, and gave her opinion for calling in a male practitioner. I accordingly went for Dr. Poignard, physician and man-midwife to the same hospital, who arrived between three and four hours after the birth of the child. He immediately proceeded to the extraction of the placenta, which he brought away in pieces, till he was satisfied that the whole was removed. In that point however it afterwards appeared that he was mistaken.

The period from the birth of the child till about eight o'clock the next morning, was a period full of peril and alarm. The loss of blood was considerable, and produced an almost uninterrupted series of fainting fits. I went to the chamber soon after four in the morning, and found her in this state. She told me some time on Thursday, "that she should have died in the preceding night, but that she was determined not to leave me." She added, with one of those smiles which so eminently illuminated her countenance, "that I should not be like Porson,"[2] alluding to the circumstance of that great man having lost his wife, after being only a few months married. Speaking of what she had already passed through, she declared, "that she had never known what bodily pain was before."

On Thursday morning Dr. Poignard repeated his visit. Mary had just before expressed some inclination to see Dr. George Fordyce, a man probably of more science that any other medical professor in England, and between whom and herself there had long subsisted a mutual friendship. I mentioned this to Dr. Poignard, but he rather discountenanced the idea, observing that

[2] Richard Porson (1759-1808), his wife had died that same year.

he saw no necessity for it, and he supposed Dr. Fordyce was not particularly conversant with obstetrical cases; but that I would do as I pleased. After Dr. Poignard was gone, I determined to send for Dr. Fordyce. He accordingly saw the patient about three o'clock on Thursday afternoon. He however perceived no particular cause of alarm; and, on that or the next day, quoted, as I am told, Mary's case, in a mixed company, as a corrobation of a favourite idea of his, of the propriety of employing females in the capacity of midwives. Mary "had a woman, and was doing extremely well."

What had passed however in the night between Wednesday and Thursday, had so far alarmed me, that I did not quit the house, and scarcely the chamber, during the following day. But my alarms wore off, as time advanced. Appearances were more favourable, than the exhausted state of the patient would almost have permitted me to expect. Friday morning therefore I devoted to a business of some urgency, which called me to different parts of the town, and which, before dinner, I happily completed. On my return, and during the evening, I received the most pleasurable sensations from the promising state of the patient. I was now perfectly satisfied that every thing was safe, and that, if she did not take cold, or suffer from any external accident, her speedy recovery was certain.

Saturday was a day less auspicious than Friday, but not absolutely alarming.

Sunday, the third of September, I now regard as the day, that finally decided on the fate of the object dearest to my heart that the universe contained. Encouraged by what I considered as the progress of her recovery, I accompanied a friend in the morning in several calls, one of them as far as Kensington, and did not return till dinner-time. On my return I found a degree of anxiety in every face, and was told that she had had as sort of shivering fit, and had expressed some anxiety at the length of my absence. My sister and a friend of hers, had been engaged to dine below stairs, but a message was sent to put them off, and Mary ordered that the cloth should not be laid, as usual, in the room immediately under her on the first floor, but in the ground-floor parlour. I felt a pang at having been so long and so unseasonably absent, and determined that I would not repeat the fault.

In the evening she had a second shivering fit, the symptoms of which were in the highest degree alarming. Ever muscle of the body trembled, the teeth chattered, and the bed shook under her. This continued probably for five minutes. She told me, after it was over, that it had been a struggle between life and death, and that she had been more than once, in the course of it, at the point of expiring. I now apprehend these to have been the symptoms of a decided mortification,[3] occasioned by the part of the placenta that remained in the womb. At the time however I was far from considering it in that light. When I went for Dr. Poignard, between two and three o'clock on the morning of Thursday, despair was in my heart. The fact of the adhesion of the placenta was stated to me; and, ignorant as I was of obstetrical science, I felt as if the death of Mary was in a manner decided. But hope had re-visited my bosom; and her chearings were so delightful, that I hugged her obstinately to my heart. I was only mortified at what appeared to me a new delay in the recovery I so earnestly longed for. I immediately sent for Dr. Fordyce, who had been with her in the morning, as well as on the three preceding days. Dr. Poignard had also called this morning, but declined paying any further visits, as we had thought proper to call in Dr. Fordyce.

The progress of the disease was now uninterrupted. On Tuesday I found it necessary again to call in Dr. Fordyce in the afternoon, who brought with him Dr. Clarke of New Burlingon-street,[4] under the idea that some operation might be necessary. I have already said, that I pertinaciously persisted in viewing the

---

[3] The death of a part of the body while the rest is living; gangrene (*OED*).

[4] John Clark (1761-1815), surgeon from General Lying-In Hospital. Known to Godwin through his association with Joseph Johnson, who published his work on obstetrics.

fair side of things; and therefore the interval between Sunday and Tuesday evening, did not pass without some mixture of cheerfulness. On Monday, Dr. Fordyce forbad the child's having the breast, and we therefore procured puppies to draw off the milk. This occasioned some pleasantry of Mary with me and the other attendants. Nothing could exceed the equanimity, the patience and affectionateness of the poor sufferer. I intreated her to recover; I dwelt with trembling fondness on every favourable circumstance; and, as far it was possible in so dreadful a situation, she, by her smiles and kind speeches, rewarded my affection.

Wednesday was to me the day of greatest torture in the melancholy series. It was now decided that the only chance of supporting her through what she had to suffer, was by supplying her rather freely with wine. This task was devolved upon me. I began about four o'clock in the afternoon. But for me, totally ignorant of the nature of diseases and of the human frame, thus to play with a life that now seemed all that was dear to me in the universe, was too dreadful a task. I knew neither what was too much, nor what was too little. Having begun, I felt compelled, under every disadvantage, to go on. This lasted for three hours. Towards the end of that time, I happened foolishly to ask the servant who came out of the room, "What she thought of her mistress?" she replied, "that, in her judgment, she was going as fast as possible." There are moments, when any creature that lives, has power to drive one into madness. I seemed to know the absurdity of this reply; but that was of no consequence. It added to the measure of my distraction. A little after seven I intreated a friend to go for Mr. Carlisle, and bring him instantly wherever he was to be found. He had voluntarily called on the patient on the preceding Saturday, and two or three times since. He had seen her that morning, and had been earnest in recommending the wine-diet. That day he dined four miles out of town, on the side of the metropolis, which was furthest from us. Notwithstanding this, my friend returned with him after three-quarters of an hour's absence. No one who knows my friend, will wonder either at his earnestness or success, when I name

Mr. Basil Montagu.[5] The sight of Mr. Carlisle thus unexpectedly, gave me a stronger alleviating sensation, than I thought it
possible to experience.

Mr. Carlisle left us no more from Wednesday evening, to the
hour of her death. It was impossible to exceed his kindness and
affectionate attention. It excited in every spectator a sentiment
like adoration. His conduct was uniformly tender and anxious,
ever upon the watch, observing every symptom, and eager to
improve every favourable appearance. If skill or attention could
have saved her, Mary would still live. In addition to Mr. Carlisle's
constant presence, she had Dr. Fordyce and Dr. Clarke every
day. She had for nurses, or rather for friends, watching every
occasion to serve her, Mrs. Fenwick, author of an excellent novel,
entitled Secrecy, another very kind and judicious lady, and a
favourite female servant.[6] I was scarcely ever out of the room.
Four friends, Mr. Fenwick, Mr. Basil Montagu, Mr. Marshal,[7]
and Mr. Dyson, sat up nearly the whole of the last week of her
existence in the house, to be dispatched, on any errand, to any
part of the metropolis, at a moment's warning.

Mr. Carlisle being in the chamber, I retired to bed for a few
hours on Wednesday night. Towards morning he came into my
room with an account that the patient was surprisingly better. I
went instantly into the chamber. But I now sought to suppress
every idea of hope. The greatest anguish I have any conception
of, consists in that crushing of a new-born hope which I had
already two or three times experienced. If Mary recovered, it
was well, and I should see it time enough. But it was too mighty
a thought to bear being trifled with, and turned out and admitted in this abrupt way.

---

[5] Basil Montagu (1770-1851), barrister, legal author, friend of Godwin.
[6] Eliza Fenwick (1760?-1840?), novelist and children's writer. The "kind and
judicious lady" could be either Maria Reveley, once an admirer of Godwin and
later friend to Wollstonecraft, or Mary Hays (1760-1843), feminist writer and
novelist who remained Wollstonecraft's champion even after her death. Mary was
also the name of Wollstonecraft's favorite servant.
[7] James Marshall, friend of Godwin and amanuensis.

I had reason to rejoice in the firmness of my gloomy thoughts, when, about ten o'clock on Thursday evening, Mr. Carlisle told us to prepare ourselves, for we had reason to expect the fatal event every moment. To my thinking, she did not appear to be in that state of total exhaustion, which I supposed to precede death; but it is probably that death does not always take place by that gradual process I had pictured to myself; a sudden pang may accelerate his arrival. She did not die on Thursday night.

Till now it does not appear that she had any serious thoughts of dying; but on Friday and Saturday, the two last days of her life, she occasionally spoke as if she expected it. This was however only at intervals; the thought did not seem to dwell upon her mind. Mr. Carlisle rejoiced in this. He observed, and there is great force in the suggestion, that there is no more pitiable object, than a sick man, that knows he is dying. The thought must be expected to destroy his courage, to cooperate with the disease, and to counteract every favourable effort of nature.

On these two days her faculties were in too decayed a state, to be able to follow any train of ideas with force or any accuracy of connection. Her religion, as I have already shown, was not calculated to be the torment of a sick bed; and, in fact, during her whole illness, not one word of a religious cast fell from her lips.

She was affectionate and compliant to the last. I observed on Friday and Saturday nights, that, whenever her attendants recommended to her to sleep, she discovered her willingness to yield, by breathing, perhaps for the space of a minute, in the manner of a person that sleeps, though the effort, from the state of her disorder, usually proved ineffectual.

She was not tormented by useless contradiction. One night the servant, from an error in judgment, teazed her with idle expostulations, but she complained of it grievously, and it was corrected. 'Pray, pray, do not let her reason with me," was her expression. Death itself is scarcely so dreadful to the enfeebled frame, as the monotonous importunity of nurses everlastingly repeated.

Seeing that every hope was extinct, I was very desirous of

obtaining from her any directions, that she might wish to have followed after her decease. Accordingly, on Saturday morning, I talked to her for a good while of the two children. In comformity to Mr. Carlisle's maxim of not impressing the idea of death, I was obliged to manage my expressions. I therefore affected to proceed wholly upon the ground of her having been very ill, and that it would be some time before she could expect to be well; wishing her to tell me any thing she would choose to have done respecting the children, as they would now be principally under my care. After having repeated this idea to her in a great variety of forms, she at length said, with a significant tone of voice, "I know what you are thinking of," but added, that she had nothing to communicate to me upon the subject.

The shivering fits had ceased entirely for the two last days. Mr. Carlisle observed that her continuance was almost miraculous, and he was on the watch for favourable appearances, believing it highly improper to give up all hope, and remarking, that perhaps one in a million, of persons in her state might possibly recover. I conceive that not one in a million, unites so good a constitution of body and mind.

These were the amusements of persons in the gulph of despair. At six o'clock on Sunday morning, September the tenth, Mr. Carlisle called me from my bed to which I had retired at one, in conformity to my request, that I might not be left to receive all at once the intelligence that she was no more. She expired at twenty minutes before eight.

WOLLSTONECRAFT'S DEATH:
THE REALITIES OF CHILDBIRTH IN THE EIGHTEENTH CENTURY

The question that haunts this chapter (and that Godwin rather poignantly never directly asks) is whether Wollstonecraft's death was avoidable. The question becomes all the more significant given Wollstonecraft's status after her death and after the publication of *The Memoirs* themselves. Almost immediately after its publication and the revelation of many of the private details of her life, she became an object of scandal, and in the eyes of her detractors, her death a fitting conclusion for a radical figure who had "wrongfully" sought to escape her gendered fate. Richard Polwhele—in the extensive annotations that accompany "The Unsexed Female," a satiric poem based on his reading of *The Memoirs*—sees nothing less than the "Hand of Providence" in a death resulting from complications from childbirth:

> I cannot but think, that the Hand of Providence is visible, in her life, her death, and in the Memoirs themselves. As she was given up to her 'hearts lusts,' and let to follow her own imaginations, that the fallacy of her doctrines and the effects of an irreligious conduct, might be manifested to the world; and as she died a death that strongly marked the distinction of the sexes, by pointing out the destiny of women, and the diseases to which they are liable. (167)

In more recent criticism, it is the *injustice* of her death that has made it so meaningful, and as Wollstonecraft has assumed her status as a prominent feminist foremother, the loss for many feminist critics has felt almost personal (Jacobus 78). Its profound irony, however, has continued to trouble discussions of her work. As Vivien Jones writes, "This particularly gendered death seems to defy so cruelly some of the most fundamental tenets of Wollstonecraft's feminism. In one of its most influential...manifestations, Wollstonecraft's humanist rationalism seeks to downplay sexual difference and to minimize the significant power of the body" (187). Wollstonecraft's death at 38 and as a result of complications from childbirth seems all the more tragic for seemingly re-enforcing a "power of the body" that she had sought to minimize in her writings.

Was then her death avoidable? Did childbirth bring with it necessary dangers? Not as much as one would expect, according to Vivien Jones. "Contrary to what has often been assumed, maternal death in the 1790s, especially in the case of home deliveries, was a comparatively rare event.... During the 1790s there were between sixteen and twenty maternal deaths per thousand births in lying-in hospitals. But, for home deliveries, the numbers are estimated at between three and six per thousand" (190). Although this number is certainly far greater than current statistics, it was considerably less than mortality rates in the late seventeenth century, when deaths were "150-160 per 10,000 births in the provinces and 210 in London" (Jones 190). So, neither Wollstonecraft's optimism (assuming she would be "coming down to dinner on the day immediately following") nor Godwin's determination to maintain his work schedule appears ill-founded or insensitive. Given Wollstonecraft's earlier successful and relatively easy labor, they had every reason to assume the best.

Was then the care Wollstonecraft received in any way deficient for its time? No, although her choice of female midwife had become somewhat exceptional by the late eighteenth century. "By the 1790s, it had become the norm for urban, middle-class women to employ a man-midwife, rather than a woman, from the onset of labour" (Jones 193). The reasons for this shift were many, including changes in technology (the use of forceps rather than hooks and crochets, for example), advertising, and availability of training. In each of these developing areas, women were either denied access or were at a clear disadvantage, and having a man midwife soon became a "social status symbol." So, in choosing a female midwife, Wollstonecraft was defying a cultural trend and remaining consistent with her own feminist principles, but she was not going against current best practices in childbirth. "By the 1790s, enlightened practice—whether by men or women—meant, essentially, nonintervention unless complications arose" (Jones 195). Mrs. Blenkensop, by all reports a competent midwife, appears to have followed this practice, until conditions required that she call in a surgeon, in this case her superior at Westminster New Lying-In Hospital, Dr. Louis Poignard. "In waiting—no doubt with Wollstonecraft's encouragement—to see whether the placenta would deliver spontaneously," writes Jones, "Mrs. Blenkensop was absolutely in line with the most up-to-date opinion.... In sending for help when it became apparent that intervention was necessary (probably because Wollstonecraft had started to bleed), she acted absolutely correctly within the gendered hierarchy of the best 1790s obstetric practice" (201).

Sadly, although midwives were not known for their cleanliness, it was this intervention that was most likely the source of her puerperal fever and her ultimate death. Yet still her care only followed current best practices. At this point, manual extraction of the placenta would have been the typical procedure, and if this failed to result in the smooth removal of the placenta, infection was almost certainly the result. Janet Todd describes it thus: " Obstetric practice had improved in the eighteenth century but, with no theory of germs, Poignard cannot have been aware of the huge danger and damage of [the placenta] breaking, especially when, as now, he repeatedly put in his hand" (451). The sad truth was that once the placenta did not spontaneously expel, there was little during this period that could safely be done. "Modern practice speeds up the expulsion of the placenta by administering the drug oxytocin at the moment of birth, and deals surgically with retained placentas" (Jones 200). Without these modern practices, Wollstonecraft's death, Vivien Jones concludes, was "unavoidable" (204). The pieces of placenta left in her womb began to decay, and the infection destroyed Wollstonecraft's internal organs.

Wollstonecraft's death was clearly horrific, even in Godwin's more sanitized version—and one can understand why her second daughter Mary Wollstonecraft Godwin Shelley would have been led to explore the horrors of creation in her own first novel *Frankenstein*—yet it was not a death for which one can assign blame or assume guilt.

SOURCES

Jacobus, Mary. "In Love with a Cold Climate: Travelling with Wollstonecraft." *First Things: The Maternal Imaginary in Literature, Art, and Psychoanalysis.* New York: Routledge, 1995.

Jones, Vivien. "The death of Mary Wollstoncraft." *The British Journal for Eighteenth-Century Studies.* 20:187-205.

Polwhele, Richard. "Unsex'd Females." In *Lives of the Great Poets III: Godwin, Wollstonecraft & Mary Shelley by their Contemporaries.* Vol. 2. Edited by Harriet Jump. London: Pickering & Chatto, 1999.

Todd, Janet. *Mary Wollstonecraft: A Revolutionary Life.* New York: Columbia University Press, 2000.

Her remains were deposited, on the fifteenth of September, at ten o'clock in the morning, in the church-yard of the parish church of St. Pancras, Middlesex.[8] A few of the persons she most esteemed, attended the ceremony;[9] and a plain monument is now erecting on the spot,[10] by some of her friends, with the following inscription:

MARY WOLLSTONECRAFT GODWIN
AUTHOR OF
A VINDICATION
OF THE RIGHTS OF WOMAN
BORN, XXVII APRIL MDCCLIX.
DIED, X SEPTEMBER MDCCXCVII.

The loss of the world in this admirable woman, I leave to

---

[8] Pancras was the same village (one mile north of London) in which Godwin and Wollstonecraft were married.

[9] Godwin did not attend; he was too upset.

[10] This graveyard no longer exists; in the nineteenth century it was removed to allow for a railway.

other men to collect; my own I well know, nor can it be improper to describe it. I do not here allude to the personal pleasures I enjoyed in her conversation: these increased every day, in proportion as we knew each other better, and as our mutual confidence increased. They can be measured only by the treasures of her mind, and the virtues of her heart. But this is a subject for meditation, not for words. What I purposed alluding to, was the improvement that I have for ever lost.

We had cultivated our powers (if I may venture to use this sort of language) in different directions; I chiefly an attempt at logical and metaphysical distinction, she a taste for the picturesque. One of the leading passions of my mind has been an anxious desire not to be deceived. This has led me to view the topics of my reflection on all sides; and to examine and re-examine without end, the questions that interest me.

But it was not merely (to judge at least from all the reports of my memory in this respect) the difference of propensities, that made the difference in our intellectual habits. I have been stimulated, as long as I can remember, by an ambition for intellectual distinction; but, as long as I can remember, I have been discouraged, when I have endeavoured to cast the sum of my intellectual value, by finding that I did not possess, in the degree of some other men, an intuitive perception of intellectual beauty. I have perhaps a strong and lively sense of the pleasures of the imagination; but I have seldom been right in assigning to them their proportionate value, but by dint of persevering examination, and the change and correction of my first opinions.

What I wanted in this respect, Mary possessed, in a degree superior to any other person I ever knew. The strength of her mind lay in intuition. She was often right, by this means only, in matters of mere speculation. Her religion, her philosophy, (in both of which the errors were comparatively few, and the strain dignified and generous) were, as I have already said, the pure result of feeling and taste. She adopted one opinion, and rejected another, spontaneously, by a sort of tact, and the force of a cultivated imagination; and yet, though perhaps, in the strict sense of the term, she reasoned little, it is surprising what a degree of soundness is to be found in her determinations. But, if this quality was of use to her in topics that seem the proper province of reasoning, it was much more so in matters directly appealing to the intellectual taste. In a robust and unwavering judgment of this sort, there is a kind of witchcraft; when it decides justly, it produces a responsive vibration in every ingenuous mind. In this sense, my oscillation and skepticism were fixed by her boldness. When a true opinion emanated in this way from another mind, the conviction produced in my own assumed a similar character, instantaneous and firm. This species of intellect probably differs from the other, chiefly in the relation of earlier and later. What the one perceived instantaneously (circumstances having produced in it, either a premature attention to objects of this sort, or a greater boldness of decision) the other receives only by degrees. What it wants, seems to be nothing more than a minute attention to first impressions, and a just appreciation of them; habits that are never so effectually generated, as by the daily recurrence of a striking example.

This light was sent to me for a very short period, and is now extinguished for ever!

While I have described the improvement I was in the act of receiving, I believe I have put down the leading traits of her intellectual character.

THE END.

APPENDIX

Gilbert Imlay
From *The Emigrants* (1793)

[*The Emigrants, or the History of an Expatriated Family* follows the fate of one English family as it seeks a new beginning (having suffered financial ruin in London) in the "back settlements" of America. Capt. Arl——ton, having been alerted to their plight by a family friend, Mr. Il——ray, joins them on their journey. He and Caroline T——N, the youngest daughter of the English family, fall in love and ultimately marry, after he rescues her from abduction by Indians. Caroline's oldest sister, Eliza, marries a wealthy merchant, Mr. F———, a fellow passenger on the ship to America, and returns with him to England. The rest of Eliza's tragic story emerges in the following letters. George, the only son in the family, returns to England, after proving too "unmanly" for the rigors of America, but in the following letters, we learn that he repents his former indolence and extravagance, and plans a return to America. On their journey west, the English family also encounter a wealthy uncle, long-thought dead (P. P——, Esq.) and it is through his financial benevolence—his own wife, Juliana, and his children having been killed by Indians—that they are ultimately established in America.]

LETTER LXIX.

Mr. Il——ray, to Capt. Arl——ton
London, April.

MY DEAR JAMES,

SUCH have been the advantages of liberty in this country, while all the rest of the world, for I will leave America out of the question, has been fettered and groaning under the most diabolical tyranny, that the extent and variety of its commerce, has tended to produce an increase of wealth, that is truly wonderful.

Every species of luxury has followed, and in the sumptuous banquets of the times, the flow of sentiment and the zest of reason, have been succeeded by sallies of false wit, and the harmonious sounds of soft music. Effeminacy has triumphed, and while the sofa has been the pleasurable seat of the lover, the toilet[1] has been the place where his manliness was displayed.

Nature has its bounds, and vigour is the concomitant of temperance, and exercise, and the charms of fine women can only be relished by men who have not been enervated by luxury and debauchery; and thus it has happened in every populous and wealthy city in the world, that the most lovely women have been neglected by men, whose impotence was as disgusting, as their caprices were unbounded.

The novelty to me, exhibited every day upon the great *theatre* of the *world*, was at first matter of surprise and astonishment: for although I had not been inattentive to the opinions of authors and travellers, still I had only an idea in theory of what was called fashionable life; and nothing short of mingling with the world, ever could have given me an adequate idea of its depravity.

The system of governments by securing their own aggrandizement have extended a spirit of venality through every fibre of their organization, while the sinews of their constituent pow-

---

[1] Can refer to either the dressing table, or the articles upon a dressing table. Here, it can mean one's general appearance.

ers, have lost their vigour and elasticity; so that the means of supporting splendour in private life, has become to the generality of the citizens of the great world, of more importance than the reputation for virtue and integrity.

The prostitution of principle has not been limited to political sentiments; but it has extended to the most tender and sacred of all the ties of a gentleman.

It has poisoned the source of delicacy and sentiment, and sapped every principle of honour, at the very moment it was offering an indignity to human nature, too gross and flagrant, not to disgrace the most contemptible reptile, that ever crawled upon the earth.

The embraces of elegant women have been bartered for, and places of *trust* and emolument, have been heaped upon wretches, who have merited the distinction of *singers*.[2]

Yes! my dear Arl——ton my indignation has been roused at a circumstance, that must chill every drop of blood in your veins when I have related it, and I am afraid will harrow up the very soul of Caroline. But while tenderness would silence me, I am actuated by considerations of humanity.

The delicate manner in which Mrs. F—— communicated to Caroline, from time to time, as you informed me, her reflections upon the turn of mind and disposition of Mr. F——, reflects the highest honour upon her prudence and discretion; but it can afford you no idea of her misery.

F——'s neglect has not been the only cause of her chagrin; for she has for a length of time, visibly seen, that he was precipitating his own ruin while she had not the power to retard it.

The habits of his life had compleatly disqualified him for domestic pleasures, and while his vanity was gratified in the *eclat*[3] of Mrs. F——'s beauty and accomplishments, he was in-

---

[2] Female performers were associated with prostitution. Typically, however, it was actresses rather than singers who were singled out as playing this role; Imlay himself—sometime after the publication of this novel but while still involved with Wollstonecraft—has an affair with an actress.

[3] "Lustre" of reputation; social distinction; celebrity, renown (*OED*).

dulging himself in every extravagance, until his finances became so deranged, that his credit at the gaming clubs, he frequented, was doubted. However he still flattered himself, that he had a resource in the charms of Mrs. F——, equal to redeem his ruined fortune, and give him permanent respectability; and as he had no belief there could be any dishonour in the proposal he meant to make, particularly as he had the example of many honourable gentlemen, he did not hesitate in consequence of an overture made him, by a nobleman in power, (who had only to charge cash expended in that way to secret service,) to propose to Mrs. F—— the prostitution of her person.

You have only to know my friend, that the mind of Caroline is the exact prototype of Mrs. F——'s, to be able to judge of the horror and indignation with which she received a proposition so ignominious.

Let me beseech you, James, to use your influence with Caroline, and Mr. P——, to endeavour to prevail upon Mrs. F—— to join them, as I am afraid, it is the only chance she has, of ever becoming happy: for independent of the mortal wound F—— has given to her regard for him, she pines from being separated from her sister.

I have given my sentiments upon the subject to Sir Thomas Mor—ly, who is a worthy and intelligible man, and an ornament to human nature; but he says "it is impossible for Mrs. F——, to be separated from the bed of her husband, without bringing an action in Doctors Commons,[4] and as she has not the power of substantiating any charge against him, it would be highly inconsiderate, to attempt to sue for a separate maintenance."[5]

I replied, that was not the object, for neither would the

---

[4] Area south of St. Paul's Cathedral where the buildings associated with the College of Doctors of Civil Law are located. The largest canon law court, responsible for handing the majority of marriage cases in the late eighteenth century, was located in this area.

[5] Support given by a husband to a wife when they are separated (*OED*). See Chapter XVII, note #2 in *Wrongs of Woman*.

disposition of Caroline, or Mr. P——, ever permit her to want, while they were abundantly rich; and indeed, he must recollect, that Mr. P—— meant to settle part of his estate upon the heirs of Mrs. F——; and though it was not very likely, she would ever have any by Mr. F——, still it was reasonable to believe, as Mr. P——was a rational and considerate man, that he would give Mrs. F——, so much of his property, as he intended to settle upon her children during her life, subject to reversion.[6] But if Mrs. F—— could be completely separated, she would then be at liberty to marry again; and certainly it was a cruel circumstance, that the pleasures of her life must be sacrificed, because she had been imposed upon by a man, who most likely the habits of life had rendered impotent;[7] particularly, as, after the flagrant indignity he had offered to her sentiments and honour, it would be impossible for her ever to be connected with him again.

Sir Thomas acknowledged that it was a cruel situation for Mrs. F—— to be in, but said it was impossible to alter the laws respecting matrimony without the utmost danger to the good order of society; and as they now existed, Mrs. F—— could not be intitled to a bill of divorce, without she could either prove Mr. F——'s impotence or infidelity.[8]

"Great God!" said I, "Sir Thomas, how can you or law-makers believe, that a modest woman would ever attempt to prove the debility of her husband? or I should be glad to know how it is possible—for absolute impotence and debilitation are too distinct things, but equally mortifying to women of sensibility; and certainly nothing can be more farcical than to attempt to prove the incontinency of any man in such a place as London, provided he wishes to avoid detection." Sir Thomas made no reply, but shook his head.

---

[6] The return of an estate to the donor or grantor, or his heirs, after the expiry of the grant (*OED*).

[7] In contrast to Maria in *The Wrongs of Woman*, Mrs. F—— does have grounds for divorce, impotence along with incest, bigamy and physical abuse being the only legal basis for such action. See Chapter XVII, note #1 in *Wrongs of Woman*.

[8] Infidelity on the husband's part did not provide legal grounds for divorce.

Such are the laws and influence of customs in a country celebrated for wisdom and virtue, that from the almost impossibility of married persons being repudiated, the practices of gallantry have totally destroyed conjugal love, and the evils government intended to have prevented, have been extended to a most lamentable pitch of licentiousness.

I have a pleasure in my friend, in informing you, in consequence of the request of that good man Mr. P——, George[9] has been liberated from his confinement, and appears perfectly sensible of the absurdities which have marked the conduct of his life, and so often disgraced his character and subjected him to misery and contempt: and I have no doubt, from the signs of compunction which he discovers, that his repentance will be lasting and sincere.

It has been said by a patriot in the British senate that, "there is a degree of wickedness which no reproof or argument can reclaim, as there is a degree of stupidity which no instruction can enlighten!" But you must recollect, this was applied to the most incorrigible and corrupt minister that ever disgraced the government of England.[10] For certainly if a man is not stupidly wicked after he has suffered every disgrace and hardship, which his follies merited, he must endeavour to regain the confidence and esteem of men by a generous acknowledgement of his former errors, and a noble ambition to acquire applause.

Sir Thomas Mor——ly desires I will express to Mr. P——, Caroline, and your self, how very much he is interested in your happiness, and that he will write to Mr. P— —as early as he can adjust the business he has done him the honour to instruct to his care.

Inclosed you have a letter from Mrs. F—— to Caroline.

Farewell,

G. Il——ray.

---

[9] The name of Wollstonecraft's youngest brother; he settles in and ultimately prospers in the United States.

[10] Unidentified.

LETTER LXIX.[11]

Mrs. F——, to Caroline.

London, April.

I Do not know, my dear Caroline, how to address you, as you only informed me of your perfect happiness, without saying by what date your expected union with Capt. Arl——ton would take place; and it is only from the information I received from Mr. Il——ray, that has convinced me it must have happened some time since; for I cannot draw a syllable from Mary upon the subject.

O Caroline! how did I tremble when Mr. Il——ray related to me the particular and horrid circumstances of your captivity with the savages, and the more wicked one of the note? but the transition of my feelings cannot be described as he proceeded in the narrative of your fortunate escape from barbarian slavery, and eternal melancholy and sorrow, which must have proved to a heart like yours, more gloomy than tedious winter in the arctic regions to the distressed and benighted ship-wrecked crew, who, when surrounded by chaotic frost, often languish unheard, and perish unknown to the world, and to their friends; and the tale of whose sufferings are buried with themselves, while the fond maid has beheld a blank in the creation, and the star that cheered her young imagination, and pointed to the haven of her wishes, has sat, never to rise again.

I have experienced from your affectionate recollection of my situation at a moment so important to yourself, the most un-bounded happiness that the feelings of sisterly love can pro-duce;—and it has been no small consolation to me to hear from Mr. Il——ray a relation of things in which you are concerned.

I have not the power to express to you the horror and dis-gust I have experienced at the late conduct of Mr. F——; and as I have found in Mr. Il——ray that warm benevolence, and deli-

---

[11] As it is enclosed within the previous one, this letter has the same number.

cate sense of dignity and honour which is characteristic of a man of principle, I have not hesitated to communicate to him the circumstances, as I found my existence, as a *woman*, depended upon my finding a refuge against brutality, and I knew not where else to seek for it.

He has written to Capt. Arl———-ton upon the subject in order that he may advise with you and our friendly guardian and uncle, whose sentiments and generosity can never be sufficiently admired, in what way it is possible for me to become extricated from a situation the most miserable into which a woman of any feeling can be placed:—and I hope, my dear sister, that you will inform me, as early as possible, of the result of the conference; for I assure you that my situation is too painful to be endured; for while I have been constrained to leave the bed of a man who appears to me in the light of a monster, I am continually receiving insults as gross as they are unmanly.

Express to my dear uncle the exalted sense I entertain of his worth, and promise him that my gratitude for his generous treatment of our family, and particularly his conduct towards George, will be as lasting as it is warm.

Mr. Il———ray has this moment acquainted me with his having written to Capt. Arl———ton respecting our brother—I hope, Caroline, he will continue to conduct himself as he has begun since his emancipation—for I am happy to inform you that he appears quite an altered man. Farewell.

I am your affectionate, but unhappy Sister,

Eliza.[12]—-

---

[12] The name of Wollstonecraft's younger sister; shortly after the birth of her daughter and while recovering from post partum depression, she flees—with the help of Wollstonecraft—her husband.

Letter LXX.

Mrs. Arl——ton, to Mrs. F——.

Bellefont, June.

I Had scarcely hurried over your last favour, when I flew with the greatest avidity to my dear Arl——ton to know the particulars of Mr. F——'s behaviour to you, and was petrified with the shocking and degrading injustice offered to your honour.

Not a moment was lost in summonsing our best friend, to know what could be done in order to rescue you from insult and wretchedness—never did he appear to greater advantage—his whole faculties for a moment seemed to have lost their energy: but the next instant, they burst forth into a blaze of manly eloquence, which defied all resistance.

"What, said he, "shall an unfeeling wretch, whose excesses in the school of corruption, where the prostitution of principle and the feelings loose their elegant elasticity, and which have destroyed in him, every *manly* sentiment, be suffered, after having offered the most atrocious insult that can be used to a delicate woman, be permitted to continue to treat her with the most aggravating contumely and petulance? shall it be said in a civilized world, beauty and virtue have received every indignity which the most depraved can imagine, and the most callous and abandoned can inflict, and that they cannot find a friend sufficiently rational, and with spirit enough, to protect them against a tyranny more odious than ever was practised by the most contemptible despot that ever tyrannized over a nation? and will it ever be believed by posterity, that in a country renowned for gallantry and honour, and which has given the most glorious proofs of its attachment to freedom, and who have set an example to all the world, of the advantages which its struggles produce, that they should have been insensible spectators of the most inhuman and nefarious oppression that ever disgraced the annals of humanity? Ah! Caroline, I blush for the degeneracy of my countrymen, and while I am confounded at the thoughts of the lowest pitch of infamy to

which a being, *for he cannot be a man*, can descend, I weep for
the sufferings of the unfortunate fair, who have not friends to
chastise the *cowards* who thus insult them with impunity.

Here he paused, and as he held me by one hand, and Arl—
—ton with his other, "My children! my life!" said he, "has been
a series of perils and misfortunes; I have learned in its vicissitudes, how to appriciate its blessings, and I know how to sympathize with the afflicted; but I should deem myself unworthy
of being called a man, was my benevolence confined to the effusions of my sensibility; my age and infirmities prevent me from
being active, and you my children, have become so dear to me,
that if any accident should happen to you in my absence, I never
could again resume my spirits; but if you will accompany me, I
will return immediately to England, and relieve my dear and
virtuous niece from all future uneasiness, and we will bring her
with us to this country, where love and joy shall compensate for
past sufferings; and for the loss of the meretricious and unsubstantial pleasures of a court. It will be but a summer's excursion,
and our felicity will then remain unruffled, for all our friends
will be concentered.

Arl——ton and myself stood for some moments so charmed
with the energy of his heroick mind, that we could make no
reply until he asked our approbation of his intention.

"It was with the most painful anxiety that I read my friend's
letter," replied Arl——ton, which confirmed Caroline's suspi-
cions of Mrs. F——'s wretchedness, but it remained for me to
understand a conduct so unnatural as that of Mr. F——'s to
experience the full force of that disgust, which a treatment, to
me, so unprecedented and depraved, could not fail to effect; and
if you will permit me, I will assure you, that the interest I have
taken in the relief of a person whom I consider as a sister, can
only be exceeded by your generosity and benevolence, and the
merits of a being so amiable and lovely as a woman, whose mind,
my friend informs me, is the exact image of the heart of the most
charming and delightful of her sex:—But it wanted not this
information to have given me the most lively concern for the

welfare and happiness of a friend and sister, whom Caroline tenderly loves. However, with every deference to your judgment, I
beg leave to submit my opinion to your consideration, respecting the propriety of your undertaking a journey of such extent at
your time of life; when it is necessary to take all possible repose,
in order to prolong that existence, which is invaluable to your
friends, who have barely had time sufficient, in their short knowledge of your talents and virtues, to know your loss would be
irreparable: And therefore I beg leave to recommend, that Mrs.
F—— may be immediately written to, and requested to put
herself under the protection of our friend Il——ray, who I know
to be a man of the strictest honour, and as bountiful as he is
friendly."

Arl——ton was going to proceed when our dear uncle
stopped him by saying:—"My dear friend, I beg your pardon,
and Mr. Il——ray's, for not recollecting at the moment I was
making my proposition, that our friend was in England:—but
as I have the highest reverence and esteem for him, so I have the
fullest reliance upon his kindness, and do most readily consent
to the adoption of your opinion."

So it has happened, my dear Eliza, that circumstances, the
most strange and inhuman, have conspired to produce us a most
certain prospect of still living together.

It is this certainty alone, that could give relief to the grief I
experienced from the knowledge of the shocking treatment you
received from Mr. F——; and I hope you will find a full recompense in our love, and in the innocent charms of this wild country, for the losses you must sustain in leaving the European world.

***

To a mind formed like yours, replete with sentiment, it is
impossible for it not to experience in this way of living, every
degree of felicity it could wish.

And as it is one of the most singular pleasures of my life, to
have it in my power to accompany my wishes with assurances,
that your happiness must be compleat, when you shall have
joined us. We all shall embrace you with one heart, and will

love you with one soul; and you will be protected by the same generous hand from insult, and that tyranny which the caprices of men in the European hemisphere inflict upon unprotected women.

God bless you my dear and fond Eliza. Put yourself under the protection of Mr. Il——ray, and fly immediately from bondage to a land of freedom and love; and here in the bosom of peaceful affection, let the effusions of our hearts drown in oblivion the recollection of former distresses. Fly upon the pinions of the wind, for your uncle and Arl——ton, will be made as happy as myself to receive you; and that the gales which ruffle the ocean that now separates us, may prove propitious to your passage, and waft you safe to its western shores, shall be the constant prayers of,

Your affectionate
Caroline.

LETTER LXX.

P. P——. Esq. To Sir Tho. Mor——ly, Bart.
Bellefont, June.

MY DEAR SIR,

THE last communications from our friends in London, have given me no little uneasiness, as they have afforded me another proof of the many miseries resulting from the crude policy of the European world.

It is not a time for me to enter into a dissertation of those evils, nor could my troubling you upon the subject, be relevant to removing them.

That you are sensible they exist, and that you have given generous and manly proofs of your abhorence at the cause, I have been well informed. But you must permit me to say, I am apprehensive, that like every other thing, by our growing familiarized with them, they in some degree lose their influence; so it has happened I presume with your opinions upon the important consideration of protecting innocence against the inhuman, I will not disguise my sentiments upon the business to which I allude.

The conduct of Mr. F—— to my niece, has not only been dishonourable and tyrannic, but it has been brutal; for which reason I have desired that she may be requested to leave him without ceremony, and accompany Mr. Il——ray to this country, provided it is agreeable to her; and if not, I desire that you will give her a suitable establishment[13] on my account.

Give me leave to assure you, that I am with every sentiment of regard,

Your sincere Friend,
P. P——.

LETTER LXXI.

Sir T. Mor——ley, Bart. to P. P——, Esq.
London, Sept.

MY DEAR SIR,

***

I have not been an insensible spectator of the sufferings of your amiable niece Mrs. F——. But to the habits of a desolate life, her late unfortunate husband, added that aspiring folly, which vainly hopes to mount to the summit of glory by the slippery ladder of princely allurements.—-

He seems to have commenced his life with error, to have continued it with shame, and to have ended it with infamy.

His attempt to sully the chastity of a virtuous woman, which is too shocking to reflect upon, and to add ignominy to sacrilege, having proved abortive, and consequent poverty having brought upon him the contempt of his associates in vice, he came to a resolution to die as cowardly as he had lived; and by

---

[13] Refers not only to a place to live, but a guaranteed income as well.

putting a loaded pistol to his head, he fell a victim to those enervating passions, which first lead to the practice of folly, and then prevent the exercise of that bravery necessary to combat the frowns of adversity; and by a feeble effort of unmanly resolution he had the presumption to aim at the reputation of dying like a hero, when he had not spirit to live like a man.

Such, my friend, is the depravity of the manners of which you so justly complain; that men who are ambitious to live with splendour exceed their income, and when they find their fortunes ruined, and themselves neglected, which is always the case, they have recourse to the dastardly practice of putting an end to their own existence.

Poor Mrs. F—— was so shocked with a series of absurdities and the atrocious actions of Mr. F——, and particularly at this last, which happened a short time before your letters came to hand, that she determined to leave England without delay and join your society in the western world, where I hope you will have the wisdom to appropriate useful truths, and thereby interdict the inconveniences which the state of Europe experience from evils, that have accumulated under the immaturity of our establishments.

Mr. Il——ray, who added to the warmest benevolence has an acute understanding, and almost, infallible penetration and judgement, has taken under his care, agreeable to your wish, both Mrs. F—— and your Nephew, who I hope will continue as he has begun, to merit the approbation of his friends.

***

The laws of matrimony, which Mr. Il——ray reprobates, as they subject women to hardships, certainly are defective; and it is a cruel consideration, that when a woman of feeling has been imposed upon and insulted, and has taken refuge in the tender solicitude of some friend or lover, and in consequence shall be subject to lose the very fortune she may have carried her husband: and it is also unfeeling and indelicate in us to suffer them in the eye of the laws of this country, to be considered in the light of property, and not as beings to whom we owe every thing, and to whom we are indebted for every felicity worth enjoy-ing.—[14]

But it is at the same time certain, if our laws, in some re-spects regarding this subject, have the complexion of barbarism and brutality, that no women in Europe enjoy so many privi-leges, or have so much consequence in the common affairs of life.

The practice of married persons being repudiated for every trifling disagreement, would be productive of endless distrac-tions in families; and which I apprehend would prove more dan-gerous to the harmony of society than the anarchy of political sentiments.

I am aware that the complication of laws at the advanced age of states will be productive of many inconveniences, and per-haps it is one of the taxes necessarily imposed by the refinement of manners. For in the infancy of every state particular codes and institutions, sometimes of a local nature, must take place, and which doubtless, in many instances, will be destitute of wisdom.

It is from the accumulation of laws and multifarious distinc-tions that distract the opinions of men, and produce that obscu-rity of ideas upon the subject of jurisprudence which tends to bewilder the understanding of the most learned; and thus it has happened in common affairs, the perplexity of laws, and the expences attending the administration of justice, which both custom and the practice of our courts have rendered necessary, that peaceable and industrious citizens have continually been the prey of licentious villain and wealthy miser, whose unpro-tected innocence has been sacrificed to avarice, impotence, and contumely.

The laws of England which are specifically good and whole-some, have multiplied to an enormity that is truly astonishing; and it is to the contradiction of the Judges that we are indebted

[14] See text box "The Feme-Covert: Marriage Laws in Eighteenth-Century En-gland" in *Wrongs of Woman*, p. 144.

for that disgraceful proverb the "glorious uncertainty of the law," which is spoken of with as much indifference as though there was no evil annexed to it:—and therefore it has happened that while the form of our government has existed the administration of justice has not only been tardy;—but it has been so heavily taxed that the great bulk of the nation has found security only from the spirit of its citizens;—while partial and cruel violations of our privileges have raised a general clamour against the excellence of our boasted constitution, which is likely to shape it to its very foundation.

***

I beg leave to assure you and your adopted children, and my valuable friend Mr. Il——ray, of the utmost solicitude for their happiness, and to subscribe myself,

Your sincere and faithful friend,
T. Mor——ley.

Letter LXII.

P. P——, Esq. to Sir Thomas Mor——ly Bart.
Bellefont, July.

My Dear Sir,

Mr. Il——ray having made a short delay in Philadelphia in order to adjust his business preparatory to his final settlement with us, necessarily procrastinated our felicity of embracing Mrs. F——, and telling her that we sincerely rejoiced to have it in our power, to prove how tenderly we were interested in all the vicissitudes of her happiness.

The delicacy of her frame, I perceive, has been not a little shattered by the shocks that have been given to her sensibility, and while I was contemplating the animation of her face which so peculiarly expresses the sentiments of a heart pregnant with virtue, moulded with feminine softness, and warm with all the social virtues, I felt the keenest indignation at the cause of her

sufferings, and silently reprobated the depredations which unnatural restraint must ever produce.

The change of her situation, and the endearments of her
friends, added to the cheerful and joyous pleasures, that spontaneously present themselves to a mind formed like Mrs. F——
's, could not fail to perfect her prospect of happiness, so far as
depended upon herself and relations; and which has been
compleated by the mutual sympathy, inspired for each other, by
her and Mr. Il——ray, and I am happy to inform you, that their
union will be solemnized as early as the rules of decency will
permit.

Suffer me to return you my most sincere thanks for the
trouble you have taken in the various arrangements that my req-
uisition must have given you; and to assure you, that while I am
surrounded by those I love, and feel all the tranquility of mind
after a long and boisterous life, which a situation so delectable,
as being placed in the center of your friends, and cherished by
the cordial interchange of the congeniality of sentiment, must
ever afford to a rational being, I am not forgetful of the friendship you have shewn me, by your attention to my unfortunate
relations, nor insensible of the honour you do me in requesting
a continuance of our correspondence.

The happy effects from changing the situation of my
nephew, is every day marked with some new feature, distinguished by manly form; and they now display the renovated
energy of a man naturally good, but which had been long dormant, and like decrepitude in the arms of beauty that views
the charms of love through the medium of a palsied frame, and
resigns the joys, it has not vigour to attain, was insensible to
the pleasures that are obtained by the virtuous exertions of a
noble emulation.

***

His understanding has not only been regenerated but his
person has already become robust, and he now has more the
appearance of an Ancient Briton,[15] than one of those fine fel-
lows, whose nerves require the assistance of hartshorn,[16] to en-

able them to encounter the perils of a hackney coach,[17] or the fatigues of a masquerade.

***

Thus you will find my friend, though all my tender hopes were blasted, and all my pleasures mutilated, while my anguish was as corroding, as my losses were severe I am now surrounded like a Patriarch of old,[18] and with my eyes fixed upon Heaven, where I expect to join my loved Juliana, and fond offspring, I am contented in administering all the good to which the limits of my capacity can extend—and if it is the rewards of my struggles, I confess I am over paid from the alleviation I feel to the pangs of a heart long since overwhelmed with sorrow.

You shall soon have my opinion upon the progress and advantages of philosophy.

Farewell.

P. P——.

The End.

[15] This reference would ascribe to him a more heroic appearance, one associated with the warrior culture of an "ancient" England.

[16] Salt of hartshorn; smelling salts (*OED*).

[17] A four-wheeled coach, drawn by two horses, and seated for six persons, kept for hire (*OED*).

[18] A scriptural reference to one of the fathers of the Hebrew people; in biblical terms, one of the fathers of humankind.

REVIEWS OF *THE WRONGS OF WOMAN*

The Analytical Review, vol. 27 (1798): 240-245
The Posthumous Works of the Author of a Vindication of the Rights of Woman. In 4 Vols. 8 vo. Abour 800 pa. Prince 14s. in boards. Johnson. 1798.

[This review immediately follows a critique of Godwin's *Memoirs.*]

These posthumous works consist of 'The Wrongs of Woman, or Maria, a fragment,' 'Lessons for Children,' letters, and miscellaneous pieces.

'The Wrongs of Woman' is a novel, in which Mrs. Godwin appears to have designed the vindication of her own sentiments and conduct. Maria, her heroine, is at first married to a very worthless man, who persecutes her in the most cruel manner, and, for the sake of obtaining her fortune, confines her in a madhouse. She there meets with a young man, who was also confined under false pretenses by those who ought to have been his friends, and his generous concern for her, and the sympathy that their condition inspired, fix her affections. They escape from confinement and live together. She is pregnant, and her husband, after persecuting her in every possible way, commences a prosecution against Darnford her lover for adultery, and obtains damages.

It was the design of Mrs. G. that this novel should consist of three parts; one of which only is completed, and part of that has not received the author's finishing touches. It is a very simple and a very probable story, founded upon daily occurrences and existing laws. It was evidently the design of Mrs. G. to represent a woman, injured by her husband, without the dissolution of the marriage, and in defiance of the laws, connecting herself with another man, bearing all the persecution that the laws in this respect authorize, and at last sinking into voluntary death, overcome with the weight of her calamity.

Mrs. G. meant to vindicate this conduct of her heroine, in the exercise of her natural and social rights; and to show, that the laws and customs which render this conduct dangerous, and expose it to suffering, are the foundation of *the wrongs of woman*, the sorrows which she now is heir to.

It makes an essential part of her plan, to assert the propriety of allowing *divorces* to take place, in many cases where they are now allowed to be obtained.

It is not easy to criticize an unfinished work. The *dramatic effect* which might have been produced, had the author finished her design, cannot now be estimated. The fragment abounds with just sentiments, forcefully expressed, and we particularly admire the justness of Jemima's story. Giving all necessary weight to the considerations of the place and condition in which they were, and the sympathy they were likely to inspire, we yet think that Maria is represented as too easily impressed; for there is nothing dignified or touching in the account which Darnford gives of himself.

When Mrs. G. employs the strong language of passion in this fragment, we think she is not always happy in the *construction of her sentences.*

They are full of sentiment and energy, but want simplicity.

(The review here gives four examples of "faulty and harsh construction.")

We heartily lament, that this work was not finished by Mrs. G., for although it might not have 'given a new impulse to the manners of a world,' we have no doubt that it would have been a pyramid on which her name might have been engraven for ages.

(The review here discusses the "Lessons for Children," also included in *The Posthumous Works*.)

We think that the letters are all in the last two volumes, that are greatly worthy of notice. Most of these letters are addressed to him, who is by his conduct to Mrs. G. 'damned to eternal fame;' and we have no scruple in saying, they will be valued as long as the language of the heart is held dear. Let no one speak of Mrs. G. who has not *seen these* letters; they form the true account of her life and character. They show, that whatever were Mrs. G.'s opinions respecting marriage, her love was pure, ardent, individual, and exclusive. We will lay two or three of them before the reader, who, however, we think will give little proof of his sensibility, if he be not induced by these specimens to read the whole.

***

The British Critic, vol. 12 (1798): 234-235
Posthumous Works of the Author of A Vindication of the Rights of Woman. In Four Volumes. 12 mo. 14s. Johnson. 1798.

[This review immediately follows a critique of Godwin's *Memoirs.*]

The preceding article exhibits the memoirs of the very singular personage whose posthumous works we are now to notice. They consist of the Wrongs of Woman, a fragment; to which are added, the first book of a series of Lessons for Children; some Letters, and miscellaneous pieces.

The first of these, the Wrongs of Woman, represents a specimen of that system of morality in which the writer displayed in her own person, but which is alike offensive to the purity of female virtue, and the precepts of our holy religion; and which fortunately the zeal of the scanty number of her proselytes has not hitherto been able to disseminate, nor the varnish of modern philosophy to recommend.

A young woman marries an undeserving husband; his cruelty and ill-treatment drive her from his house. She attaches herself to another, who is in all respects congenial to her; and, as far as the tale is continued, her sufferings are deplorably afflicting. These are the wrongs of women. But what a short-sighted view of things is displayed in the moral, meant to be deduced from this narrative. As if man was to expect, without interruption, the gratification of his wishes; and as if it were not far, very far nobler, and more generous, rigidly to obey the claims of duty, than, like our puny moralist, to whine and complain, because her own frail and fallible views of things are checked by obstacles, and opposed by disappointments. Besides, it will not fail to be observed, that this paltry system puts the hopes and consolations of religion out of the question; and the idea of this being but a probationary state, is never permitted to intervene. It is hardly worth while to oppose argument to such weak and preposterous speculations; their own absurdities will soon sink them beneath the level of popular notice, and the author, if remembered at all, will excite only pity in some, and scorn in others.

The Lessons for Children, subjoined to the end of the second volume, might perhaps have been acceptable to Mr. Newberry, but how they could be deemed worthy of the distinction they have here found, we are at a loss to imagine.

The third volume consists of Letters, many of them of the most impassioned kind, and might well have been denominated the English Eloisa. We must confess that Mr. Imlay appears to have treated his Roxalana with no common coldness. But we suppose him to have been a plain man of business, who had no objection to see the article *wife*, in the invoice of his other goods; but when she began to exclaim so very vehemently about flames and darts, and the other combustible matters in the vocabulary of disappointed passion, he literally took fright, and put from the cup so little suited to the temperature of his constitution, and habits of his life. There are many without doubt of the young, the ardent, and the dissipated, who will peruse these epistles with eagerness and delight; but, in our cold and sober opinions, who are proud and anxious to avow principles diametrically opposite to the editor of these volumes, greater honour would have been done, and more genuine esteem evinced to the memory of the author, by destroying than by publishing them.

The latter part of the fourth volume is that alone which we can read without disgust; and, if we could separate it from the rest, would, but not too warmly, recommend. Some of the remarks on poetry are novel and ingenious, and display much power of thinking, although the strange prejudices which poisoned the mind of the author, do not fail occasionally to show themselves.

Upon the whole, as our opinion of Mrs. Godwin will probably be required, and may have some efficacy, we give it without scruple. She was a woman of strong intellect, and of ungovernable passions. To the latter, when once she had given the rein, she seems to have yielded on all occasions with little scruple, and as little delicacy. She appears, in the strongest sense, a voluptuary and sensualist, but without refinement. We compassionate her errors, and respect her talents; but our compassion is lessened by the mischievous tendency of her doctrines and example; and our respect certainly not extended or improved by her exclaiming against prejudices, of some of the most dangerous of which, she was herself perpetually the victim; by her praises of Virtue, the sanctity of which she habitually violated; and by her pretences to philosophy, whose real mysteries she did not understand, and the dignity of which, in various instances, she sullied and disgraced.

The Anti-Jacobin Review, vol. 1 (1798): 91-93
Maria, or the Wrongs of Woman. By Mary Wollstonecraft Godwin. Being Part of her Posthumous Works. In 4 Vols. small 8 vo. About 800. pp. Price 14s. Johnson. 1798.

To this work there are prefixed too prefaces; one by Godwin, editor of the author's posthumous works—the other by herself.

Maria is in the form of a novel. Its object is to shew the miseries to which women are exposed, owing *to the inferior state which they occupy in society*. It is a tale intended to illustrate the doctrines which Mrs. W. had attempted to establish in her "Rights of Woman." Besides illustration of her own opinions, the principles supported and the practices recommended have a very great coincidence with those inculcated by the philosopher himself, in that part of his "Political Justice" in which he describes the promiscuous intercourse of the sexes, as one of the highest improvements to result from *political justice!* The editor regrets that this work is only a fragment of a plan which "if it had been filled up in a manner adequate to the writer's conception, would perhaps have given a new impulse to the manners of the world."—The *purity* of the lady's *conception of female excellence*, and the usefulness to society of the conduct to the adoption of which she exhorts her sex, our readers may, from the following sketch, be able to comprehend.

(The review here summarizes the events that lead to Maria's confinement in a private madhouse and her friendship with Jemima.)

The pleasure of political discussion is not the only comfort which Maria derives from the kindness of Jemima. There happened to be confined in the same house, in his full senses, a Mr. Darnford, in whom, on seeing him from her window, Maria recognizes a very great favourite. He had been kidnapped also, so that, according to her own story, women are not the only persons placed unjustly in madhouses; and *her argument* concerning the WRONGS OF WOMAN, founded on that species of imprisonment, *is destroyed by herself.* A principle often inculcated by the author, both in Maria's character and her own, is, that there can *exist no duty unless prompted by feeling*; that, therefore, if a woman feel herself disinclined to her husband, the feeling constitutes a dissolution of every obligation to fidelity: and also, that when she feels herself inclined towards another man, she has a *natural* right to follow that inclination; that the prohibition in the present state of society to unrestrained compliance with the dictates of the passions, constitutes one of the greatest WRONGS OF WOMAN. Jemima, attentive to the *rights* of the sex, affords Maria an opportunity of reducing her theories to *practice* by permitting Darnford to spend his nights in her apartment. To assist the reader's imagination, *the virtuous Maria*, whose writings and example were to give so *beneficial an impulse to the manners* of the world, informs us that she was a very *voluptuous* figure, that Darnford was a handsome man, but peculiarly remarkable for *muscular strength*,—Maria, by no means of the same opinion with Square the philosopher, that "things are fitting to be done which are not fitting to be boasted of,: having with her paramour escaped from confinement, openly and boldly manifests her conduct.—The husband prosecutes her gallant for criminal conversation. The lady appears in court herself, and pleads her feelings, not as her apology, but as her justification. This was indeed a conduct, according to Godwin's own heart. It avowed a disregard for the institution of marriage, an institution so strongly reprobated in the new system of political justice; it banished concealment, the only evil, according to the philosopher, that can detract from the political and moral blessings of a promiscuous intercourse of the sexes, guided by the feelings of the parties. On the trial, the judge (England being the scene) retains the old system of morals; and does not admit Maria's plea of her feelings as a vindication of her adultery, however comfortable it may be to the new philosophy. *The restrictions upon adultery* constitute, in Maria's opinion, A MOST FLAGRANT WRONG TO WOMEN. Such is the moral tendency of this work, such are the lessons which may be learned from the writings of Mrs. Wollstonecraft; such the advantages which the public may derive from this performance given to the world by Godwin, celebrated by him, and perfectly consonant to the principles of *his* Political Justice.—But as there have been writers, who have in theory promulgated opinions subversive of morality, yet in their conduct have not been immoral, Godwin has laboured to inform the world, that the theory of Mrs. Wollstonecraft was reduced to practice; that she lived and acted, as she wrote and taught. But this communication of an admiring husband respecting the conduct of his wife, as well as the remarks of the Analytical Reviewers on the publication before us, will come under consideration in the succeeding article.

REVIEWS OF *MEMOIRS OF THE AUTHOR OF*
"A VINDICATION OF THE RIGHTS OF WOMAN"

The Analytical Review, vol. 27 (1798):
Memoirs of the Author of a Vindiction of the Rights of Woman. By
William Godwin. Small 8vo. 199 pa. Price 3s. 6d. boards.
Johnson 1798.

(The review begins with a summary of the chief events of
Wollstonecraft's life as recorded in the *Memoirs*.)

Such is the narrative here offered to the public of the life of
this very extraordinary woman. We feel ourselves impelled to
make some observations both on these memoirs, and on the character of Mrs. G.

The narrative is easy, and we believe very faithful and true,
so far it is entitled to praise. But it is obvious, that Mrs. G.
entertained singular opinions, and reduced them into practice.
This circumstance will invite many severely to criticise, and some
to censure her character. As this is the case, we think it was due
to Mrs. G., to have stated *how* those opinions were formed, and
the *reasons* by which she supported them.

It is indeed a bald narrative of the life of a woman, very
eventful and touching. We think it entitled to very limited praise.
In another respect it is deficient. It gives us no correct history of
the formation of Mrs. G.'s mind. We are neither informed of
her favourite books, her hours of study, nor her attainments in
languages and philosophy. She contemplated nature with rapture we are told, and enjoyed much of it's inspiration. Of this
there can be no doubt; but as the chief use of biography is to
teach us to attain to eminence in virtue and knowledge, we think
too little is told us concerning the subjects of Mrs. G.'s study,
and her manner of studying: but, perhaps, instead of censuring,
we ought to lament the paucity of the means of information.

We conceive exceptions will be taken to her conduct in three respects; and we think too little attention is given to such prob-able exceptions in the narrative.

1st, Mrs. G.'s notions and practice respecting marriage will meet with violent objection.

Without offering to vindicate her in these respects, we must be allowed to observe, that we think them questions of prudence rather than morality. He, who is not bewildered and lost in the mists of superstition, must be obliged to acknowledge, that there is something more necessary to render the sexual connection between man and woman pure, than the public ceremony of marriage; and that it is very easy for the vilest prostitution to exist under the sanction of this ceremony.

***

And if the ceremony of marriage cannot protect from the just charge of prostitution, in any case where a mental attach-ment has not preceded the sexual intercourse, neither can the neglect of the ceremony of marriage make that intercourse im-moral, when that neglect has flowed from motives of benevo-lence, or the convictions of immoral imposition. The ceremony of marriage performed or neglected alters not the morality of the thing, but it is essentially and solely a question of prudence, as it is the legal tie by which the laws of men compel to certain atten-tions and responsibilities. When, therefore, we consider the present very corrupt state of man, we are inclined to conclude Mrs. G's confidence too great, and her conduct imprudent and hazardous. That marriage ought to be an *indissoluble union*, where the parties prove wholly incompatible, we do not believe; and we think, not withstanding the powerful reasoning of Hume on this subject, that Milton was right, and that divorces should be allowed in many cases, where they cannot in this country be obtained.

Superficial minds will be apt to say, that the experience of Mrs. G. is the best refutation of her theory: but we dare not say this, as long we see, which we daily do, thousands married, whose union is as *unhappy* as the union of this lady and Mr. Imlay.

If any think that, without accusing Mrs. G. of *immorality*, a charge of *indelicacy* will fix, on account of her neglect of the established rules of the community; we have only to observe, that Mrs. G was an original thinker, differed from the vulgar in most things, had long reflected on this subject, and drawn decisive conclusions, and entered upon this connection with Mr. Imlay, *in France, and at a moment when the difficulties of the subject of marriage agitated the national councils, and when a new system of thinking on that point almost universally obtained.* That, therefore, may appear to us in our circumstances indelicate, which *there* would not have appeared to be so.

We have however observed, that we think her conduct *imprudent*, while men continue as corrupt as they now are, as we are far from holding it up for imitation. Her nature was generous in the extreme, and inclined to place confidence, when it ought, perhaps, to have cherished suspicion.

2. The next charge we expect to hear advanced against the character of Mrs. G., is the versatility of her attachments. It will be said, to-day she loves Mr. Fuseli, to-morrow attaches herself to Mr. Imlay, and, the moment Mr. Imlay finally abandons her, we find her in the arms of Mr. Godwin.

But what is there in all this? Those, who feel powerfully one impression, are, no doubt, the most easily susceptible of another.

Rochefocault, in his maxims, the result of a profound study of mankind, asserts, that the heart, which is torn by a disappointed affection, is the best prepared to form a new one. *But did Mrs. G. ever renounce an attachment?* He who reads her letters will declare, that the possibility of such a conduct did not exist in her nature. Her love was more lasting than it's object.

***

3. Her attempts to destroy herself, when she had a child deserted by it's father, will be thought worthy of censure. To this we can only say, that we possess not the scale of suffering by which to estimate what every one ought to endure before he seeks relief in death. We see Mrs. G. struggling with an overwhelming sorrow, and we have no power to throw an arrow at

one so sadly pierced. We wish her character and conduct to be seriously and candidly examined, and we would protect it, if we could, from the freedom of licentious tongues. She appears to us another Heloise; and it is a reflection upon men, that Abelard should have possessed the first, and Imlay the second of these illustrious women.

A head of Mrs. G. is prefixed to these memoirs, which exhibits at once a striking likeness, and a very interesting figure. We think every one who reads these memoirs ought, in justice to Mrs. G., to read her letters; and we wish, indeed, that they had not been separately printed.

Imperfect as these memoirs are, we have no fellowship with him, who can read them without a tear.

***

Mary Wollstonecraft Godwin, farewel! Thou hast asserted the rights, and received an uncommon portion of the wrongs of woman. Thy life was imbittered by those whose duty it was to succour and sooth thee. Thy name is pursued by the censures of the licentious and malignant. But better times approach, and thy vindication is secure. Thy name shall yet be mentioned with those, who have been distinguished for virtue and talents; and under this persuasion we are contented, that for a time thou shouldst suffer the reproach of married and unmarried prostitutes.

The British Critic, vol. 12 (1798): 228-233
Memoir of the Author of the Vindication of the Rights of Woman. By William Godwin. 12 mos. 199 pp. 3s. 6d. Johnson. 1798.

(This review immediately precedes that of Wollstonecraft's *Wrongs of Woman*.)

To such persons as are capable of unbiased reflection, this performance, extraordinary as it is, may prove instructive. Of the authenticity of the tale no doubt can be entertained; for, as the author was the husband of the heroine, he had access to the best information, of which he appears to have assiduously availed himself. It is well known, that both Mrs. Wollstonecraft and her biographer spent much of their time in labouring to eradicate from the minds of their readers all respect for establishments deemed venerable for their antiquity, and to inspire them with enthusiastic admiration of daring and untried theories in morals, in politics, and in religion. In the narrative before us, we have an opportunity of contemplating the effects of such theories on their own practice.

The first thing recorded of Mary, as Mr. Godwin constantly calls her, which is peculiarly worthy of notice, was her rotted abhorrence of her father. Mr. Wollstonecraft it seems,

"was a man of quick, impetuous disposition, subject to alternate fits of kindness and cruelty. The conduct he held toward the members of his family, was of the same kind as that he observed toward animals. He was the most extravagantly fond of them; but when he was displeased, and this frequently happened, his anger was alarming."

In some instances of passion exercised by him "to one of his *dogs*; his dutiful daughter was accustomed to speak of her emotions of *abhorrence*, as having risen to agony."

It is very possible that the old gentleman's conduct on this occasion may have been such, as to excite in any feeling mind a momentary abhorrence at once involuntary and just; but Mary *was accustomed to speak of it,* and her enlightened biographer *has given it to the public at large,* for the perpetuating the disgrace of the parent of her who was "the object dearest to his own heart that the universe contained." But we beg Mr. Godwin's pardon. It is only among those who believe themselves bound by an antiquated law to "honour their parents," and to be silent when they cannot speak of them with respect, that this *custom* of Mary's will meet with general disapprobation; and we need not be told how little he values the approbation of men who are under such prejudices, and strangers to *political justice.*

If Mary abhorred her father, she seems not to have had any

great degree of dutiful regard for her mother. She is represented as having considered her attention to that parent on her death-bed, as a wonderful effort of kindness. She had some time before left her father's house, as it appears to us in a fit of peevishness, because all her caprices were not humoured.

"But, true to the calls of humanity," says Mr. Godwin, "she felt in the intelligence of her mother's illness an irresistible mo-tive, and eagerly returned to the paternal roof. At first, every attention was received with acknowledgment and gratitude; but as the attentions grew habitual, and the health of the mother more and more wretched, they were rather exacted than received."

Were they given without reluctance? We suspect not; for, we are told, that the last words her mother ever uttered were, "a little patience, and all will be over!" words which can hardly be accounted for, but on the supposition that the daughter become impatient of her duty.

(The review here summarizes her relationship to Fanny Blood, her employment as a governess, her association with Jo-seph Johnson, and finally her feelings for Henry Fuseli.)

In about four months after her arrival at Paris, she was in-duced to banish Mr. Fuseli's merits from her memory, and to enter with another "into that species of connection, for which," says her biographer, "her heart secretly panted, and which had the effect of diffusing an immediate tranquility and cheerfulness over her manners." Mr. Imlay felt no objection to gratify *all* her desires; and she now enjoyed that "happiness of which her ar-dent imagination was continually conjuring up pictures, during her intercourse with the celebrated painter." To screen her from the cruelty of the French Convention, she found it expedient to assume the *name* of Imlay, and pass for the wife of a native of the United States of America; but she refused to be actually married to her lover, "because she would not," says Mr. Godwin, "in-volve him in family embarrassments, or expose him to pecuniary demands that existed against her."

If this was really her reason for objecting to a legal marriage, she had no cause to be surprised or offended at being afterwards deferred; for how could Mr. Imlay *keep* a woman as his *wife*, without embarrassing himself more or less with her family; and even paying her debts? During the first months, however, of her sensual delirium, she appears to have been under no apprehension of future desertion; but considered herself as "arrived at the situation, which, for two or three preceding years, her reason had pointed out to her as affording the most substantial prospect of happiness!" In the language of Eloisa, she seems to have said to herself,

> Not Caesar's Empress would I deign to prove;
> No, make me mistress to the man I love.

This dream of happiness was not of long duration. *** Mary tried every method to recover his affection, and, when she did not succeed, attempted to drown herself! In all this she acted with great inconsistency. Imlay was a philosopher of the same school as Godwin, and saw "the absurdity of expecting, that the inclinations and wishes of two human beings should coincide through any long period of time." ***

*** Her connexion with Imlay was finally broken off in the month of March, 1796; and, in the succeeding August, she entered into a new one, in all respects similar, with the paradoxical author of *Political Justice*, who had publicly ridiculed and censured the rites of marriage, and from whom therefore she could not reasonably expect greater constancy than she had experienced from her former lover. She determined however to run the risque of a second desertion "It was her maxim," we are told, "that in the intercourse between the sexes, the imagination should awaken the senses, and not the sense the imagination;" but whether this was actually the process in her own mind or not, it appears that her senses were now so *completely awakened*, that she could not exist without their gratification; and she was prevented from quitting England, only by finding in Mr. Godwin a man able and willing to satisfy her desires. She became pregnant; and, after seven months of sexual intercourse, she had acquired such an ascendancy over her lover, that she prevailed with him to marry her, though he had, not long before, declared to the world, that "so long as he should seek to engross one woman to himself, and to prohibit his neighbour from *proving* his *superior desert*, and *reaping the fruits of it*, he would be guilty of the most odious of all monopolies."

One consequence of this marriage was such as might have been expected, in a country where female virtue is still valued. Mrs. Godwin was deserted by many ladies who had courted the acquaintance of Mrs. Imlay; and though her biographer affects to wonder at this, and to turn what he calls their squeamishness into ridicule, his wonder is certainly groundless, and his ridicule much misplaced. *** To their minds the following beautiful lines of Milton were more likely to occur, than the ravings of the author of *Political Justice*.

> Hail, wedded love! mysterious law, true fount
> Of human offspring, sole propriety
> In Paradise of all things common else.
> By the ADULTEROUS LUST was driven from men
> Among the BESTIAL HERDS TO RANGE; by thee,
> Founded in reason, loyal, just, and pure,
> Relations dear, and all the charities
> Of father, son, and brother, first were known.

Mary did not live long as the wife of Mr. Godwin. On Wednesday the 30th of August, 1797, she was delivered of a daughter, and died in great agony on the 10th of September, though her husband, with the good sense of a modern philosopher, "*intreated* her to recover," and though, with the same good sense, she had *promised* "not to leave him."

In the account of her last sufferings, which seem to have been indeed uncommonly severe, her husband does not scruple to specify the exact circumstances of the case, which, though more suited to a medical statement than a book of memoirs, intended for general perusal, is exactly conformable to the *Elements of Morality* written by Mrs. G. herself; in the introduction to which she urges the propriety of making young persons, particularly girls, intimately acquainted with certain parts of anatomy, generally thought to be unfit for their contemplation.

The reader of the *Vindication of the Rights of Woman*, will perhaps be surprised when he is informed, that, during her last illness, no religious expression escaped the author's lips. In that work, the grand principle is, that woman is not the inferior of man, but his equal in moral rank, walking along with him the road of duty, in which "they are both trained for a state of endless improvement." The biographer of Mary affirms, that she had made greater progress than her neighbours. Her hopes therefore should have been better founded. Prospect of success in a greater and favourite pursuit, usually animates the heart, and shows itself; but alas! if this narrative be correct, she, whom the author calls the greatest ornament of her sex, gave no signal of that hope, "she died and made no sign." She had long discontinued her attendance on public worship: she preferred the faint glimmerings of a false philosophy to the glorious light of the gospel; and she could not be animated with those hopes, which the gospel alone can excite.

The Anti-Jacobin Review, vol. 1 (1798): 94-103
Memoirs of the Author of the Vindication of the Rights of Woman. By Wm. Godwin. 12 mo. Price 3s. 6d. Pp. 199. Johnson, London. 1798.

(This review immediately follows that of Wollstonecraft's *Wrongs of Woman*.)

"There are (the author says) not many individuals with whose character the public welfare and improvement are more intimately concerned, than with the author of A Vindication of the Rights of Woman." Mr. Godwin, indeed, considers her as a model for imitation, and her life as *peculiarly* useful on account of the *precept and example* it affords. We coincide with him in his opinion of the *utility* of a life of Mrs. Wollstonecraft; though for a very different reason. Intended by him for a beacon, it serves for a buoy; if it does not shew what it is wise to pursue, it

manifests what it is wise to avoid. It illustrates both the sentiments and conduct resulting from such principles as those of
Mrs. Wollstonecraft and Mr. Godwin. It also in some degree
accounts for the formation of such visionary theories and pernicious doctrines.

(The review here summarizes the early life of Wollstonecraft
and "the intellectual process by which Mary was led to her extravagant, absurd, and destructive theories.")

The substance of Mrs. Wollstonecraft's moral sentiments and
history were briefly this—the creature of impulse, some of her
propensities were benevolent, and frequently operated to the
good of those were placed within the sphere of her actions. Not
directed, however, by sound principles, she considered herself as
exempted from those restraints on inclination, which are necessary to the welfare of society. Prompted by the feeling of the
time, she even in her friendly acts proceeded much farther than
virtue, guided by reason, would dictate. Intent on one object
only, she disregarded other relations, to which it was her duty to
attend. She was evidently totally unused to that balance of affections in which the soundest philosophers and wisest men have
placed the supreme good of man. From love to Miss Blood, Mary,
when she was in bad health, left her engagements and duties at
home to accompany her abroad: to her feeling (benevolent we
allow) she sacrificed the good of the pupils who had been en-
trusted to her care. ***

Her constitution, as the philosopher, her husband, bears
testimony, was very amorous.*** She entered (says Godwin)
into that *species of connection*, for which *her heart* secretly *panted*,
and which had the effect of diffusing an immediate tranquility
and cheerfulness over her manners." The state to which he at-
tributes such beneficial consequences, to the mind of her who
he afterwards made his wife, was *concubinage*. She became the
concubine of Mr. Imlay, an American. The biographer does not
mention many of her amours. Indeed it was unnecessary: two or
three instances of action often decide a character as well as a
thousand. *** Here, we must observe, that Mary's theory, that

it is the right of women to indulge their inclinations with every man they like, is so far from being new, that it is as old as prostitution.

(Here the review summarizes the events leading up to her abandonment by Imlay and her subsequent suicide attempt.) But being restored to life, she transferred her love from an *absent* to a PRESENT man—from the adventurer Imlay, to the philosopher Godwin. Although they at last married, yet, as the *philosopher himself bears testimony, they lived for several months in a state of illicit commerce.* The biographer, in speaking of their intercourse, is much more particular than decency permits us to state. (The review then quotes Godwin's philosophical reasons for why he and Wollstonecraft did not immediately marry.)

The reader is to observe, that the biographer afterwards married the lady. Soon after her death, *to do honour to the memory of his wife, and himself in choosing such a wife,* he records her adventures. The moral sentiments and moral conduct of Mrs. Wollstonecraft, resulting from their principles and theories, exemplify and illustrate JACOBIN MORALITY.

***

Having thus considered the character and tendency of these works, and having, we trust, formed such an estimate of the effects which these notions, principles, and conduct would produce as precepts and example, as will coincide with the opinions of the soundest friends of morality, religion, order, and the British constitution, we proceed next to examine the account given of Mrs. Wollstonecrafts's works and history, by the friends of the new philosophy.—Analytical Review, for March, Art. II . and III.—*** (The Analytical Review's discussion of *The Wrongs of Woman* is here quoted.)

These are opinions and sentiments, which, whilst the Analytical Reviewers continue to publish, we shall not cease to attack. It is, and shall be, the business of the Anti-Jacobin Review, to expose attempts to abuse a most beneficial engine, by employing the press as a vehicle of Jacobinism.

COMBINED REVIEWS OF *THE WRONGS OF WOMAN*
AND *THE MEMOIRS*

The Monthly Mirror, vol. 5 (1798): 153-157.
*Memoirs of the Author of a Vindication of the Rights of Woman, by
William Godwin. Small 8 vo. 3s. 6d. boards. Johnson, 1798.
The posthumous Works of the Author of a Vindication of the Rights of
Woman; containing the Wrongs of Woman—Maria, a fragment,
Letters, and Miscellaneous Pieces, 4 vols. small 8 vo. 14 s. in bds.
Johnson. 1798.*

The first of these productions begins with the life of the
celebrated author, written by her husband, Mr. Godwin, who,
venerating no doubt, the amiable virtues and eminent talents of
Mrs. G. has thought fit to give this volume to the world, compiled principally from written memorandums and careful in-
quiries, respecting the remarkable incidents of her life. It must
be confessed, that this morsel of biography does not teem with
much variety of anecdote, or dignity of sentiment. If we take
out of the account her intimacy with Mr. Imlay, there is little to
interest the feelings: her labour and the circumstances attending
her death, are too minutely described; not to say, that, in some
places, there is a frequent repetition of the same occurrences:
this gives that sort of *ennui*, which, to the generality of readers,
must render its perusal very desultory and insipid. It is easy for
many minds to comprehend the nature of a dangerous and trying labour; and when once we are led into all the minutiae of
this state, our pity for the afflicted object is divided between our
astonishment at the cool precision of the person who describes
it. This observation holds particularly in the present instance—
for as Mr. G. was her husband, he might, with as much credit to
himself, have left all the minutiae of the case for memorandums
to the medical men who attended her. Surely it is not necessary
in a plain simple biographical composition to alarm one's readers with a recital of circumstances not immediately understood

by every head, and not sufficiently dignified to heighten the awful catastrophe of the scene.

Upon the whole, the life of Mrs. Godwin leaves no very considerable impression upon the feelings: had it pleased heaven to prolong her days, and extend her labours, the world, by and by, might probably have been in possession of facts which would have redounded more to the celebrity of her name: we should not then have merely read an account of *moving from this place to that*, which at present occupies nearly one half of the volume: but should have discovered her ardent and vigorous mind busied every day in fresh pursuits for the amelioration of mankind.

Of the posthumous works, the first in rotation, is, "the *Wrongs of Woman*;" containing nearly two volumes; upon this, as it is left in so mutilated a state, criticism has little to advance. The injuries inflicted on "the fairest and dearest part of creation," are very lively and energetically displayed. Both Jemima and Maria seem not only to have continually partaken of the bitter cup of misfortune, but to have swallowed its very dregs. What catastrophe would have ensued, it is impossible now to conjecture: the author of the work has had *her* share of afflictions, and is now gone, we hope, to that retreat "where the wretched may have rest."

The story is written in a very uneven, and, in some places, very inflated manner: the beginning is a sufficient demonstration. (The review then cites the opening paragraph of *The Wrongs of Woman*).

Mrs. G's description, however, of Maria, drawn with considerable truth and freedom, affords some compensation for the preceding extract. It is too long for quotation; but certainly possesses great merit.

(The review then comments on the *Letters to Imlay* which constitute a volume and a half of the *Posthumous Works*, and finds them "only inferior to those of *Werter*.)

The rest of the works, notwithstanding their detached condition, partake fully of the lively sensibility and instinctive sagacity of Mrs. Godwin. They do honour to the memory of her who now "sleeps with her fathers," and will for ever remain "a splendid and deserving monument of female worth and female renown."